Redevelopment and Race

Great Lakes Books

*A complete listing of the books in this series can be found online at **wsupress.wayne.edu***

Redevelopment and Race

Planning a Finer City in Postwar Detroit

June Manning Thomas

Wayne State University Press • Detroit

Originally published 1997 by The Johns Hopkins University Press.
Paperback edition © 2013 by Wayne State University Press, Detroit, Michigan 48201. All rights
reserved. No part of this book may be reproduced without formal permission. Manufactured
in the United States of America.
17 16 15 14 13   5 4 3 2 1

Library of Congress Control Number: 2013930905

ISBN 978-0-8143-3907-7 (paperback)
ISBN 978-0-8143-3908-4 (ebook)

For the Metropolitan Detroit Bahá'í community,
tireless workers for racial unity and
the vision of a world at peace

Contents

Preface
to the Paperback Edition

This book is as important today as it was when first published. We need to have a clearer understanding of the roles of racial change, planning, and redevelopment in the modern evolution of cities like Detroit—cities that have struggled to retain primacy in their regions. As explained in the original preface, I wrote the book to explain what had happened to Detroit's physical, economic, and social fabric in spite of decades of local efforts, in the field of urban planning and development, to protect that fabric. One goal was to document what role city planning had played in the evolution of this fascinating city over a major portion of its twentieth-century history. Of concern were questions such as why planning tools had not "revitalized" the city, and how their use affected people's lives, particularly those of low-income minorities located in the path of redevelopment and social change. The purpose was not to write another narrative about the rights or wrongs of urban renewal, but rather to highlight redevelopment as a partially quixotic campaign in the context of a city undergoing massive deindustrialization and racial conflict. Many books, articles, and commentaries had elaborated on U.S. cities and their social and economic change during similar eras, but relatively few had looked specifically at the role of purposeful governmental action in attempting to remake modern U.S. cities through planning and redevelopment in the midst of such change.

Rereading this book again only highlights how dramatic Detroit's evolution has been. This is a story filled with hope, vision, heartbreak, and frustration; it is a story of both heroic acts and villainous deeds, but mostly good intentions. The short version of the book's story is that urban planners and related professionals tried to encourage development and growth in a city rent apart by industrial change and racial conflict, all in the context of metropolitan decentralization more pronounced in this region than almost anywhere else in the U.S.

For a few decades the city pursued its redevelopment agenda in the bright light of optimism and with a sense of civic righteousness, but it soon became clear that this model of redevelopment was more conflictual and limited than anyone had anticipated. Although that agenda generated several laudable successes, defined as places within the city that survived socially and economically in spite of difficult times, it proved utterly inadequate to halt the decline in population size and economic primacy. The real pathos of the story is that such limitations were a surprise to many planning professionals, who had seen themselves as crucial reformers but increasingly realized they were making at best improvements at the margins.

The era of blacks' "civil rebellions" in the mid-1960s exacerbated an exodus of white citizens that had already begun years before. This took place in a metropolitan area characterized to an unusually high degree by numerous small suburban governments, lack of open housing in such suburbs for racial minorities, and a flawed, car-driven regional transportation network that discouraged centralization and helped empty out the city. Efforts under several Detroit mayors to create an urban growth agenda faltered in many ways, in part because the redevelopment projects selected fought against the tide of market forces and emerged without critical connections among themselves. The book's latter portion noted major triumphs—such as the winning of Empowerment Zone designation under Mayor Dennis Archer—but also described a severely fragmented region, bifurcated by race and income, with many metropolitan area residents openly hostile to "black Detroit."

This book, along with other books and articles about Detroit, provides some answers to the question of why Detroit is economically distressed, focusing in these pages on matters related to partially successful planning and redevelopment. A newly written postscript at the end of the book offers a very brief overview of what has happened since the book was first written, possible only by describing a few key highlights. In addition, the postscript will briefly suggest considerations for future improvements in the city and region.

The original narrative remains compelling, vaguely disturbing, yet simultaneously uplifting. With the additional postscript added, the book now explains that professionals in at least one field have been steadily working for the betterment of the people of the city of Detroit and its region, with greater or lesser success, for at least three-fourths of a century. Their story deserves to be told.

June M. Thomas
August 2012

Preface

The primary purpose for this book was to discover why one city has suffered decline and abandonment, what urban planners had to do with the situation, and what the experience can teach us about other cities. The reader might like to know why the author chose to look at these issues.

A major motivation was concern for family and friends in Detroit and the urban suburb of Highland Park. My husband had grown up in the Brewster-Douglass housing project, but he soon escaped to the relative security of, first, the Marines and then Michigan State University. Other close relatives, however, lived in the very sections of Detroit and Highland Park that were suffering the most from joblessness, poverty, abandonment, and crime. One young niece had to walk next to dangerously weeded and undeveloped urban renewal lots to get to school. My mother-in-law donated years of effort to her block club, seemingly to little avail, as her once-lovely street lost its families and houses one by one.

Naomi Oden, a major mentor during my adult years, was an inspiring warrior for social progress during her lifetime. She fought a constant battle against abandonment of the elderly, drug addiction, and youth estrangement, both in her neighborhood in Highland Park and in the drug rehabilitation clinic and nursing home that she and her husband owned and operated in Detroit. She saw these as natural extensions of her deeply felt belief in the need for a new spiritual transformation in inner cities. Even as Naomi taught me to seek spiritual solutions to social problems, she would challenge me: it's wonderful that you are an urban planner, especially a professor. What can you do to help us in this situation?

Part of the effort to help has been to work in and for Detroit periodically. This book project began at the tail end of a sabbatical leave from Michigan State University in 1985–86, when, as a planner for the Michigan Department of Commerce, I worked with several unsuccessful redevelopment projects in Detroit. These included refurbishment of Tiger Stadium, anticipated development of the Michigan Central Railroad Depot, attempted resolution of several issues concerning the Ambassador Bridge and entry to the city for Canadian tourists, and an aborted effort to persuade General Motors executives not to close down the Cadillac Fleetwood and Clark Street assembly plants.

Another fruitless assignment during that period was as consultant for the Governor's Urban Affairs Adviser, Terry Duvernay, who was also head of the Michigan State Housing Development Authority. Duvernay struggled to develop a sense of responsibility for Detroit and other urban areas among heedless state government department officials. Unless I was a jinx, it seemed that redevelopment was indeed very difficult.

This time period came just after completion of another book, *Detroit: Race and Uneven Development* (Philadelphia: Temple University Press, 1987), written with my co-authors Joe Darden, Richard Child Hill, and Richard W. Thomas. Although that book explained much about Detroit's state, and my contributions on redevelopment and metropolitan governance included important information, on the whole the project did not silence the nagging concern and puzzlement that assailed me every time I stepped foot in Detroit, and every time I opened the morning newspaper.

It appeared a more focused effort was needed, to try to understand more fully the historical background of what was happening, and to help identify solutions. As a professor of urban and regional planning, in love with the profession and with cities, my attention turned to my colleagues' role in this nearby city's fortunes. What were they doing all of this time? The perhaps naive thought that they were doing anything but their best soon died upon immersion in this project.

Poring over the collective reports, memos, letters, and sketches created by the city's planners and development staff, over a period beginning in the 1930s, was a revelation. This research revealed a fifty-year history of missteps and miscalculations, as expected, but also uncovered dreams of a better city, noble visions stilled by the realities of social and economic transformation. The decline of the industrial sector and the government-sanctioned flight to suburbia meant that planners fought uphill battles against market forces. Racial disunity and conflict, even in the face of growing political power for the city's African Americans, brought a particular kind of devastation. The telling of these events sometimes came dangerously close to making corrective efforts seem futile. Yet the struggle for improvement continued, as it should today.

This book relates the results of a process of self-education that hopefully will prove useful to readers as well, but the author is still searching for answers. Part of that search has required working with those who are building solutions. It is important to believe in, and respect, the efforts of those who have not given up, who continue to fight to improve urban organizations, communities, and governments.

Occasionally I am able to offer some small assistance to these efforts. Spurred by Naomi Oden's unforgettable query, I sought out research and outreach projects—such as an evaluation of the state's Neighborhood Builders' Alliance, association with M.S.U.'s partnership for economic development assistance, and work with Wayne County on assessing its urban policy initiatives—that helped assist social reformers in the Detroit region. In the early 1990s I began working with urban planning classes, first as a visitor with the University of Michigan, and then with my own Michigan State University students, to identify neighborhood planning projects in Detroit for which we could donate student labor as we simultaneously trained students in the planning profession. The resulting projects—in Corktown and Hubbard-Richard, with the Northwestern Goldberg Community Association, Fellowship Inc., New Hope Housing Development Corporation, Hubbard-Richard, West Warren Business Association, and others—were seminal experiences, both for me and for many urban planning and landscape architecture students. These Detroit experiences tempered scholarly perspective with practical reality.

New initiatives took place in 1993–94, well after the first drafts of most of these chapters were written, but just in time to provide insight into revisions and into the last few chapters. For that sabbatical leave year I worked as a faculty coordinator for training of community housing development organizations in Wayne County. I also coordinated training for a dozen faith-based community development organizations in Detroit. And for a time I worked for the City of Detroit, as one of several staff members working for a citizen group which organized the city's application for Empowerment Zone designation. This was a career highlight because the city that I had studied for so long actually trusted me to do something important for it. What a truly humbling situation that was, as I struggled to do my best for them!

Academic purists might ask if one could do all that and remain an objective scholar. But how can one remain an aloof academic, given such crying needs, without offering assistance as well? And what good is the theory of urban planning without the practice? I hope the reader will find that my personal passions and concerns are tempered but reflected in this book in the best possible ways.

Acknowledgments

Numerous people provided the support necessary to write this book. Prominent among these is certainly Joe Darden, Dean of Urban Affairs Programs at Michigan State University, who donated graduate assistant time, secretarial time, travel funds, some of the production costs, as well as encouragement over a number of years. Conference travel and moral support also came from Roger Hamlin in Urban and Regional Planning, my major academic appointment, located within the Geography Department.

Extremely helpful were the librarians at various archival libraries, particularly the Burton Historical Collection of the Detroit Public Library, a fine institution that manages to excel in spite of periodic budget crises. Tom Cocozzoli, librarian of the Barr Planning and Design Library at Michigan State University, served as watchdog and scout for historic planning documents, and greatly exceeded the requirements of his job in his efforts to assist this research. The Walter Reuther (Detroit) and Bentley (University of Michigan, Ann Arbor) librarians also provided important assistance.

Since the gestation period for this book lasted many years, it is difficult to list all of the Urban Affairs Programs graduate assistants who aided the research efforts. But special thanks to them and to students in the former introductory history course for Urban and Regional Planning, who tolerated early drafts of various chapters.

Among outside readers the most supportive have been two men: historian/planner/social worker Barry Checkoway, University of Michigan, who read early drafts when they were barely legible; and most especially my husband, historian/race relations expert Richard W. Thomas, who read, commented, encouraged, and propped me up in untold ways. Planning historian Larry Guerckens's reading provided pithy comments that greatly influenced the last chapter. Special thanks go to stalwart scholars/reviewers Chris Silver, Robert Catlin, and Chuck Connerly; urban planners Marsha Bruhn, Quintus Green, Harold Bellamy, Hilanius Phillips, and Mel Ravitz, who read and commented upon selected chapters; and several anonymous scholars. George F. Thompson, president of the Center for

American Places and my editor at Johns Hopkins University Press, pulled it all together. Thanks to colleague and super friend Mim Rutz for telling me about him.

Actual production of the document depended absolutely on graphics whiz Ellen White, whose office does things with computer-generated maps and illustrations that most of us only dream about. Special thanks to her assistant Nat Evans. Carol Croop, my spiritual sister, also contributed important graphics, lovingly drawing these by hand. Fran Fowler of Urban Affairs Programs provided the most essential secretarial support, handling the bulk of formatting, printing, and mailing tasks. Dawn Brown of Urban Planning contributed early versions of graphics and much moral as well as clerical support, as did Barb Dewey.

It is important to acknowledge those whose story is told here, particularly those planners who worked for so many years to improve the city, and who donated written archival materials to libraries accessible to scholars. Those who let me interview them helped bring the planning documents to life. Planning Director Blessing has since died, and so I am especially grateful that he took the time from a busy retirement to sit for two interviews.

Over the past few years I have grown to know several activists and planners working in Detroit. Thanks to Bill Lontz, formerly with the Michigan Department of Commerce, for giving me my first professional planning assignment in Detroit; Lillian Randolph, for letting me organize parts of her community development training workshops, through Wayne County and World Vision; Gloria Robinson, for asking me to work for Wayne County and for the City of Detroit; and countless other friends in the planning and development community, who continue to offer insight that no book could provide. And for sheer dedication to the cause of racial unity and city improvement, few can match the Bahá'í community, particularly Detroit area members such as the late Naomi Oden and James Oden, who have given me constant inspiration throughout my adult life.

Last, but really first, special thanks to my father and mother, who set superior standards for excellence, service, and triumph over adversity in their roles as college president and college professor, respectively, accomplishing marvelous things in racially segregated South Carolina; to my daughter Kemba and son Ali, who donated precious time for me to go to Detroit and work in various libraries and attend community meetings; and, again, to my husband Richard, a Detroit native, fellow scholar, and as fine a companion as anyone could hope to have.

I wish to acknowledge permission to use material previously published in my "Racial Crisis and the Fall of the Detroit City Plan Commission," *Journal of the American Planning Association* 54 (1988): 150–61; "Planning and Industrial Decline: Lessons from Postwar

Detroit," *Journal of the American Planning Association* 55 (1990): 297–310; and "Designing a Finer City," in *Planning the Twentieth-Century American City*, edited by Christopher Silver and Mary Corbin Sies (Baltimore: Johns Hopkins University Press, 1996).

All errors of fact or interpretation are, of course, my own.

Acknowledgments
───────────────

Abbreviations

AIP	American Institute of Planners
AME	African Methodist Episcopal
ASPO	American Society of Planning Officials
CBTU	Coalition of Black Trade Unionists
CCR	Commission on Community Relations
CDBG	Community Development Block Grants
CEDD	Community and Economic Development Department
CRP	Community Renewal Program
DCPC, or CPC	Detroit City Plan Commission
EZEC	Empowerment Zones/Enterprise Communities
FHA	Federal Housing Administration
GM	General Motors
HHFA	Home and Housing Finance Administration
HOLC	Home Owners Loan Corporation
HUD	U.S. Department of Housing and Urban Development
LISC	Local Initiatives Support Corporation
MACO	Michigan Avenue Community Organization
MSHDA	Michigan State Housing Development Authority
NAACP	National Association for the Advancement of Colored People
NAREB	National Association of Real Estate Boards
NOF	Neighborhood Opportunity Fund
OEO	Office of Economic Opportunity
PNC	Poletown Neighborhood Council
PWA	Public Works Administration

RDI	Regional Development Initiative (SEMCOG)
RenCen	Renaissance Center
SEMCOG	Southeast Michigan Council of Governments
SEMTA	Southeast Michigan Transportation Authority
STRESS	Stop the Robberies, Enjoy Safe Streets
TAP, or TAAP	Total Action Against Poverty
UAW	United Automobile Workers (sometimes known as the International Union, United Automobile, Aircraft and Agricultural Implement Workers of America)
UDAG	Urban Development Action Grants
ULI	Urban Land Institute
VA	Veterans' Administration
WCO	West Central Organization

Redevelopment and Race

Introduction

Surely one of the great mysteries of twentieth-century American civilization, one that puzzles native and visitor alike, is how one of the world's great powers could let its older, larger cities decline so. In some quarters, even to raise the issue is traitorous. The rallying cry of civic boosters is that American cities are on a comeback, that the appearance of decline is merely the reality of adjustment to changing times. Loyalty to one's own municipality demands fierce optimism. Cities are not in such bad shape, this view holds; witness their new waterfronts, their viable downtowns, their many attractive and fine neighborhoods.

For some cities, however, even the most partisan booster must question: What went wrong? Consider the example of Detroit, Michigan. How could a city that for so many years enjoyed livable neighborhoods, healthy commercial strips, a bustling downtown, and beautiful parks turn into what exists today? How could a city that once symbolized opportunity for the working class become so troubled by crime, poverty, declining services?

Different experts answer such questions in different ways. Economists explain that the economic base declined and that economic incentives led businesses and commuters to abandon the city. Experts in American culture address the collective mentality of the U.S. middle class, which values newness, single-family homes, and large lawns: the life reflected on prime-time television. Political scientists point to government incentives that encouraged exodus and political fragmentation. Each approach provides an aspect of the truth.

In this book I will try to answer a slightly different set of questions: How could a city that for so long enjoyed prosperity turn into what exists today, given that so many people tried, for so many years, to improve it? For years, municipal politicians and staff fought the tide of decline, trying to recreate a viable and livable city. Their efforts to carry out "redevelopment"—a deliberate effort to rebuild decayed or declining areas—began as early as the 1940s and have continued to the present. Were their efforts completely in vain? Why were they not more successful?

It takes a conceptual leap to assume that civic reformers had the ability to improve the city since social, political, and economic forces were so overwhelmingly against their efforts. If one considers that they focused on *targeted* reforms, however, one can analyze the results. Detroit's leaders and their staff supported many positive developments, and these provide visible areas of beauty and attraction. In fact, one could visualize the riverfront and central third of Detroit as a patchwork quilt, where some patches show great physical distress and others do not. Virtually every patch containing new or moderately new housing, well-designed community facilities, hospital or museum complexes, or other civic improvements bears some mark of the more than fifty years of service by the city's urban planners and other development staff. They could not do more than they did for two basic reasons which provide the two main themes for this book.

The first reason was that city politicians and staff, particularly urban planners, did not have the implementation tools and administrative structures necessary to ward off the city's deterioration. Federal urban policies were weak and ineffective, and the federal government did as much to build up the suburbs as they did to buttress central cities. Local leaders had to use urban planning tools that were not designed to address population and economic decline, such as traditional comprehensive plans and urban design initiatives, and they also struggled with less than optimal redevelopment operations.

The second reason for ineffective action was that racial bias stunted efforts. White preference for racial segregation warped the city's public housing program, slowed down its redevelopment efforts, and blocked neighborhood upgrading. The ultimate symbol of city destruction was the 1967 rebellions, directly linked to the climate of racial injustice and intolerance. Even in the relatively quiet years of the 1970s and 1980s, racial estrangement kept the region fragmented and alienated. This context of alienation counteracted whatever improvement programs the city initiated.

These two issues strike at the core of today's tasks for many distressed central cities and their metropolitan areas. The ravages of industrial change, population decline, and federal policy have already taken their toll, but other lessons have yet to be learned. Understanding the evolution of redevelopment and race relations can point the way to more effective policies for today. The experiences of Detroit can offer lessons instructive for other cities.

In the next two sections I will briefly expand on these concepts, but first it is important to note the basic theoretical perspective of this book. The governing values of this work are these: that no real and lasting progress can come for America's urban regions without certain fundamental reforms. These reforms include the elimination of the extremes of wealth and poverty dividing metropolitan communities, the expansion of social progress and economic opportunity for the region's poorest citizens, and the eradication of the lingering effects of racial disunity and injustice. Urban professionals have a special responsibility to help implement these goals.[1]

The call for social justice in the metropolis is not new. A significant body of theoretical literature has focused on just this issue. In *Social Justice and the City,* for example, David Harvey urged society to discard its preoccupation with making a profit, a fixation that built many cities, and to turn instead toward concern for social justice.[2] This study of Detroit uses a normative theory to carry out a historical methodology. A normative theory proposes what should be, based on certain norms or values.[3] One succinct label for the normative concerns expressed here could be "social justice in the city," but this study of Detroit looks at specific aspects of such justice: the relationship between redevelopment and planning practice, with a focus on race relations.

This approach owes much to the concept of "equity planning" promoted by practitioner-scholar Norman Krumholz. Krumholz has developed a consciously proactive theory for bringing about justice in the city. Equity planning is rooted in the logical positivism of urban planning and in the writings of such social philosophers as John Rawls. Using his own career as example, Krumholz suggests how to develop local policies that promote social justice. He also gives practical guidelines about how to fight for social reform, yet remain effective within city bureaucracies. Thus equity planning bridges the gap between the theory and implementation of social reform.[4]

Although most of the work related to equity planning is contemporary rather than historical, it is not difficult to adapt this model to a historical perspective. Equity planning suggests that the ends do not justify the means and that city improvement that shuts some people out is insufficient. Used as a historical construct, equity planning judges previous policies by the standard of how well they promoted redistributive justice. This work builds on the base of equity planning but argues that racial disunity adds another dimension to the need for just and effective local policy. Society's failure to address the most fundamental dilemmas of racial injustice tainted Detroit's improvement efforts in overt and subtle ways. If the Detroit experience is any example, progress will not be made until society resolves these issues and successfully promotes an agenda of racial unity for the metropolitan area.

The Tools of Redevelopment

The first major theme of this book is that weak federal and local policy tools and structures stunted redevelopment. Federal programs such as public housing, urban renewal, and Model Cities suffered because of poorly conceived legislation, antagonistic private interests, congressional or presidential indifference, and erratic funding.

These shortcomings posed significant barriers and in their own way shaped local redevelopment policies. Yet local decisions, made by local political leaders, growth coalitions, and bureaucrats, were important as well.

Research on redevelopment decisionmaking in cities such as Chicago, New York, San Francisco, Boston, Hartford, and Houston presents a fairly consistent composite portrait. In the period beginning after World War II, city leaders used redevelopment to advance their political and economic interests. The growth coalition—elected officials, private sector interests, and appointed commissioners and staff—aimed for very specific goals. Using federal urban renewal funds, they aimed to eliminate low-income neighborhoods located near central business districts or important local institutions and to replace them with "higher" uses. Since relocation funds and low-income housing programs were ludicrously inadequate, the poor suffered in the process.[5]

Just before the urban renewal era faded, some control over redevelopment passed, temporarily, to the residents of distressed neighborhoods. The federally funded community action and Model Cities programs helped local residents determine social, physical, and economic development priorities for their own neighborhoods. But the empowerment was short-lived; local political leaders regained control with the advent of community block grants. Political leaders consolidated their partnership with local economic leaders and refocused attention on their particular vision of urban improvement.

Many scholars disagree about the specifics of this broad picture, especially which group dominated local redevelopment policies. In general, political and economic leaders prevailed, but which of the two had more power is a matter of debate. Some scholars argue that economic forces dominated all action. In their view, cities carry out the bidding of market forces or the corporate elite.[6] Political scientists emphasize the importance of local political decisionmaking, whether this is pluralist, elitist, or a combination. John Mollenkopf, for example, proposes that politicians shaped redevelopment by putting together growth coalitions based on political considerations.[7]

It is most likely that economic and political forces work together. Cities are "political economies," where economic considerations dominate the political state.[8] This relationship has varied over time, however. In the 1950s and early 1960s, growth coalitions dominated land-use decisions and skewed redevelopment toward downtowns. By the mid-1960s, aroused neighborhoods made it more difficult to centralize decision-making. The rise of federal block grants in the 1970s further changed the nature of alliances and bargains, as did the era of the 1980s and 1990s, when the paucity of federal assistance forced cities to turn to strong "public-private partnerships."[9]

Local political leaders determined the direction that city redevelopment policy took, but their decisions depended upon federal policies and local political and economic realities. In addition, city staff played an important role. In Detroit, for example, city planners—defined here largely as staff members of city planning agencies, although their voluntary citizen-based planning commissions also played important roles—helped visualize, support, and implement policy decisions.[10] This was possible in part because of the peculiar nature of decision-making in American cities. For certain decisions and during certain time periods, city bureaucrats, for all practical purposes, run the government.

Urban government can be so disorganized that nominal leaders do not govern. Mayors may not control their bureaucracies, and high-level administrators may not control street-level employees. Instead, many political, administrative, and community interests interact, making "street-fighting pluralism" reign supreme. Only with a narrow range of problems or policies is centralized control possible. This range includes problems involving only a few participants and problems exhibiting low instability or uncertainty.[11]

For many years, urban planners operated within that range of problems for which control was possible. From the 1930s until the early 1960s, power was centralized and goals were clear. Just before and after World War II, planners used comprehensive plans and zoning ordinances to guide construction of public and private housing and community facilities. After 1954 the federal urban renewal program required a local "workable program," which included a statement of goals, development priorities, and implementation strategies. Cities needed planning expertise to write these statements. Planners were effective because "renewal required expertise, long-range planning, and intricate negotiations with the federal government; it was a kind of policy making that an energetic mayor and his professional planners would naturally and easily dominate."[12]

But the influence of planners changed over time. The 1940s and 1950s were a time of great ambition for the potential of master plans, traditional land-use tools, and redevelopment. In the 1960s planners continued to pursue urban renewal goals but dealt more directly with social programs. Project development became more important than long-range planning in the 1970s and 1980s, and planners became less useful. Detroit planners' identification with the oppressive urban renewal program—and difficulty using traditional planning tools to solve contemporary problems—caused their credibility to plummet with the city's growing minority electorate. They fell out of favor with a powerful African-American mayor and lost even more influence. The trauma of the transition is palpable, a story in itself.

Several books written about American cities during these decades investigate either the federal government's role or the local political and economic context. Less attention has been given to urban planning professionals. Yet city planners formed a unique group: They were trained visionaries, full-time staff that municipalities hired to help them prepare for the future through orderly development. Their vision of how cities should develop is important to understand, even though planners, as employees, usually carried out the will of their employers. They could not implement policy goals which local political and economic leaders did not support. The result was a tug of war between planners as visionary reformers and planners as lackeys.

Race and Change

The second theme is that although redevelopment negatively affected racial justice, a fact that has been well documented in many studies, race relations in turn negatively affected redevelopment. Most studies explore only the first part of this reciprocal relationship. They have examined which racial groups suffered the most from clearance projects or analyzed the racial dimensions of public housing, relocation, and resettlement decisions.[13] The case of Detroit confirms that redevelopment had strong negative repercussions for racial minorities, here represented by African Americans, but offers additional insight into the way racial prejudice and conflict impeded efforts to stop city decline.

In Detroit, as in other cities, the growth of the Black population helped spur postwar redevelopment efforts, because the city leaders' desire to contain people of color in well-defined ghetto areas shaped their decisions about public housing and redevelopment. But here is a partial list of other, less obvious connections: Racial prejudice was a critical factor in the slow start of inner-city reconstruction efforts and in the failure of neighborhood rehabilitation projects. Racial conflict generated an era of civil unrest and helped shape contemporary mayoral politics and redevelopment policies. The lingering effects of racial antagonism and injustice are primary reasons that redevelopment failed to revitalize the modern city of Detroit.

Race was not the only factor to influence redevelopment success. So did other social forces, particularly economic decline and suburban growth. In each case, however, race offers an important added dimension.

Economic decline was an especially important force. Economic decentralization hit Detroit harder than most cities. The city's high-wage, low-skill industrial jobs had supported hundreds of thousands of workers. These workers lost the base of their livelihood when the automobile industry began to close down its older, central city manufacturing operations. While some of these manufacturing jobs went to suburban sites in the metropolitan region, some left the state or the country completely. Simultaneously Detroit's central business district declined, killing many city retail jobs.

African-American workers had been highly dependent upon central city manufacturing and retail jobs. The oldest factories were often the ones with the highest percentage of Black workers. A wide range of social and economic problems arose because the shrinking industrial economy had formed the financial backbone for the Black community. Its members often found suburban jobs inaccessible because of housing and job discrimination, lack of public transportation, or higher educational requirements than inner-city schools prepared them to meet.

Another significant social force was the growth of metropolitan area suburbs. Two reasons for that growth were the suburban housing boom, financed with federal home mortgage insurance programs and tax policies, and heavy reliance on automobiles, financed by federal support of highways. Another reason was the attractive amenities of suburban life. But racial change within cities speeded White exodus to the suburbs. Suburban housing and quality of life were the primary "pull" attracting urban Whites, but Black entry into formerly White residential areas was a major "push" encouraging many to leave. Since national policies encouraged racially selective suburbs, growing concentrations of economically displaced racial minorities arose within inner cities. This perverse situation inevitably affected efforts to improve Detroit.

Thousands of African-American families came to Northern cities during and after World War I and World War II, attracted by work in the area's industrial plants. Discrimination forced them to live in the most deteriorated sections of town. Racial barriers to better housing were lifted only slowly, and Blacks pried open previously White neighborhoods a block at a time. Because Whites refused to accept mixed neighborhoods, the arrival of Black residents led to White exodus and neighborhood instability.

Detroit's leaders could not or would not resist the tide of racial prejudice, and it influenced their decisions about public housing and neighborhood clearance. They found it difficult to attract Whites back into the inner city because of social taboos against housing integration. Their neighborhood rehabilitation programs floundered because the remaining White residents could not wait to leave their racially changing neighborhoods for more attractive suburbs. Meanwhile, lack of open housing kept Blacks pinned in cities, and city leaders alienated the increasingly restive Black community with burdensome decisions, laying the groundwork for extensive, transformational social protest.

The ultimate symbol of racial conflict was the civil disorder of the mid-1960s. A few years later, a strong mayor and a champion of the Black community took over city government. Coleman Young promised to rectify racial wrongs and to redevelop the city effectively. But even for him, the cumulative results of industrial and commercial decline, population loss, increasing poverty, and racial conflict proved difficult. He sponsored a series of redevelopment projects which brought piecemeal success but failed to heal the deep wounds that racial hatred had caused.

Early in the postwar period, one astute observer warned that it was impossible to redevelop cities without promoting social justice for racial minorities. Catherine Bauer Wurster was a creative and dedicated advocate for enlightened urban policies. In the 1950s she predicted: "To some future historian, the most significant fact about housing and city planning policy in the United States in our time may be the extent to which it promoted racial integration or conversely strengthened the pattern of discrimination and segregation."[14]

Even earlier, in 1946, Bauer had urged those attending a national planning conference to consider the racial effects of burgeoning suburban growth. She asked, "must we continue that fearful trend toward segregated one-class, one-type, one-use, one-race ant-heaps which we sometimes have the nerve to call 'planned neighborhoods'?" She told her audience that it was necessary to link redevelopment policies with broader social reforms, or risk certain failure:

All of this merely dramatizes that last illusion inherent in all the connotations of the phrase "urban redevelopment"—the notion that it can really be done on a town-by-town basis by dealing solely with blighted areas as such. If we had been thinking of urban redevelopment in dynamic terms—population movements, density, the quantity and quality of new homes, class and race relations, community and regional integration—and not just in terms of a lot of unpleasant old buildings, declining values and tax rates (the City Beautiful fallacy in reverse), we should have never thus deceived ourselves.[15]

At least one respondent at that conference protested the "pessimistic picture presented by Miss Bauer," and doubtless other planners were skeptical as well [16] but "population movements," "class and race relations," and "community and regional integration" were indeed pivotal issues affecting postwar Detroit. Not peripheral concerns, as they have seemed at times, they shaped the urban region, and they shaped the success of redevelopment.

Detroit in Context

Other authors have written case studies of American cities that discuss the two themes covered here: the effectiveness of local planning and redevelopment tools and the link between race relations and redevelopment. This book is both similar to and different from these other studies.

As mentioned above, most historical case studies of redevelopment in American cities give little attention to professional urban planners, except as a peripheral subject. Notable exceptions include Carl Abbott's study of Portland, Oregon, Christopher Silver's study of Richmond, Virginia, and John Bauman's study of Philadelphia.[17]

Abbott found that planning was a key theme in Portland's government decision-making throughout the twentieth century. City economic and political leaders tended to prefer private planning consultants. They brought in outside experts at periodic intervals to guide city development, often ignoring local planning agencies in the process. Nevertheless, planning was able to reshape the city, in part because of its manageable size and the active participation of the private sector.

Silver noted similar results in twentieth-century Richmond. There, too, dominant private interests influenced municipal planning and redevelopment decisions. Local planners failed to live up to their rich reform heritage, and their definition of the "public good" catered noticeably to the interests of local economic elites. Bauman looked at planning in Philadelphia from 1920 to 1974 mainly through the prism of public housing and urban renewal. According to his study, planners did live up to their reform heritage, but failed to block efforts to subvert their visions to the will of political and real estate interests.

The second theme, race relations, also provides important source material for several authors. Silver linked planning decisions to the desire of Richmond's White leaders to limit Black residential areas and to maintain racial segregation. He presents little evidence that city planners objected to this role. Blatantly racist planning policies in Richmond changed, instead, because of the rising voice of Black neighborhood activists and the collapse of the urban growth coalition.

John Bauman's description offered another view. Bauman presented Philadelphia's planners as visionary promoters of enlightened, well designed public housing for the poor. Although they helped consolidate the downtown, they also fought for housing for the city's low-income Black residents and encouraged residential integration. The planners became less effective in these goals as federal policies changed and the climate of racial segregation and social protest escalated.

Hirsch and Catlin documented deliberate efforts to subvert the progress of African Americans. Hirsch's study of Chicago from 1940 to 1960 highlighted the insidious nature of city leaders' schemes to isolate Black citizens in the "second ghettos" of Chicago's public housing projects. Catlin's study of Gary, Indiana, which examined the 1980s, chronicled the tribulations of planning a central city in a regional context of racial prejudice against Gary and its mayor. He demonstrated that regional racism distorted decisions about municipal planning and development, metropolitan governance, and airport site location.[18]

This study focuses on the fifty years following the closing days of World War II, allowing for a longer-range perspective than Hirsch and Catlin addressed and a more targeted time period than Abbott, Silver, and Bauman attempted to cover. Like the books by Abbott, Silver, Bauman, and Catlin, this study examines the way the profession of urban planning shaped city development. It is also similar to books by Bauman, Hirsch, and Catlin in that it examines the link between race and redevelopment. But we find the relationship among redevelopment, urban planning, and race more complex than most. Detroit's planners did not belong completely on the side of oppressor, as in Richmond, or reformer, as in Philadelphia. They actually walked back and forth between both sides. And at various times planners were themselves the victims of racial prejudice, because it so strongly counteracted the redevelopment gains they were able to make.

This book explores why Detroit's urban planners failed to "save" more than a few targeted areas of the city and how the social environment of race relations connected with their actions. This requires fresh insights into how planners approached the tasks of each era, how the racial context influenced events, and how the African-American community viewed them.

As one example, the 1960s were important not only because civil disturbances and neighborhood protests brought changes in the postwar redevelopment agenda but also because they generated important efforts in social planning and citizen empowerment, redefined the role and self-concept of professional city planners and designers, and witnessed the rise of an alternative tradition of social protest by newly hired Black urban planners. As another example, the 1980s and 1990s were important because of the cumulative effects of decades of social and economic decline, because of the revelation that a mayor's brown skin did not guarantee community-based redevelopment policy, and because both the Black electorate and the corporate elite discovered that, for all its shortcomings, planning offered a useful model for city and neighborhood improvement.

Those who are trying to improve today's cities can learn much from urban reform efforts of yesterday. Unfortunately, it is easier to describe the evolution of problems than it is to use a purposeful understanding of that evolution to create more effective solutions. Yet as one scholar has suggested, "fruitful social science must be very largely a study of what is not, a construction of hypothetical models of possible worlds which might exist if some of the alterable conditions were made different."[19]

In an attempt to be fruitful, this study of Detroit will end on a prescriptive note, suggesting two things. First, the profession of planning offers valuable skills needed to improve cities, but it will have to become a different kind of planning, one characterized by social equity, participatory strength, and tools appropriate for the challenges of today. Second, urban problem-solving requires that society develop more deliberate methods to overcome the barriers built by the ongoing effects of racial prejudice, discrimination, and disunity. Not until then will better cities be possible.

The
Optimistic
Years

I

Roots of Postwar Redevelopment   1

Near the end of World War II, American cities were seriously deteriorated. Housing built during the early part of the century was beginning to age, and central cities were showing the ill effects of middle class exodus. When Sir Ernest Simon, a British planner, visited Detroit in 1943, he saw the following:

One Sunday morning I walked less than half a mile from my hotel, in the very centre of Detroit, and saw my first "blighted" area. [I saw] a considerable proportion of open space, sometimes used for parking, sometimes covered by debris and the typical American city weed about three feet high. Roads and alleys were often unpaved and uncleansed, and there was garbage everywhere in streets and courts. We saw a man walk out along a flat roof and throw an armful of debris into the street somewhere near a garbage bin. There was no crowding on the land; there was plenty of room, but neglect and decay everywhere. A Detroit citizen described the downtown (skyscraper) centre of the city as a "desert island in a swamp of blighted areas." I saw many blighted areas afterwards, but nothing quite so bad as this district in Detroit, which is in fact one of the richest and most rapidly expanding cities in the world.[1]

That Detroit contained the most blighted area in the United States is doubtful; Philadelphia, Chicago, Baltimore, and many other cities also contained districts suffering from decay. Certainly Detroit suffered from blight, as well as other difficulties. City revenue had declined, and the city was losing commerce and industry. The middle class had begun to leave inner-city areas, and housing conditions were poor. The search had already begun for ways for the municipality to rectify some of the problems at hand; two potential solutions were public housing and regional planning. But first, what were the problems city leaders faced?

Stark Realities

One problem was the city's lack of financial resources to make municipal improvements. Detroit had gone on a capital improvement spending binge during the 1920s. Then the Great Depression and the war, following each other in breathless succession, obligated the

TABLE 1.1   POPULATION OF DETROIT, 1900 – 1950

Year	Population	Percentage Increase over Previous Decade
1900	285,704	38.8
1910	465,766	63.0
1920	993,678	113.3
1930	1,568,662	57.9
1940	1,623,452	3.5
1950	1,849,568	14.0

Sources: Carl Wells, "Proposals for Downtown Detroit" (Washington, D.C.: Urban Land Institute, 1942), p. 15; U.S. Census of Population (1950 data).

city to defer needed construction and maintenance. By the mid-1940s, past financial indiscretion and neglect of the physical infrastructure lay upon the city like a hangover. Detroit spent, on the average, $25 million a year in capital improvements from 1920 to 1933, and it increased its bond indebtedness by $299.9 million. Between 1933 and 1944, average annual expenditures for capital improvements plummeted to $3.8 million. By 1945, Detroit had only $5.5 million for annual capital improvements.[2]

Population changes made this situation even worse. The population was still growing, and would continue to grow until the 1950s, but by 1940 more middle-class people were moving out of Detroit, markedly slowing the city's rate of population growth (see table 1.1). With every improvement in transportation the middle class became more mobile. While the city's population increased by only 3.5 percent during the 1930s, the population of the urban areas adjacent to the city grew 19.3 percent.[3]

Downtown decline was a related problem. Signs of decline appeared early in the century. Between 1919 and 1929, New York City gained seven times more office space than Detroit, and Chicago gained 2.3 times more. Detroit's office construction per capita ranked last among major cities.[4] The number of people entering the central business district daily fell by 16 percent between 1925 and 1940, but the number of entering passenger cars rose. As early as 1930, 33.8 percent of passengers traveling to and from Detroit's central business district used automobiles, compared with only 21.9 percent of Chicago passengers and 20.8 percent of Philadelphia passengers. Among American cities with populations over 1,000,000, only Los Angeles was more dependent upon cars than Detroit, but Los Angeles was a relatively new city built largely during the highway era. Detroit's relative lack of public transportation placed even more burdens on its insufficient street system, and automobile dependence caused chronic traffic congestion (see fig. 1.1).[5]

Two-thirds of Detroit's central business district buildings were over fifty years old in 1940, and a high percentage of land was taken

Fig. 1.1. Congestion on Gratiot Avenue, a main thoroughfare leading to and from the central business district, during the 1941 transit strike. Courtesy Michigan Historical Collections, Bentley Historical Library, University of Michigan, George Kennedy Collection.

up by vacancies or obsolete buildings. In most areas of the city, the market value of property matched assessed value dollar for dollar. In Detroit's downtown area, market value declined to only one-half of the assessed value, indicating a severe devaluation of property. This too was related to the steady decrease of middle and upper income people living near the central business district. As the Urban Land Institute's Carl Wells explained, "people who constitute the best market for the central business district are moving farther and farther away from it." [6]

Downtown decay was a major problem, but so was industrial decline. At a 1945 national conference of city planning officials, presenters from Dayton, Miami, Newark, and New York all acknowledged that the end of the war would bring substantial employment changes. But staff in these other cities had defined the problem largely as one of rebuilding neglected physical facilities and providing jobs for returning veterans. Detroit's representatives feared most the devastation of their manufacturing sector. They calculated that 300,000 fewer people would have jobs after the war than held jobs during the war, even after women war workers left the labor force. [7]

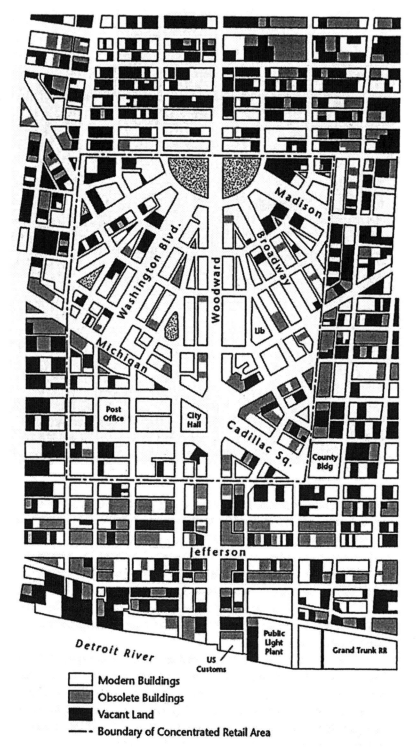

Fig. 1.2. Map of central business district, 1940, showing the extent of deteriorated property. Note the street pattern of the riverfront section at the foot of Woodward Avenue that the city later cleared to create the Civic Center. The half-circle near the top is Grand Circus Park, remnant of an early, plaza-based city plan. Carl Wells, "Proposal for Downtown Detroit" (Washington, D.C.: Urban Land Institute, 1942), p. 8. Courtesy Urban Land Institute.

Detroit's manufacturing sector was in a serious state of decline. Fifty percent of the city's labor force was employed in manufacturing, making industry and the location of industrial plants "a basic factor in the pattern of the whole city."[8] Yet some older industrial firms had already moved out of the inner city, further reducing the tax base.[9] Almost half of the area's manufacturing employment was located outside of the city limits of Detroit. Few tracts of undeveloped land suitable for industry survived within the city, and those that did were too small for practical use. A 1944 planning report concluded that "if decentralization is not to be accelerated, areas for future industrial development must be designated, and some means for land assembly found."[10] This was the beginning of an ongoing effort to graft industrial needs onto redevelopment actions, an effort that did not have practical implications for the city until the early 1950s.

The connection between financial decline and problems in the commercial and industrial sectors was obvious. City leaders needed to support the downtown and buttress the industrial sector in order to improve the tax base and protect local jobs. An important part of the strategy was to eliminate areas of concentrated deteriorated housing. These areas contributed to central business district decline and cost the city more in expenditures than they produced in tax revenue.[11]

The housing problem was, of course, more than one of lost revenue: inner-city residents suffered from chronic overcrowding and physical deterioration of their environment. The end of the war worsened the situation, because the return of veterans and pent up demand created a housing shortage. But not all suffered equally. At the end of 1944, over half of all dwelling units occupied by the city's African-American residents were substandard, although only 14 percent of White dwelling units were substandard.[12] By the end of 1948, 43 percent of Black veterans' families in Detroit lived "doubled-up or in rented rooms, trailers or tourist cabins." Although this number was not quite as bad as in other cities—53 percent in Cleveland and New York City and 51 percent in Newark—it was bad enough.[13]

In addition to these problems, race relations in the city had become volatile. In the race riot of 1943, White crowds attacked innocent Blacks, Blacks fought back, and battling mobs took over the streets. Thirty-five people lay dead when the riot ended. Twenty-nine of the dead were Black, and policemen had killed seventeen of them. In a post-riot analysis, Walter White of the national office of the National Association for the Advancement of Colored People (NAACP) blamed the riot on prejudice within the police department, conflict over war-related jobs, and the pressures of inadequate housing and residential segregation.[14]

How was the City of Detroit going to address all of the problems of deteriorating community facilities, loss of the middle class, downtown decline, clogged streets, industrial exodus, inadequate housing, racial conflict? Mayor Edward Jeffries, Jr., began to develop a strategy. Spurred by evidence that the federal government awarded public works funds to those municipalities with plans in hand and by the Michigan legislature's appropriation of money to support public works planning at the end of the war, Mayor Jeffries organized a special postwar improvements committee. He appointed Planning Director George F. Emery as chair of the postwar improvements committee. He directed all city departments to give the committee lists of capital improvements they wanted funded.

In 1944 the mayor's postwar improvement committee issued "Post-War Improvements to Make Your Detroit a Finer City in Which to Live and Work." It is from a phrase in the title of this report that we take part of the subtitle of this book: *Planning a Finer City in Postwar Detroit*. The main purpose of the report was to inventory necessary improvements in the city's physical stock, particularly those that were the responsibility of government, but in doing so it provided a snapshot portrait of how city leaders planned to improve Detroit after the austerity years of World War II. The committee indicated that, of all the projects, "none is of greater importance to Detroiters" than a proposed system of expressways and wider streets, a statement that would unfortunately come true. But the plan included other items as well.

A new civic center would "symbolize our dynamic Detroit," anchor the central business district, and house the city's departments. A new city airport, a new medical center, new "places to play," and additional community facilities were also important. Although few strategies addressed industrial decline directly, public improvements would provide a better city "in which to live and work," and construction projects would supply much-needed jobs. Building more public housing was also an important part of the agenda, according to the committee, because the war had interrupted the city's efforts to house poor citizens.[15] In future years, the city carried out the report's suggested improvements by means of an array of plans and activities.

In addition to postwar city improvements, Jeffries had a regional strategy. As mayor of the metropolitan area's central city, Jeffries was defense coordinator for the Metropolitan Detroit Defense Area. The Regional Defense Planning Committee was formed in February 1942 to advise the mayor. Represented on the committee were housing commissions, planning commissions, special authorities, bureaus, and municipal offices from four area counties. The committee consulted about ways to provide adequate housing, utilities, and transportation to serve area armament plants. This dialogue laid the groundwork for rethinking regional relationships and even the city's boundaries; Jeffries soon appointed key staff to explore the possibility of creating satellite cities, which would allow Detroit to expand into the suburbs.[16]

Of all the problems previously listed—deteriorating community facilities, middle-class flight, downtown decline, industrial exodus, inadequate housing, racial conflict—the only one not yet addressed was racial conflict. For this problem, Jeffries's approach was extremely modest.

In the wake of 1941 racial skirmishes, the Common Council and an emergency committee had urged the mayor to create a permanent committee and give it authority to attack racial discrimination problems. Six days after the 1943 riot, the mayor finally created a permanent committee. Although practically powerless, the Mayor's Interracial Committee set up a division of labor within city government, freeing other, more traditional departments—with the notable exception of the housing commission, which supervised public housing—to conduct their affairs with little conscious thought about racial matters. For most of its existence, that committee only investigated discrimination complaints. Later in this book I will describe the results of the efforts begun by Mayor Jeffries and by his postwar public improvement committee, and I will indicate how the racial context influenced those efforts. The remainder of this chapter, however, will focus on public housing and regional planning, two areas of reform that had strong potential in the 1940s. If either of these two movements had succeeded, the City of Detroit would be far different from what it is today.

The program that advocates of public housing reform first proposed ended up much different from what they had hoped. Reformers wanted to improve the lives of low-income urban residents and simultaneously revitalize inner-city areas. Housing for defense industry workers, known as "war housing," and more permanent housing built by local public housing authorities, known as "public housing," did improve many lives in the short term. In the long term, however, the program became a potent tool for the enforced segregation of the city's African-American population.

The second reform movement, regional planning, aimed to reconfigure the urban region. American proponents of the concept argued that lasting reform could only come through new styles of metropolitan settlement and governance. Influenced by these ideas, Detroit planned to set up satellite cities by purchasing outlying land or annexing adjoining territory. But the lack of consistent support for regional restructuring and the growing number of municipalities doomed their efforts to failure.

Housing the Masses

The first major reform movement was the public housing program. This movement failed to solve cities' problems because the federal government did not support it consistently, because the program suffered from internal dilemmas and external opposition, and because cities misused public housing to perpetuate racial segregation and oppression.

Federal construction of housing for low-income people appeared to be a good path to urban reform because it directly attacked the problem of decrepit housing. Several people lobbied hard for such a program. Notable among these were Edith Elmer Wood, who wrote

Fig. 1.3. Boys playing on construction site of Brewster Homes, a housing project built for African Americans and located just north of the central business district (ca. 1939). Bentley Historical Library, University of Michigan, Josephine Gomon Collection.

one of the first critical studies of housing in the United States, and Catherine Bauer, social reformer and strategist. Bauer was particularly adept at organizing a national network of unions and college-educated women to adopt public housing as their social cause. Another boost for the program was the Great Depression, which threw millions of people out of work, pressuring the federal government to build housing for "a new, submerged middle class."[17]

The Housing Act of 1937 allowed local housing authorities to acquire land, construct low-income units, and maintain them. Some of the earliest public housing projects reflected commendable principles of community building, including low-density townhouses and walk-up units, and close access to recreation and community service facilities. But soon the original coalition that had lobbied for public housing fell apart. White unionists, benefiting from the mortgage insurance programs of the Federal Housing Administration (FHA) and Veterans' Administration (VA), moved to suburban single-family housing. The influence of reformers such as Wood and Bauer declined, and the quality of public housing plummeted.[18] Financial support for public housing vacillated widely; in some years, Congress appropriated no funds at all.[19]

Detroit's experiences unfolded in the context of these national events. In 1933 the City of Detroit established the Detroit Housing Commission, its local public housing authority. When the Public Works Administration approved site construction in 1937, work began on two projects: Brewster, near the center of the city, and Parkside, in the northeast section. The first units built were clean and sturdy, a remarkable improvement for those who had lived in dilapidated tenements. Rents were reasonable, pegged at an amount affordable for the average war worker, and major sites were located near the central business district or scattered throughout the city near major industrial employment centers. At Brewster Homes, one of the first project sites, 701 fortunate Black families moved into the first units in 1938. The first few years brought enthusiastic lawn care and cooperative efforts by tenants to furnish recreational facilities and organize social events. On an outlying site, Parkside Homes offered comparable benefits to 785 low-income White families. Both project sites soon expanded, and the city built additional public housing complexes.[20]

Unfortunately, the city could not build enough units to meet housing needs. In 1938, Carl Bradt, secretary-director of the housing commission, reported that the city contained 58,061 substan-

Fig. 1.4. Brewster Homes: playground in an area located near the original two-story "rowhouses" and walk-up apartments, looking toward the Black commercial district along Hastings Street, 1946. All businesses on Hastings were eventually razed for the construction of the Chrysler Expressway. Bentley Historical Library, University of Michigan, Emil Lorch Collection.

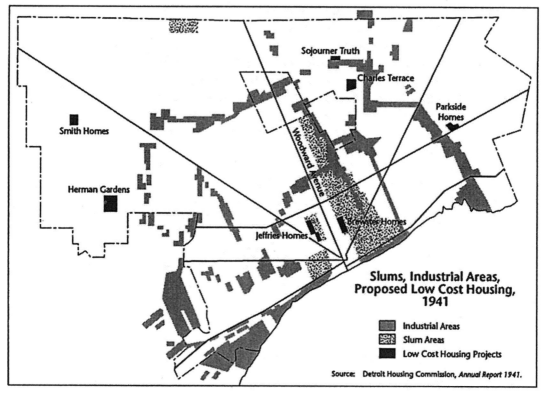

Sojourner Truth

Charles Terrace

Parkside
Homes

Smith Homes

Woodward Avenue

Herman Gardens

Brewster Homes

Jeffries Homes

**Slums, Industrial Areas,
Proposed Low Cost Housing,
1941**

Industrial Areas
Slum Areas
Low Cost Housing Projects

Source: Detroit Housing Commission, *Annual Report 1941.*

Fig. 1.5. Slums, industrial areas, and public housing in the 1940s. Several public housing projects were located close to industrial areas, in order to house workers. At first, those projects open to African-American families included only Brewster, Jeffries, and Sojourner Truth Homes. Permission, Detroit Department of Planning and Development.

dard units. A 1940 analysis uncovered close to 70,000 substandard dwelling units, with 48,000 of them housing low-income families.[21] Wartime placed even more demands on the housing stock, as workers flooded into Detroit, "the industrial defense capital of the nation."[22] At the end of 1942, George Emery, the director of the Detroit City Plan Commission, calculated anticipated housing needs. Federal agencies expected a total of 96,000 migrants to move into the region. With conversion of private homes, new housing financed with FHA backing, and projected public housing, the area would still lack 29,000 family dwelling units.[23]

Between April 1940 and the summer of 1945 more than 250,000 people moved into the Detroit area, including Wayne, Macomb, Oakland, and Washtenaw counties. Many of these people were the workers and families of workers employed at Ford Motor Company's Willow Run "bomber plant."[24] The results were predictable. Desperate families doubled up and accepted residence in unacceptable dwellings. It became more difficult to build public housing; there was no place to put people during construction. Detroit's commission decided to build on vacant land adjacent to existing projects and to place new projects on outlying vacant land.[25] It built Frederick Douglass Homes, the largest of several extensions to the Brewster Homes projects, and the Jeffries Homes close to the central business district. All other permanent housing projects of the era, including the Parkside, Charles Terrace, Herman Gardens, and John

Fig. 1.6. Aerial photograph of Parkside Homes, built for White tenants only, early 1940s. Courtesy Burton Historical Collection, Detroit Public Library, Detroit News Air Photo.

Smith Homes, went into outlying areas of the city. (See figs. 1.5, 1.6.)

Building public housing on vacant land in outlying sites caused another, very serious problem which arose because of racial segregation. Detroit's African Americans were rigidly segregated in central areas of the city; housing on sites outside of the central core was not open to them. Since the nineteenth century, their major residential areas lay to the immediate north of the central business district and east of Woodward Avenue, the city's great commercial thoroughfare.[26] These areas suffered from overcrowding and poor housing conditions, yet because of the perverse effects of enforced segregation, landlords could demand and get high rents for bad housing.[27] (See figs. 1.5, 1.7.)

Pent up demand from the African-American community led to pressure on surrounding White neighborhoods to "turn" racially. Nearby White working class neighborhoods reacted violently when Black communities spread. This was one of the points of tension leading to the 1943 riot. Long after that riot, White residents continued to attack Black "intrusion" into White neighborhoods. This undercurrent of White violence was a hallmark of urban racial conflict during the war and for some years afterward. Arnold Hirsch, writing about similar violence in Chicago, called these sporadic outbursts "a pattern of chronic urban guerrilla warfare."[28]

This was the social context within which Detroit's housing commission had to build public housing. It is small wonder that the city's 1942 Sojourner Truth housing project provoked violent reaction. Frustrated by lack of housing, civil rights leaders lobbied the federal government to designate a new defense housing project for

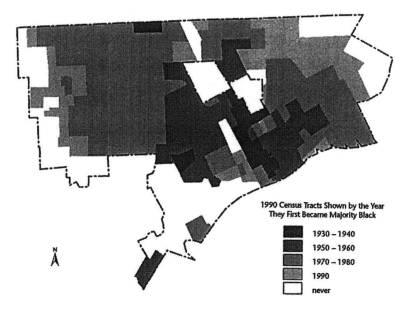

Fig. 1.7. Growth in majority African-American areas, 1930–90. Early settlement patterns forced Blacks to move into the areas designated, according to figure 1.5, as "slums." Courtesy Southeast Michigan Council of Governments.

1990 Census Tracts Shown by the Year
They First Became Majority Black

1930–1940
1950–1960
1970–1980
1990
never

Blacks. Amazingly, civil rights leaders "won" Black occupancy for a site located in a White neighborhood. They weathered strong opposition from neighbors, a U.S. congressman, and the majority of the housing commission. When the first few Black families tried to move into the project in early 1942, they met first irate picketers and then a riotous crowd. The incident proved to be only the first spark of what would become more serious racial clashes, including the 1943 riot.[29]

A less violent but similar reaction came from central business district interests, who tried to use public housing to replace Black residents with White. The Wider Woodward Association—a collection of merchants, business owners, and real estate interests—wanted Whites to occupy a new public housing project located close to the central business district. They hoped that a housing project open only to Whites would reverse Black encroachment. Black leaders opposed clearing out low-income members of their community to make room for low-income Whites. These leaders instead lobbied for opening all projects to all races.[30]

The battle between integration and segregation did not last long. The housing commission quickly formalized its informal policy of racial segregation through a strange bargain dreamed up by the city's first housing director. Ironically, Director Josephine Gomon had been criticized for her apparently "radical" ties to the unions.[31] At a critical moment, however, Gomon engineered a decidedly conservative compromise. She met with local Black leaders and told them bluntly that they would have to accept either a segregated public housing project or none at all. Desperate for housing, they chose a segregated project.

Fig. 1.8. Eleanor Roosevelt, during a 1935 visit to Detroit, with Josephine Gomon, early city housing director and designer of segregated neighborhood policy. Bentley Historical Library, University of Michigan, Josephine Gomon Collection.

Gomon then devised an infamous policy: "No housing project shall change the racial characteristics of a neighborhood." Projects built in Black neighborhoods would only accept Black tenants, while projects built in White neighborhoods would only accept Whites. In 1943 the housing commission formally adopted the segregationist policy. In vain, civil rights leaders collected letters and news clippings from around the country showing that integrated defense and public housing were working elsewhere.[32] Not until 1952 did the housing commission rescind its policy. Not until a 1955 order from the U.S. Court of Appeals did the commission claim to begin assigning tenants without regard to race. Years after that, the city's Community Relations Commission (descendant of Jeffries's interracial committee) found deliberate segregation practices in public housing.[33]

The city continued to build public housing in outlying, White neighborhoods, housing that was closed to African Americans even

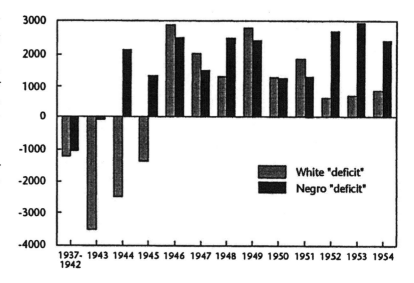

Fig. 1.9. Public housing deficit chart shows that during 1937–54, the years for which the city kept records by race, the number of eligible Blacks applying for public housing far exceeded their number of placements. In contrast, for several years a surplus of available housing existed for White family applicants. Courtesy Detroit Department of Planning and Development.

though their housing crisis was most critical. An observer writing in one of Detroit's Black newspapers claimed that "Negro housing and resulting racial tension are the Number One problem of metropolitan Detroit."[34]

From 1937 to 1954, the Detroit Housing Commission published data on housing applications and placement by race. Throughout this period, as figure 1.9 shows, the number of eligible applications that the commission received from Blacks far exceeded the number of their placements in commission dwelling units. Whites did not suffer such a "deficit," however. Only during the years when veterans returned from World War II did the number of White applications far exceed the number of White placements.

The city's response to the need was simply to reinforce patterns of racial segregation. In 1950 Detroit added more public housing units onto the already large inner-city complexes, Brewster-Douglass and Edward Jeffries Homes. These units became concentrated foci of poverty. As public housing declined in quality, so did community life. The city abandoned the architecture of earlier phases and began stacking housing units on top of each other in elevator buildings. This style of housing was cheaper but severely challenged low-income families, who could monitor neither children playing outside nor unwelcome intruders. The federal government compounded problems by failing to provide sufficient funds for maintenance. Government income limits forced successful wage-earners to move out, discouraging ambition and leaving only the poorest families. Eventually, relaxed tenant rules allowed problem-ridden households to move into the units and stay there. Thus, inner-city projects became warehouses of despair.

Detroit's experiences with public housing were repeated throughout the country. Chicago's council, controlled by White ethnics, assured that all sites built after 1949 were located in ghetto areas. Like

Detroit, Chicago tended to expand existing public housing projects rather than build upon new sites. Gradually Chicago built a "second ghetto," vast tracts of gargantuan, multistoried public housing. These projects, or prison cities, practically incarcerated the city's low-income Black population and preserved new redevelopment sites for middle-class residents.[35]

The story of Philadelphia's experience with public housing was just as sad. Philadelphia housers and planners had first envisioned public housing as an integral part of redevelopment. Philadelphia's first projects also featured rowhouses rather than multistoried monoliths. But redevelopment and public housing became intertwined in what author John Bauman calls "the invidious process of ghetto building." Money constraints and the lack of vacant sites in Black neighborhoods pressured the city to build elevator buildings. Persistent obstacles to integration and high-problem households soured the dream of enlightened public housing.[36]

Chronic housing shortages, relocation problems, and racial conflict all tempered dreams that public housing could improve Detroit. Congressional underfunding killed the vision. Great Britain and other European countries constructed large housing developments for their working and middle classes; the United States grudgingly provided relatively few housing units, first for the "deserving poor," and then for the poorest of the poor. Financial neglect reduced the quality of American public housing, which local officials

Fig. 1.10. Jeffries Homes scene, July 1957, showing difference in scale of rowhouses and walk-up apartments, built first, and high-rise units, built later. The high-rise units reinforced isolation by race and income and reduced informal supervision over children and youth. Bentley Historical Collection, University of Michigan, Emil Lorch Collection.

misused to confine the poor and solidify ghetto lines. Simultaneously, the federal government made suburban homes easily affordable to White working-class families. Its FHA and VA mortgage subsidy programs financed a mass exodus outward even as they discriminated against Black home seekers. Expanding but segregated suburbs became the norm.[37]

Regional Planning

The second reform initiative to reconfigure the American metropolis also faltered. In Detroit, as elsewhere, several earnest reformers tried to develop new ways to reorganize the metropolitan area but found their pathway blocked.

If this movement had succeeded, American cities and their regions would be far different from what they are today. Effective regional planning could have helped forestall many contemporary problems. It could have controlled the constant dispersion of industry, commerce, and tax-paying citizens from the central city. It could have created more unified metropolitan areas, characterized by cooperation rather than conflict.

The term "regional planning" has several definitions. One definition is planning either for a multistate or similarly large region or for a metropolitan area that includes several localities. But as used in the 1930s and 1940s, the term often referred to bolder schemes for restructuring the metropolis. Advocates aimed to construct new communities, of limited population size, in selected areas outside of existing cities. These communities were supposed to contain semi-autonomous economies, and thus reduce the need for long commutes. Carefully planned on a regional scale, they would have allowed a metropolis to grow in an orderly fashion rather than develop as fragmented, competitive sets of municipalities.

One of the earliest advocates for metropolitan restructuring was the Regional Planning Association of America, a small but influential group of like minds who began to meet in 1923. Members Clarence Stein, Henry Wright, Benton MacKaye, Edith Wood, Catherine Bauer, and Lewis Mumford promoted such diverse causes as townless highways, the Appalachian Trail, public housing, community planning, garden cities, and socially conscious architecture. Lewis Mumford was particularly active in promoting garden cities, as defined by Great Britain's Ebenezer Howard, and regional restructuring, as described by Scotland's Patrick Geddes. Mumford urged federal and local governments to resist the process of amorphous decentralization and to channel growth more deliberately.[38]

Ebenezer Howard, one of Mumford's ideological mentors, first proposed garden cities in 1898. Howard despised the overcrowding and disorganization of large industrial central cities such as London. His new urban invention was the orderly construction of new cities limited in size to just over 30,000 people, and surrounded with a permanent greenbelt of open land. Residents would work within the city, reducing the need to commute. The municipality would own all land, lease it to residents, and use the profits to support community facilities and social welfare programs for the elderly, widows, and orphans. Howard built two prototype garden cities, hoping to show the practicality of his utopian idea.[39]

Several governments and private developers adopted parts of the garden city model. Their variations were called new towns, satellite cities, greenbelt communities, or greenbelt cities. Most versions did not implement Howard's ideas about community land ownership or social welfare. Imitations of the real thing often became no more than pleasant residential subdivisions, a far cry from the economically self-sufficient cities Howard promoted. But in modified form, Howard's basic concept for garden cities was the foundation of Great Britain's post–World War II "new town" policy.

In the 1930s, as part of Franklin Roosevelt's New Deal, the United States came close to adopting garden cities as a model for urban growth. Rexford Tugwell administered a greenbelt city program based on Howard's ideas. Yet Tugwell's Resettlement Administration only managed to build three small greenbelt communities in Maryland, Ohio, and Wisconsin, in part because of an adverse U.S. Supreme Court ruling.[40] The Roosevelt administration did encourage other forms of regional planning. The Urbanism Committee of the National Resources Committee urged central cities to expand their boundaries through annexation.[41] The federal government promoted planning agencies set up for multistate river basins, such as the Tennessee Valley Authority (TVA). Although the TVA did not live up to expectations, it gave respectability to the concept of planning beyond municipal and state boundaries.[42]

These were bold, sweeping visions of regional planning. They aimed to divert new urban growth into planned, self-sufficient communities, or to consolidate urban regions under one government. The push soon came, however, to develop milder models of regional planning.

Detroit's push in this direction came in the form of a crisis at the gargantuan bomber plant at Willow Run. Ford Motor Company's Willow Run plant was built almost literally in the middle of nowhere, 3 miles east of the town of Ypsilanti and 28 miles west of Detroit.[43] Since many workers lived in Detroit, the necessarily long commute led to massive road congestion, because local roads were completely inadequate for the job.

Employment at Willow Run exploded from just under 2,490 at the beginning of 1942 to a peak of 42,331 in mid-1943. Long before that date the housing shortage reached critical levels. The government eventually built 5,000 "war housing" units for defense workers, but as noted by two outraged sociologists who studied the situation, Lowell Carr and James Stermer, the unlucky others had to live "wherever they darned pleased in trailers, chicken coops, or tents."

Many families had to cope with poor sanitation facilities and unsafe water supplies. On one occasion county health authorities dramatized the problem "by dropping purple dye into a particularly choice collection of outdoor toilets and then returning a few hours later to pump purple 'drinking water' from the nearest family wells."[44]

Some good things came out of the experience. The situation at Willow Run—which one federal official described as "the worst mess in the whole United States"—became so bad that after 1942 the federal National Housing Agency routinely provided temporary "war housing" at newly established munitions factories and shipyards.[45] The other result was that municipalities in the Detroit metropolitan community began to consult about Willow Run and other issues of mutual concern. This was the genesis of Mayor Jeffries's Regional Defense Planning Committee.[46] That committee was the first of a series of regional planning groups and coordinating committees, most of which conducted studies and fostered cooperation.

The regional defense committee could have made bolder regional planning schemes unlikely. Nevertheless, one proposal emerged shortly after the defense committee began to consult. Detroit's planners had discussed several metropolitan reconstruction schemes when they began to prepare for the city's new master plan in 1942. At that time, as an exercise in creative thinking, they laid out what the city would look like if they followed the alternative recommendations offered by Frank Lloyd Wright, Ebenezer Howard, Thomas Adams, and Clarence Stein.[47] But it was a prominent labor union that pushed the city to develop satellite townsites surrounded by permanent greenbelts, based on Howard's garden city idea.

The International Union of the United Automobile, Aircraft and Agricultural Implement Workers of America (UAW) proposed that the city construct five satellite cities outside of its existing corporate limits. They proposed that a permanent greenbelt of land, held in trust for recreational or agricultural use, surround each new city. The union noted that several European cities had already purchased outlying lands: Stockholm owned five times the area of the city proper outside its corporate limits, and Helsinki, Oslo, Copenhagen, Berlin, and Zurich had each made major acquisitions. Furthermore, the British Parliament was at that time considering new towns as the basic land policy for postwar reconstruction of Great Britain.[48]

Detroit's Mayor Jeffries urged the planning staff to explore the possibilities. As the planners reported in the first progress report on "city expansion," uncontrolled fringe development would eventually cause problems. Not only was the city losing tax base and "citizen leadership," but at some point, staff expected, it would have to "step in and clean up the haphazard mess" caused by unplanned suburban growth.

The planning staff recommended that the city develop one or more greenbelt communities in undeveloped areas. They found two potential annexation sites, to the west and north of the city, in

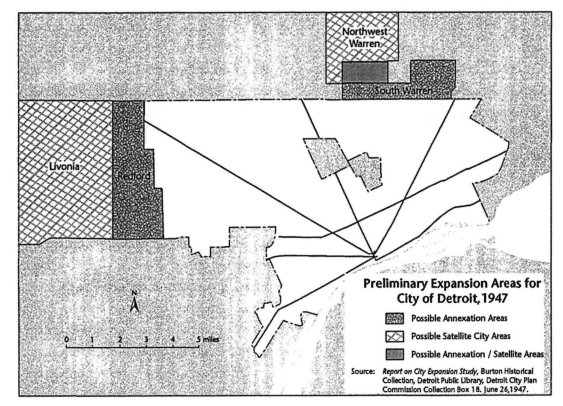

Fig. 1.11. This map shows potential expansion areas that the city's planners recommended for additional annexation or for development of satellite cities in the late 1940s. Permission, Detroit Department of Planning and Development.

what are now the cities of Redford and Warren. Settlements at these sites could easily accommodate 294,000 more people, they suggested. Satellite city sites, in what are now Livonia and Warren, could accommodate 244,000. Detroit could then keep people and commerce that it would otherwise lose, and gain much-needed large open tracts for industrial expansion. Such a policy could also facilitate "soundly planned," stable communities rather than unplanned, mushroom growth. (See fig. 1.11.)[49]

Detroit's efforts to develop satellite cities was one of the first indications that city tools did not match city needs. Detroit legal counsel found that the union proposal for satellite cities went beyond the current authority of the city and would require enabling action by the state legislature, perhaps even a state constitutional amendment.[50] Mayor Jeffries asked the planning commission to continue its research, but eventually the project died.

The heart of the problem was state law. Because of U.S. constitutional law, cities have only those powers which their states choose to give them. Michigan set up home rule laws which facilitated incorporation and limited annexation. The seminal act in Michigan dated back to 1909, but this was amended several times, in 1929, 1937, and 1939.[51] It was largely because of this legislation that the City of Detroit's boundaries stopped expanding in 1926 (see fig. 1.12). As territories surrounding the city incorporated, it became increasingly difficult to enlarge the city.

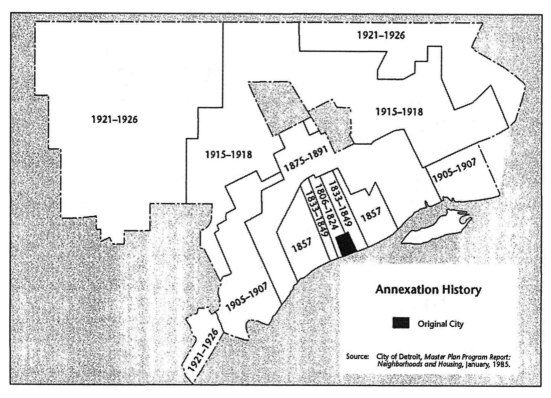

Figure contents:

1921–1926

1921–1926

1915–1918

1915–1918

1875–1891

1833–1849
1806–1824
1833–1849

1857

1857

1905–1907

1905–1907

1921–1926

Annexation History

◼ Original City

Source: City of Detroit, *Master Plan Program Report: Neighborhoods and Housing*, January, 1985.

Fig. 1.12. Actual annexation pattern for the City of Detroit, which shows no new growth after 1926, and thus no chance to retain tax base or keep decentralizing populace within city boundaries. Permission, Detroit Department of Planning and Development.

It would have required a major legislative campaign to change state law. Such a campaign would have been very difficult for Mayor Jeffries, whose political reputation had suffered from conflicts over public housing and the race riot of 1943. Jeffries could not save his own mayoral position, much less launch a territorial campaign. By the time the planners issued their final "city expansion" report in the fall of 1947, Jeffries was only warming the mayor's seat until 1948, when Eugene Van Antwerp, a man with no recorded interest in the satellite cities or annexation proposals, won the office.[52]

The issues of annexation and metropolitan governance came up time and time again in subsequent years. In 1967 Mayor Jerome Cavanagh ordered city planners to study the possibility of annexing a suburban satellite in an area ten miles from Detroit. The new community would have housed up to 100,000, carving out from 3 to 9 square miles from Northville and Plymouth Townships. The city already owned two major parcels of this land, including that on which the Detroit House of Corrections stood. The plan failed because of state annexation laws and because the city did not have the money to pursue it without federal help. A short-lived and underfunded federal "new town" program fizzled in the 1970s.[53]

The difficulty of annexation haunted Northern cities for years to come. The regional reconstruction schemes of the 1930s had little chance in the national political context. Yet with annexation, cities could have created buffers against their own decline. By the 1970s, comparisons of those American cities that had grown geographically and those that had not showed clearly that expanding cities kept their tax base. American cities in the South and West were able to annex new territory, but Northern state laws made incorporation easy and annexation difficult.[54]

Detroit abandoned the idea of satellite cities and settled into "active support" of the regional planning commission, created from the remnants of the wartime regional advisory committee. The commission had only research, analysis, and advisory functions, with no power to regulate or control. Its successors offered valuable services to the region, but these were a far cry from metropolitan governance. One succinct statement summarizes the limitations of postwar regional planning from the perspective of the central city. In 1956 Detroit's planning director, Charles Blessing, responded to a man who had asked what the city was doing about "urban sprawl." Blessing described the city's efforts to keep residents and industry and noted its support for the regional planning commission. Apparently the main value of the regional commission, however, was that it "has been very successful in getting the many suburban communities to cooperate in meeting their common problems."[55]

Tempered Visions

Both public housing and regional planning were good ideas that turned out to be extremely difficult to implement. City politicians, commissioners, and staff had to fight against the considerable handicap of poor federal policies and inadequate implementation techniques. With public housing, they also confronted early effects of racial hostility. In chapter 3, we will revisit the lingering problems caused by the forcible segregation of, and uneven federal and local support for, Detroit's public housing program.

Detroit's mayor and planners tried to find ways to expand the boundaries of the central city, but could not do so with existing state legislation. Mayor Jeffries's weak political position left him unable to pursue necessary legislative changes in the 1940s, and conditions had only grown more difficult by the time Mayor Cavanagh proposed an updated satellite city proposal in the 1960s. As in other Northern states, annexation and home rule legislation hemmed Detroit into a confined geographic area. There it remained, vulnerable to the flight of people and commerce.

One of the most eloquent statements of the direction American cities should take after World War II came from the UAW. The union warned that low-income housing and regional planning were tightly interconnected. According to their 1944 "Memorandum on Postwar Urban Housing," the country needed to create "an adequate, economically sound and socially desirable living environment" for its citizens.[56] The memorandum labeled housing the key to creating such an environment, but it cautioned against indiscriminately tearing down substandard housing. The need for housing, slum clearance, and regional planning were intimately tied together:

In the early postwar period there may be a clamor to "do something" about slum clearance right away and let the rest of the program wait awhile "until we can get around to it." Undertaking a slum *clearance program* without the guidance of a *master plan for the entire urban area* is like starting out on a long trip into unfamiliar territory without a road map. Without an extensive program of *home building* for low income groups, slum clearance simply cannot function effectively.[57] [Emphasis in original]

According to the union group, the proper approach would be to build as much low-income housing as was necessary *before* clearing out dilapidated housing, and to locate much of that housing in new, planned communities on "inexpensive outlying land." To create healthy American cities, it was necessary to plan for the orderly growth of the entire metropolitan area.[58]

No appropriate regional body existed to implement such a regional strategy. According to federal legislation, each municipality could choose to participate or not to participate in the public housing program. Many suburbs chose not to participate. Each local public housing authority maintained control only over sites within its boundaries. It would have taken some form of regional government to do things any differently, but political and legislative realities made this impossible.

As the UAW had suggested, subsidized low-income housing—open to all races—ideally should have been established on a regional basis. Then the government could have built new housing for low-income residents on vacant land throughout the region before clearing housing in the inner city. A regional plan could have guided all construction, with full consideration given to community services and affordable transportation. Failing this regional approach, smaller housing projects should have been dispersed throughout the central city, without racial segregation, and with enlightened construction and design so as to provide a healthy living environment and avoid the stigma which came to haunt public housing in later years. Failing this, at least public housing should not have been used for perverse purposes such as racial segregation. Unfortunately, all the ideal situations failed, and the surviving remnant of the dream became in some ways more of a problem than the decrepit housing it replaced.

Postwar Planning 2

Obviously, the visions of regional restructuring and humane public housing did not come to pass. The satellite cities–annexation option was practically dead in the North, and signs of life were already fading for public housing. Municipal leaders turned to two interconnected devices for city improvement. The first of these was city planning, a professional activity that promised to lay out the physical framework for a rebuilt Detroit. The second was redevelopment, a process of clearance and reconstruction.

In the 1940s, the city created local implementation tools that would last for decades. Detroit planned to use its new master plan to control growth and direct public and private investment. It also planned to launch a locally financed redevelopment strategy, independent of potential federal legislation. As the city responded to the realities of its political economy, it laid the groundwork for a more elaborate effort to redevelop the city.

City planning seemed especially promising. Municipal leaders saw planning as a way to improve Detroit's infrastructure and bolster the declining residential and economic sectors. City planners, believing strongly in the efficacy of traditional planning tools, expected to make a positive impact on the central city. They never had that bold, swaggering confidence again. For a brief period, planners emerged as the new professional heroes, guides to a better society, experts in saving cities from their own decay.

During this period city leaders also began to conceptualize a program for redevelopment that was, for the first time, independent of public housing construction. They helped create a state law giving localities the legal authority to acquire and clear land and offer it for reconstruction. In the process, they laid the groundwork for a policy haunted by social inequity.

Planning the City

Efforts to use urban planning to improve the City of Detroit had been made before World War II, but the results were mixed. In fact, the whole field of urban planning, a relatively new profession, not yet firmly defined, had been in a state of flux for years. As Harland Bartholomew complained in 1932, urban planning had tended to leap from one phase to another, first emphasizing the City Beautiful, then zoning, then street and traffic planning, then regional planning. These phases were not random, but related somewhat to changes in conditions and somewhat to changes in the profession's perspective of its role in alleviating those conditions. At various times those in control of cities—leaders of business and industry, as assuredly as political leaders—needed to remove different barriers to production, circulation, and freedom of commercial enterprise. The only consistent trend is that planning became increasingly identified as an important component of municipal reform.[1]

Planning had received national support under President Franklin Roosevelt and his New Deal administration. Tugwell's greenbelt city program, the National Resources Planning Board, and the Tennessee Valley Authority were three manifestations of that support. At the local level, however, planning had become more dispensable during the hard times of the Great Depression. In 1932, the U.S. Department of Commerce issued a list of 828 American cities with planning departments, but a large proportion of these agencies were inactive.[2]

In the 1940s, local planning still had only tenuous support. Walter Blucher, executive director of the American Society of Planning Officials (ASPO), testified about the need for postwar planning before the U.S. House of Representatives in 1944. He described an ASPO survey which showed that almost half of responding members felt that "little or no" recognition existed locally that planning was a necessary part of local government.[3] Another example of the slow growth of support for planning was the skeptical reception prominent planner Alfred Bettman met during the same congressional hearings. Bettman had to argue defensively for master planning as an important component of any program of postwar improvement.[4]

The position of planning in the City of Detroit was hardly better than it was in the rest of the country. According to some criteria, it was much worse. The city had commissioned five city plans between 1900 and 1918. Yet a 1927 publication called these plans "interesting from a historical standpoint but worthless for other purposes" and complained that "they now occupy valuable storage space in the city garage."[5] Creation of the Detroit City Plan Commission (DCPC) in 1919 led to a number of useful products, including a 1919 "building zone plan" and an officially adopted master plan of major "thorofares" in 1925.[6] But Detroit lagged far behind other cities in adopting a comprehensive plan or a zoning ordinance. The Detroit Common Council did not approve a zoning ordinance until 1940, after twenty-two years of effort, and it did not publish a complete master plan until 1951.

Detroit Embraces Planning

The story of why it took Detroit so long to get a zoning ordinance helps explain why zoning and antiblight action became so important in the 1940s. Detroit's lack of strong planning tools in the period before 1940 and revival of planning in the years following 1940 were alternate sides of the same coin.

Zoning had become a popular legal tool for controlling land use. New York City established a zoning ordinance in 1916, and the U.S. Department of Commerce promoted a model state zoning enabling act beginning in 1922. A zoning ordinance designated appropriate areas for residential, commercial, or industrial land use, and regulated construction within these areas. Zoning was therefore a powerful tool for shaping new growth, particularly if linked with a comprehensive or master plan for future land use. By 1940, nearly every state had a zoning ordinance in at least one of its cities, and three-fourths of the nation's urban population lived in zoned communities.[7]

Detroit lagged far behind in this movement. Studies for a zoning ordinance began in 1919, but progress was delayed because of the lack of state enabling legislation (finally passed in 1921) and because of a rapid series of annexations, each one of which made previous draft zoning maps obsolete. When planners finally prepared new maps and a proposed ordinance for the council's consideration, they faced strong antizoning agitation from opponents interested in keeping up land speculation. These opponents called zoning regulation Prussian and socialistic, among other epithets.

At that time, the 1920s, new subdivisions within city limits were so popular that plots were sometimes sold out immediately. Downtown business became increasingly valuable, as common wisdom held that each new subdivision required new blocks of downtown businesses. One 1927 map labeled almost one-third of the city as Detroit's future downtown. Property owners thought that high demand would create high prices for central city property and that regulation would decrease the value of that property. Their opposition helped defeat a proposed zoning ordinance in a 1927 referendum.[8] The Depression of the 1930s led to drastic staff cuts. By the 1940s, growth had slowed considerably. Business interests became concerned about protecting property values and attacking blight. On the flip side of the coin, business owners then led the effort to approve a zoning ordinance and redevelop deteriorated areas near the central business district.[9]

Other groups also supported greater planning activity. Foremost was the UAW-CIO, which promoted unified slum clearance, housing construction, and regional planning. The Detroit Citizens' Housing and Planning Council, a small group of reformers, challenged the city to follow the example of Mayor LaGuardia and public infrastructure czar Robert Moses in New York City. New York had already spent millions of dollars in public improvement projects such as the Triborough Bridge, Central Park, and the Lincoln Tunnel. Detroit's planning advocates credited these accomplishments to Thomas Adams's 1928 plan for New York.[10] Other proponents of an aggressive city policy included Walter Blucher, executive director of ASPO and former Detroit planning director, who visited Detroit in 1943. In widely publicized comments he urged city leaders to rebuild Detroit by improving the transportation system, schools, parks, and recreation facilities.[11]

Perhaps the most important impetus for planning came from the federal government, which provided Works Progress Administration assistance for the staff work necessary for municipal projects. Mayors all over the country, including Detroit's Mayor Jeffries, realized that such projects let cities simultaneously hire the unemployed and improve city facilities. Since cities needed to plan public improvements in order to receive federal assistance, political pragmatism joined with the support of downtown business interests to create a climate for planning.[12]

In 1940, within a few months of each other, Detroit's council passed a zoning ordinance and the mayor appointed a "blight committee" composed of "downtown property owners and business men as well as leaders of various civic groups and interests."[13] This blight committee decided that the city needed state legislation to enable it to redevelop Detroit's core areas. It persuaded the Michigan legislature to adopt a state law that facilitated creation of urban redevelopment corporations. The committee also recommended to the mayor that the DCPC develop a master plan, which Jeffries directed them to do.[14]

The mayor's office also issued two important statements of policy in the 1940s. Both of these were predecessors of its more complete master plan, issued in 1951. In the last chapter we mentioned the mayor's Postwar Improvement Committee's report, "Post-War Improvements to Make Your Detroit a Finer City in Which to Live and Work." As an extension of this document, in 1947 the mayor's office issued "The Detroit Plan: A Program for Blight Elimination," a statement of the city's redevelopment plans. This document was very short, sixteen pages long including appendices, and laid the groundwork for a more elaborate 1951 master plan.[15]

A consensus was growing that the major tasks were to protect Detroit's central business district and industrial areas from encroaching blight, to rebuild its public facilities, and to clear residential slums. The *Detroit Free Press* urged the city to use planning to help accomplish these tasks. The *Detroit News* called Planning Director George Emery "the single individual on whom blame can be heaped if the war's end should find Detroit unprepared with public works and constructive plans to carry it into a new era of peace."[16] The mayor's postwar improvement committee noted that a master plan was necessary to prepare for postwar public improvements. In 1944, at the urging of the postwar improvement committee, the mayor increased the number of planning staff in order to finish the plan for Detroit's physical development. All of these activities, proponents hoped, would significantly improve Detroit.[17]

A Master Plan

Expectations were high, as was faith in the ability of planning to help prepare the city for the postwar world. The 1947 comments of a planning commissioner reflect that optimism: "the postwar situation has telescoped our planning program and has become a near emergency that requires every community . . . to meet opportunities and problems that are sprouting like mushrooms." Admiring the possibilities of the relatively new (to Detroit) concept of master planning, the commissioner admitted that "ten years ago, practically none of us here in Detroit had any but the foggiest notion of what a Master Plan could be [or] how to go about getting one. We have crawled a little way out of that slough and have, under [consultant Ladislas] Segoe's tutelage, worked our way through night school. It has taken time, too much in my opinion in view of the postwar situation."[18]

Planning thought in the 1940s made ambitious claims for master plans. The standard planning reference text, written in part by Segoe, argued that a master plan could provide "the inspirational force that will foster civic interest, devotion and loyalty essential for building better cities." The master plan presented "a picture in outline form of the future community . . . by seeing to it that every new building erected and every improvement makes its full contribution toward the gradual transformation of the present city into an increasingly better one."[19]

Master plans are formally adopted public documents that indicate what kinds of land uses are anticipated and where future public improvements will be located. The map that often accompanies a master plan designates specific areas for residential, commercial, industrial, and other uses. If implemented before development takes place, a master plan can help a municipality reserve certain land areas for designated uses before anything at all is built. If implemented after major development has already taken place, however, the potential power of a master plan declines.

In spite of its limited ability to shape land use within a mature city, a master plan can be a powerful tool for directing future public investment. It was this aspect which was of most use to cities of this era. By understanding the population growth, economic base, and land use of a municipality, Segoe's text instructed, a planner could determine several important things: where the city should build new streets or widen old ones; whether other forms of transit needed to be encouraged or supported; and where to locate new public utilities, low-rent houses, parks, or other community facilities. If done in an orderly, synchronized fashion, planning for such improvements could in the long run save money. For example, a city could thereby avoid building a street before installing a sewer.

When Detroit finally adopted a master plan, its planning for community facilities did help create a "finer city in which to live and work." The plan laid out a carefully constructed agenda for postwar civic improvements that served the city well for decades.

The framework of that plan, published in 1951, focused on two major concepts: developing broad swatches of industrial and commercial corridors, and organizing residential areas around neighborhood units. A later chapter will describe the industrial and commercial areas. The concept of neighborhood units, originally developed by Clarence Perry, was to provide community self-sufficiency. An early sketch of Perry's "neighborhood unit subdivision" showed houses grouped around parks and playfields, circuitous routing of major automobile arterial roads and a curved design for interior streets so as to give highest priority to pedestrians, and clusters of commercial shops around the unit's perimeter. Extensive landscaping provided green spaces and street trees.[20]

With its more idealistic ambitions tempered, the concept of neighborhood units was firmly entrenched within mainstream planning by the 1940s. Segoe's planning text suggested that planners could stabilize and support neighborhood units by insuring that each had its own schools, churches, clubs, recreation areas, and shopping centers. Each should provide an elementary school accommodating up to 1,000 pupils, meaning that the neighborhood itself could support from 4,000 to 6,000 people. As the concept became used in practice, even some of these essential elements were missing, however; neighborhood units came to be defined via population guidelines and elementary schools.[21]

Detroit's planners used the organizing concept of neighborhood units to plan an equitable distribution of schools and recreation facilities. First they excluded those areas of the city used or recommended for commercial or industrial purposes, even if they included existing neighborhoods. (For example, many existing neighborhoods in Detroit's industrialized southwest were excluded; see fig. 2.1.) They divided the remainder of the city into 150 neighborhood units, using existing street patterns as boundaries. They also clustered anywhere from six to twelve neighborhood units into a total of sixteen "communities," the basis of larger service areas.

The city and private developers had already built most Detroit neighborhoods with grid-patterned streets, leaving little room for creative design. The plans that resulted for public facility location were impressive, however. Working with staff of the Detroit Board of Education, for example, planners identified for each neighbor-

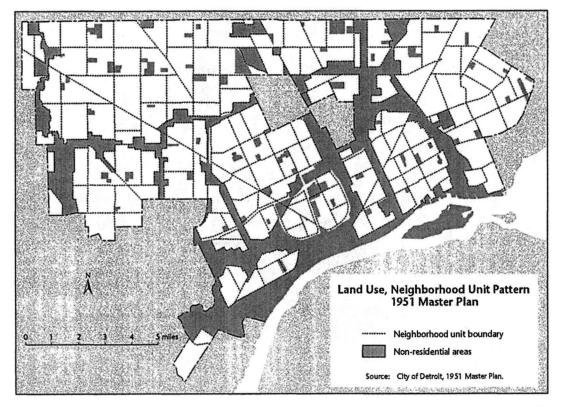

Land Use, Neighborhood Unit Pattern
1951 Master Plan

┈┈┈┈ Neighborhood unit boundary

▓ Non-residential areas

Source: City of Detroit, 1951 Master Plan.

hood whether an elementary school was to be demolished or retained and where new schools were needed. They placed all of this
information in an easy-to-read map, then created similar maps for
intermediate schools, high schools, and special schools (see fig. 2.2).

The planners consulted with other line agencies as well, including the police and fire departments, parks department, and public
library system. They used the same procedure of identifying existing facilities, consulting with the line agency providing the service,
and clarifying future actions. This led to a series of graphic representations of the city's plans to retain, eliminate, or build municipal
facilities throughout Detroit. A partial list of such facilities, each
with its own separate map, includes parks, playgrounds, public libraries, public health centers, welfare offices, police and fire stations
and buildings, water supply facilities, lighting plants, public housing, and city produce markets. In conjunction with detailed plans
for improving the city's expressways and other thoroughfares, grade
railroad crossings, and motor freight terminals, the results offered
an impressive road map for postwar reconstruction of public facilities and buildings.

This planning undoubtedly saved the city millions of dollars by
coordinating civic improvements. Because the line agencies had
participated in the planning process, they followed the plan's guidelines when they built new municipal facilities. For years thereafter

*Fig. 2.1. Land use, neigh-
borhood unit pattern, 1951
Master Plan, showing
areas that the City of Detroit intended to protect for
semi-autonomous residen-
tial neighborhood units.
Courtesy Detroit Depart-
ment of Planning and
Development.*

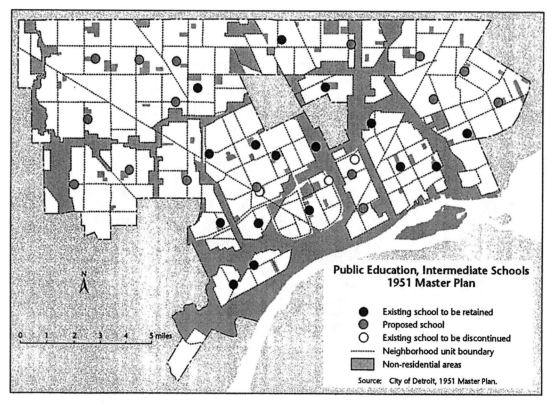

Public Education, Intermediate Schools
1951 Master Plan

● Existing school to be retained
◉ Proposed school
○ Existing school to be discontinued
-------- Neighborhood unit boundary
▨ Non-residential areas

Source: City of Detroit, 1951 Master Plan.

*Fig. 2.2. Public Education,
intermediate schools, 1951
Master Plan, showing ex-
ample of how the city
matched plans for commu-
nity facilities—here intermediate school openings
and closings—with neigh-
borhood unit pattern.
Courtesy Detroit Depart-
ment of Planning and
Development.*

the city's Common Council kept a copy of the master plan in council chambers and referred to it for all major land-use and public facilities issues. In these ways the plan served the city for decades.[22]

As for control of the private sector, however, the plan was only
marginally effective. At that time, primary tools for enforcing a master plan were subdivision controls and a zoning ordinance. Subdivision controls require private developers of new subdivisions to
meet certain standards and install improvements such as streets or
utilities. But so little vacant land existed that subdivision control
could not significantly affect postwar Detroit. Zoning, too, was limited. Zoning ordinances give municipalities the legal power to require certain land uses within designated areas. But many cities like
Detroit had adopted a zoning ordinance earlier than the master
plan. Once the master plan was adopted, it often did not match the
land-use designations indicated on the zoning ordinance maps.[23]
Both subdivision controls and zoning ordinances were ineffective
tools for improving deteriorated inner-city neighborhoods, where
new construction was merely a memory.[24]

Local planners also wrongly diagnosed the roots of obsolescence. Noting that the population had burgeoned from 250,000 to
1,750,000 during the first forty years of the century, planning staff
commented in one report that "it is a harsh truth that as a city
grows, its problems multiply progressively. And this applies not

only to its physical problems but to its social problems as well."[25] Expanding on this theme of uncontrolled growth, the report concluded that, "despite the fact that Detroit has many fine, well laid-out neighborhoods, the unpalatable truth is that no less than a third of the city is marred by serious physical defects. How did it get this way? The answer is simple. Together with most American cities, it got this way through lack of comprehensive planning. Like Topsy, Detroit 'just growed,' with an almost complete absence of restraint."[26] Once the new master plan for land use was completed, the planners assured readers, planning tools could resolve these problems.

They also wrote that regulating land use would allow the city "to do away with overcrowding and bad housing which results from it; to eliminate the confused jumble of business, industry, and dwellings and so stabilize property values and the tax base; to lessen the impact of noise and dirt and smoke on residential neighborhoods; to reduce traffic congestion; . . . to eliminate all these ills by attacking them at their source." Land-use regulation, the planners said, would develop a better community life for Detroit's living, shopping, and working areas. Assuredly, they argued, "the problems involved can all be solved by sensible planning, by guiding the nature and location of public and private improvements so that the city, as it is rebuilt over the years, will grow into a predetermined design for better living."[27]

Since the city's planners assumed that the city's problems came from uncontrolled growth, they assumed that controlled stability would eliminate them. The statements also reveal an exaggerated faith in the powers of planning, specifically master planning, zoning, and subdivision regulation. These opinions were not unusual for the era, however. During 1944 congressional hearings on postwar planning, at the same time that ASPO's Alfred Bettman argued for redevelopment and master planning, he also suggested that poor land use caused slums:

Mr. Manasco: Is not the cause of slums the economic status of the persons who occupy them?

Mr. Bettman: No, sir.

Mr. Manasco: Then, what is it? We have been trying to find that out for four years in this committee but have not found the answer yet. What causes slums?

Mr. Bettman: . . . obsolescence of the lay-out—the lot lay-out; and the obsolescence of the type of use to which the area is put. Of course, the mere age of the building is itself, you may say, a cause of the slum; but if one merely removes that by substituting a new building for the old, one simply starts a new period of blight, as long as one keeps the present lay-out and the present type of use.[28]

Mel Scott has commented that urban planners during this era "were somewhat like generals preparing for the next war by planning to

refight the last one."[29] Publications targeted to municipal officials and planners continued to urge improved lot layout, proper recording of subdivision plats (plans), building codes, and planned development as solutions, even though many municipalities had long before adopted these measures with no noticeable deterrence of urban expansion or inner-city decay.

Detroit's problems in the 1940s came from other sources besides uncontrolled growth and lack of planning. It was true that lack of regulation had led to poorly mixed land uses, most notably in the form of unnecessarily close association between industries and residential neighborhoods. It was also true that lack of a master plan hindered the ordered development of the city and that such a plan could have greatly improved community life. But some of the tools that planners expected to use were best suited to control growth, which had already slowed and would soon reverse. Many problems resulted from phenomena that planners would be hard-pressed to counter: flight from the city boundaries of middle-income White people, businesses, and industries; crowded and deteriorating central city housing; and an especially bad ghetto environment for Black residents.

In spite of planners' optimistic claims for planning tools, many realized that new approaches were necessary. Even as Detroit's planners promised that control of subdivision layout would improve the environment, they also noted that decentralizing forces were steadily pushing the urban settlement farther out, leaving miles of older areas in "a blighted condition."[30] On Walter Blucher's 1943 trip to Detroit, the former planning director urged city leaders to rebuild the area of the city extending from the heart of central business district to the semicircular Grand Boulevard. Blucher's call for redevelopment meshed with the concerns that downtown interests on the mayor's blight committee had already expressed.

By the end of World War II, therefore, Detroit had begun to plan for the postwar rebuilding of the city, a rebuilding which would include public improvements, master planning, land-use controls, and blight elimination. Planning for public improvements proved helpful, but recognition began to dawn that eliminating "blight" would require more direct action. The locus for such action, it seemed, should be the central portion of the city surrounding and including the downtown.

The Redevelopment Solution

All over the country urban observers were contemplating redevelopment as a postwar strategy. Yet different proponents had different ends in mind. Factions clustered at two poles. Those most concerned about "slums," the term commonly used for deteriorated housing, also supported public housing programs and tended to come from liberal or philanthropic backgrounds. Those concerned about "blight," which connoted economic deterioration, were often landowners and downtown business owners more worried about falling property values than about the fate of the poor.

John Bauman has called the program of Catherine Bauer, Dorothy Rosenman of the National Committee on the Housing Emergency, and R. J. Thomas of the UAW the "Bauer-Rosenman-Thomas cure." This "cure" prescribed massive rehousing programs and regional restructuring as necessary preconditions for urban redevelopment. This was the perspective presented in the UAW's "Memorandum on Postwar Urban Housing," the 1944 pamphlet written under R. J. Thomas's supervision. A different slant came from the National Association of Real Estate Boards (NAREB) and the Urban Land Institute. These groups, most concerned about economic decline, safeguarded the interests of private developers and investors. NAREB insisted that private enterprise alone handle the rebuilding of slum areas, a concept that planning consultant Ladislas Segoe called "a great boon to private investors" that would benefit neither poor families nor municipal treasuries. NAREB also led a campaign against congressional funding for public housing.[31]

Between these two poles lay a range of opinions and proposals and, until passage of Title I legislation in the 1949 Housing Act, no common agreement about how to proceed. Catherine Bauer, advocate of public housing and regional planning, argued that it was too late to save central cities and that the best course of action was to control suburban development. But she warned that if central city redevelopment were to take place, public housing would be essential. Alfred Bettman, representing the American Institute of Planners, disagreed. Bettman argued for legislation attacking urban blight, but against limiting redevelopment to replacing or rebuilding low-income housing.[32] This position placed the national body of professional planners somewhere in the awkward middle of the two redevelopment poles: not overly concerned with the protection of private investment, but not overly concerned with the needs of the poor either.

While various proponents and opponents debated the issue at the national level, local actors were trying to work out their own vision of redevelopment. Diverging opinions at the national level only reflected divergence at the local level. Some saw slum clearance as a humane activity benefiting existing residents, but the most influential advocated clearance for the sake of business interests.

In Detroit, controversy over who would benefit from redevelopment appeared early. Some, including a few planners, wanted to use redevelopment primarily to eliminate blight. Others, including civil rights and labor leaders, wanted to protect and rehouse the poor. The first group prevailed, and so countering economic blight became the focus rather than assisting the poor.

The triumph of antiblight sentiment was first evident in debate over state enabling legislation for redevelopment. In the mid-1940s planners sought a redeveloper for the area east of the central business district. They began to work with a developer who promised to clear out decrepit housing bordering Gratiot Street and replace it with affordable rental units. Several developers had proposed projects for this Gratiot Street area, including one who blatantly claimed that his project would "serve as a first step towards limiting areas to a certain class of people, and avoid the [racial] infiltration into other areas now occurring."[33] The most promising proposal, however, came from Eugene Greenhut of New York City. Greenhut wanted partial funding from the City of Detroit, raised by means of revenue bonds that the housing commission would issue.[34]

In order to carry out such a project, the city needed state enabling legislation. In 1945 the planning commission debated various versions of a proposed state bill. The "blight elimination bill" debate gave a strong indication that concern about property values and clearance would prevail over concerns about the needs of existing residents.

Three aspects of the bill proved to be of lasting importance. The first was whether to rely upon private enterprise to reconstruct the sites once they were cleared. The second issue was whether to require a municipality to rehouse former residents. The third was how to handle racial discrimination. In general, most commissioners and planning staff responded to these issues with cautious conservatism, with the exception of Commissioner Otis Winn. Winn was a "labor man," one of the three researchers for the UAW's 1944 "Memorandum on Postwar Urban Housing." In that publication, the union had strongly warned policy-makers not to let business interests shape redevelopment but to rehouse minority relocatees in "a healthful living environment."[35]

Although Winn raised these issues with the backing of labor, the building industry had greater influence. Detroit's planning commission let both the Detroit Real Estate Board and the Builders Association help draft the legislative bill. These business groups argued that the legislation should require sale of acquired land to private individuals. Commissioner Winn unsuccessfully argued against the city forcibly taking land from individuals in order to sell it to private developers.[36]

The planning commission chose not to build safeguards for existing site residents into their proposed state legislation. In spite of vocal support from the Detroit branches of the NAACP and the National Urban League, motions to prohibit discrimination or segregation failed. The bill that finally passed the state legislature did require adequate rehousing, even though the planning commission had tried unsuccessfully to kill that provision.[37]

Why did the planning commission take these positions? Perhaps they saw relocation and antidiscrimination safeguards as unnecessary because a major purpose of that legislation was to facilitate Greenhut's proposal. Greenhut planned to rehouse 7,500 residents of blighted areas "in decent, sanitary, fire-proof, garden-type apartment developments" with parks and playgrounds.[38] Greenhut had also contacted the National Urban League, and through them the Detroit Urban League, to build interracial support for the project, an enlightened step that other potential developers had not bothered to take. It therefore appeared that Mr. Greenhut was a man with financial resources, concrete plans, and some degree of sensitivity to the racial issues involved. The folly of relying upon individuals, however, became clear when at some point Greenhut dropped out of competition, leaving the city with a designated project but without a project developer.

Another reason for the planners' position could have been their director. In a 1944 newspaper interview, Director Emery called planners "a bulwark against declining real-estate values, a stabilizer of city finances, and a kind of insurance for the better elements of the status quo."[39] This statement reveals more concern for propertied interests than for social reform. Neither does Emery appear to have been a proponent of public housing. This is in marked contrast to the situation in Philadelphia, for example, where planners and housers developed a strong working relationship.[40]

Director Emery argued that providing adequate housing for displaced residents would be "an impossible obstacle" for cities. Consultant Ladislas Segoe countered that such a provision would be "an excellent thing," and that "any rational and realistic broad-scale program of redevelopment should, in my opinion, be accompanied by a vigorous parallel program of providing housing on vacant land."[41] Yet Emery continued to disparage relocation requirements. In 1948 he complained that the 1945 state law slowed potential progress because it required the city to provide housing for displaced residents.[42]

At least one of Emery's staff planners realized the hardships relocation of site residents would cause. Donald Monson, in one of the few Detroit planning documents of this era that mentions race, commented in 1947 that "any practical program of rebuilding the deteriorated sections of Detroit is complicated by the fact that the bulk of the deteriorated area is east of Woodward Avenue and presently occupied largely by Negro families. However, the bulk of the public housing program must be for White occupancy even after due allowance is made to the fact that the Negro people are in greater need of housing."[43] The planning director did not let this situation change his opposition to requiring the city to help relocatees.

Similar battles took place in other cities. Chicago proponents gained passage of the Illinois Redevelopment and Relocation Acts of 1947. Several groups hailed that act, shaped in large part by downtown corporate interests, as a "hallmark," a model for the 1949 Housing Act passed by the U.S. Congress.[44] The 1947 Illinois legislation and the 1945 Michigan legislation were similar in several ways. Both declared slum clearance a public purpose; both limited the use of redevelopment land for public housing; and both provided for relocation with but little attention to enforcement.

The debate over the state's blight elimination bill was an important harbinger of city policy drift. A second indication came with the city's "Detroit Plan," published in 1947. This short policy document, not a master plan but rather "A Program for Blight Elimination," provided the original mandate for locally sponsored clearance and reconstruction. The process later came to be called redevelopment, but the city's original label, "blight elimination," probably accurately reflects its intent: to eliminate unsightly residential, commercial, and industrial blight.

Under the terms of the 1947 Detroit Plan, the city planned to declare a district blighted, acquire and clear properties, and sell the razed land to developers at one-fourth or one-fifth of the cost of acquisition. The city expected to finance this plan itself, initially by using $2 million a year of general funds, recouped through in-

Fig. 2.4. Gratiot redevelopment area, a view of the neighborhood before demolition. Burton Historical Collection, Detroit Public Library.

creased tax revenues on newly redeveloped land. At this rate, the city expected to clear approximately 100 acres a year, or 10,000 acres in 100 years.

The ambitious Detroit Plan laid out a process for local sponsorship of slum clearance and redevelopment. The first project to be funded under the plan was to include low-cost new housing, but Mayor Jeffries declared that the city would not let housing dominate its redevelopment projects. That philosophy "overlooks the fact that the would-be commercial or industrial developer of a blighted area finds himself confronted with the same practical barriers which have so effectively halted the efforts of the home planner."[45] Housing commission staff, rather than champion public housing as the primary path to postwar reconstruction, fully supported the Detroit Plan; their office, as a matter of fact, had written the document. Detroit Housing Commission Director-Secretary Charles Edgecomb described the benefits of the Detroit Plan to a 1947 annual meeting. The purpose of the plan, he said, was to remedy the blight which had struck areas surrounding the downtown commercial district, "surrounded by an ever increasing zone of slum property," and then to attack commercial and industrial blight.[46]

The pro–central business district, pro–industrial sector bias of the 1947 Detroit Plan is not surprising, given the process involved in its

Fig. 2.5. Gratiot redevelopment area, before demolition, showing density of development close to central business district, far right. Burton Historical Collection, Detroit Public Library.

preparation. When city staff completed rough drafts of the plan, they called in the Construction Industry Council and the Detroit Metropolitan Association of Home Builders "to act as critics and co-operators with the City officials in the drafting of a final program."[47] Since city leaders were just as worried about downtown and industrial decline as they were about housing, it was predictable that their postwar redevelopment plan would focus on economic decline.

Edgecomb's description of the plan stood in marked contrast to Catherine Bauer's approach. Arguing for public housing, Bauer identified what she called "one great central illusion of the urban redevelopment movement—the notion that urban redevelopment could be successfully promoted and achieved quite apart from housing issues and housing policy." She warned the planners that they would have to take sides, that it was an illusion to expect that "somehow, some day, pure reason and enlightened common sense and the civic welfare would triumph in even the hardest heart, and bold city planning receive the full support of property interests without the vulgar necessity of unpleasant controversy." It is, she suggested, "politically naive to expect property and business interests ever to take bona fide initiative for any real change or reform."[48]

This warning had no noticeable effect. Redevelopment would begin with slum clearance, but the primary purpose of that clearance would be to help eliminate the economic decline of the city's central business district and to improve industrial districts. Housing for the poor was a secondary consideration. If the rights and needs of slum dwellers could not be guaranteed during this process, the city had apparently decided, so be it.

In Detroit, therefore, city leaders defined the basic parameters of postwar redevelopment policy several years before Title I of the federal Housing Act of 1949 passed. This definition of development policy was not divorced from the national dialogue. The proposals by local developers arose in large part because debate among national redevelopment interest groups created a certain facility with the issues at the local level. Planners and interest groups discussed many of the same things at the local level as they did at the national level, creating a sort of shadow dialogue. But the nature of decisions made at the local and state level does suggest that future strengths and weaknesses of federal legislation could not be entirely responsible for the strengths and weaknesses of local action. The federal legislation legitimized local inclinations, reinforcing them with the power of federal money and administrative control.

The Early Postwar Agenda

In summary, policy-makers turned to planning to help them cope with the postwar morass. Early efforts to implement planning had failed because central business district and real estate interests were afraid that land-use regulation would limit their profits. But by the end of World War II the central areas of the city were showing the effects of decay, and business interests became newly enamored of the potential of planning to protect property interests. Joining them were various citizen groups calling for major postwar improvements.

Traditional planning tools were inadequate for the tasks at hand. A new master plan helped put in place much-needed municipal improvements, as the plan carefully mapped out which facilities needed to be updated or built. But the master plan and other tools such as zoning and subdivision regulation could not eliminate blight. These tools were more useful for guiding city growth than reversing city decline. Redevelopment arose as an alternative way to attack urban decentralization and central city decay. Redevelopment was in keeping with new federal initiatives, and it answered business interests' concerns about the blight surrounding the central business district.

A series of official city documents verbalized the hopes that Detroit could rationally plan the postwar improvement of the city. The 1944 "Post-War Improvement to Make Your Detroit a Finer City in Which to Live and Work" documented local needs for new and improved public facilities. The 1947 Detroit Plan expressed Mayor Jeffries's vision for rebuilding the central city, even without assistance from the federal government. The 1951 Master Plan more completely described these needs and organized them into a clearly visible agenda for city improvement.

These documents, when compared with the UAW's memorandum on postwar housing, show how drastically visions of postwar city development differed. To the union group, the basic components of the improved city were subsidized housing, built on the edges of existing cities, and humane slum clearance, all within the context of regional planning. To the mayor's postwar committee, "a finer city" meant a city buttressed by adequate public facilities and beautiful civic symbols, with a moderate number of public housing projects to take care of the less fortunate. According to the mayor's 1947 Detroit Plan, the city planned to remove poor housing but also to undertake commercial and industrial development.

This was no contest, of course, but if it were, the city documents would have won handily. Although the authors of the UAW document were most familiar with the situation in Detroit, they addressed the nation as a whole, and their document simply had no policy-making standing in any level of government. Several of its suggestions countered established federal, state, and local policy. The City of Detroit had no control over its region and could only address issues within its boundaries. Local policy-makers began to reshape the city in the image of its dominant economic interests, particularly those associated with the central business district and major institutions.

At this time planners, who helped carry out this postwar agenda, appeared insensitive to the needs and rights of slum dwellers. Planning Director Emery and most planning commissioners actively resisted attempts by the unionist commissioners and civil rights leaders to safeguard the rights of slum dwellers and to prohibit racial discrimination. But, then, Detroit's planners were not the only ones estranged from a progressive social agenda. Tracy Auger, a planner closely associated with the Tennessee Valley Authority, had complained in 1940 about planners' blind faith in private enterprise. He advocated instead "a union of city planning and housing both thoroughly imbued with the [true] public interest," which he defined as involving the poor as well as the well-to-do. What happened instead was that planners became identified most closely with the pro–business growth coalition.[49]

Renewal and Loss

II

Eliminating Slums and Blight

3

Title I of the Housing Act of 1949, later known as urban renewal, breathed life into Detroit's redevelopment plans by providing federal money to finance what the city itself had expected to pay for. Unfortunately, this legislation was the ungainly child of political compromise. Public housing advocates made sure that the housing act included financial support for public housing, referred to the need to protect displaced families, and funded only predominantly residential redevelopment projects. But the real estate and financial institution lobby insured that the bill favored private developers and did not require construction of public housing.[1] Nationally prominent planners could neither temper the housing orientation of redevelopment nor insure control of suburban development, although they did succeed in getting the act to require planning.[2] Civil rights groups lobbied for provisions guarding against racial discrimination but managed only to exclude racially restrictive covenants, which were not legally enforceable anyway.[3]

The principals of this uncomfortable group marriage gave birth to perhaps the most important U.S. urban program of the century. Since some of its provisions were incomplete or contradictory, the offspring was bound to disappoint. The legislation did not protect the interests of low-income city dwellers, but neither did it offer an unparalleled boon to private business interests. The results were much more complex.

In the 1950s and 1960s Detroit's redevelopment strategy depended in large part upon urban renewal. The first part of the strategy was to clear out deteriorated housing in the central business district's eastern flank and replace it with new housing in Gratiot Park. The second part was to improve the central business district and complete economic redevelopment projects in downtown's western flank. This two-part attack on slums and blight appeared to be an elegant solution. Shortly, its limitations became very clear.

A Residential Strategy

Gratiot Park, later expanded to include, and then renamed, Lafayette Park, was the first phase of a complex that now encompasses over five hundred acres. In some ways the total complex is a premier success story for Detroit in that it fulfilled a simple but important function: replacing bad housing with good. But the experience raised grave questions about whether redevelopment was a solution or a problem. The city's first redevelopment project showed enormous potential for both good and evil.

Soon after the 1949 act passed, Detroit began to work on the Gratiot project. The city had identified the Gratiot area as its first redevelopment site in its 1947 Detroit Plan, which had even included preliminary sketches for reconstruction. To organize its renewal effort, the city turned to its housing commission because that agency had previous experience with slum clearance and relocation.[4] The city's urban planners made several important contributions, however. They insured that reconstructed uses were well planned and well designed, based on a physical concept of community.

The design contributions came about largely through the efforts of Charles Blessing, who became Detroit's planning director in 1952. Blessing directed his planning staff to draw cul-de-sacs, a park in the middle of the project site, and pedestrian walkways for the Gratiot site plans. Planners also suggested locating community schools, shopping, and medical facilities within easy walking distance of complex residents, building on the concept of clustered neighborhood units laid out in the master plan.[5] The developer's architect and city planner, Ludwig Mies van der Rohe and Ludwig Hilberseimer, adopted the basic design principles advanced by Blessing's planners. Of the results, architect and planner Roger Montgomery proclaimed that "Gratiot joins Radburn, that other incomplete monument, as one of the few triumphs of American urban design." Another critic, British architect Peter Smithson, said that "the essence of what one is searching for is missing from all large-scale developments all over the world, but it can be smelt at Lafayette Park [Gratiot]" (see fig. 3.1).[6] After initial problems marketing the housing units, their enduring popularity confirmed the justice of their early accolades. City planners insured that later phases—Elmwood Park I, II, and III—exemplified at least the basic qualities that distinguished work by the Mies team.

The major flaw with this project was its effect on the original residents of the sites. Like early clearance projects throughout the United States, the Gratiot project eliminated more low-income housing than it produced, and it abused and alienated Black inner-city residents in the process. It also could not significantly improve retention of the middle class in the inner city, for all its design innovations.

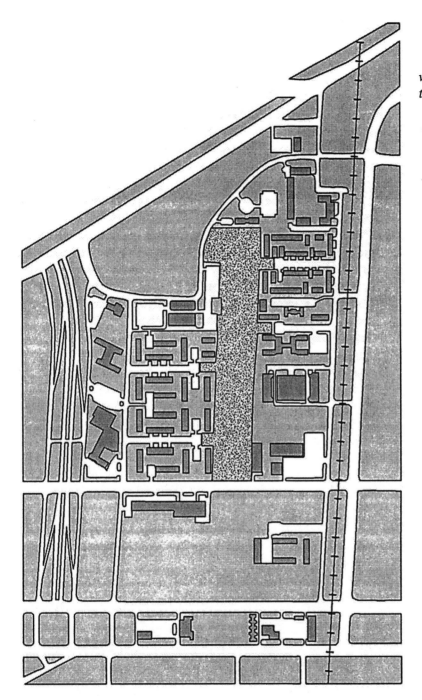

Fig. 3.1 Lafayette (formerly Gratiot) Park redevelopment project as developed, 1964. Designed in the form of a neighborhood unit, the development includes housing in the form of attached townhouses and apartment buildings, surrounding a middle park area that provided pedestrian access to an elementary school and a shopping center. Courtesy Journal of the American Institute of Planners.

Clearance and the Black Community

From the city's perspective, the core issues were basically quite simple. The Gratiot area formed an unhealthy, unprofitable, and unsightly eastern flank for the central business district. This was bad for business and bad for existing residents. From the Black community's perspective, at first, Gratiot offered the promise of clearing out poor housing and replacing it with something better. "Slum clearance" in the 1940s, however, often meant clearance for public housing. Detroit's local Black press so regularly championed clearance as a route to new low-income housing that it was almost a continuing story: Negro Housing Desperate, Where is Slum Clearance and Public Housing?[7] The truth soon dawned that redevelopment and rehousing of low-income dwellers were not necessarily connected.

As sociologist Louis Wirth phrased it, slum clearance was "complicated by the problem of race relations." Writing Detroit's Mayor Albert Cobo in 1950, he commented that "you are probably familiar with the difficulties that we have met with here [Chicago] in this connection."[8] Wirth did not specify how race relations "complicated" redevelopment, but several problems had arisen. One was that such projects often targeted Black neighborhoods for clearance. A second was the problem of how to relocate and where to rehouse former residents in racially segregated cities. A third was that some projects barred former site residents, because of race or income, from new housing built in their former neighborhoods. All of these problems affected Chicago's Lake Meadows development, for which Chicago had leveled a South Side Black residential area.[9]

Detroit's selection of the Gratiot site may have been racially motivated. One retired planner has recalled that several areas were similarly blighted, including housing west of downtown. The difference? "I guess the practical difference was that the west side was predominately White and the east side was predominantly Black."[10] In addition, Planning Director George Emery had stated, at a national planning conference, that in the "colored sections" of the city "there may be less likelihood of organized opposition."[11] Perhaps this was true, because at first selection of the site caused no outspoken protest. Instead, conflict arose after it became clear that rehousing options were limited because of the policies of Mayor Albert Cobo.

Cobo was the victor in a 1949 election campaign against a candidate of the liberal-labor coalition, George Edwards. Edwards had been the director of the housing commission during the 1942 Sojourner Truth incident, when the city placed Black occupancy "war housing" in the middle of a White neighborhood. This fact did not endear him to White voters. Those voters backed Albert Cobo, who touted himself as anti-Communist, pro-police, a champion of private enterprise, and a protector of homeowners, key words associated with a pro-White—as opposed to Edwards's liberal White, or pro-Black—image. White working-class voters broke with their liberal labor leaders and supported Cobo, who easily won the election.[12]

This election was a pivotal point for postwar housing and redevelopment in Detroit. Cobo served during seven critical years, from 1950 to 1957, and stamped an indelible mark on local policy. He supported public housing only for "honest, sincere families" of low income. Even before he took office Cobo pledged to stop scattering public housing projects throughout the city and to build them only at segregated, inner-city sites. His opposition to other locations was so strong that he even tried (unsuccessfully) to sell one large public housing complex, the fully built and occupied Herman Gardens, because it was located outside the city's older core.[13]

Criticism of Cobo's housing and redevelopment policies arose quickly. National housing expert Charles Abrams urged the new mayor to build public housing rather than simply tear down private housing. Wayne State University professor Orville Linck blasted the mayor's decision to drop non–central city public housing projects, charging that "private builders and real estate operators are trying to ghettoize the Boulevard areas. With no decent place to move, 9,000 people are going to have to crowd into already overpopulated old houses and shacks."[14] Local civil rights groups, vocal proponents of the African-American community, also had misgivings. At the urging of the mayor's interracial committee, housing commission director Harry Durbin talked to several such groups about the city's public housing program and the Detroit Plan. One of the more prominent, the NAACP, charged that Cobo's public housing policies "resulted from the organized opposition of [White] improvement associations against any developments which might cause Negroes to move into the outlying sections of the city." Furthermore, these policies would "produce more segregation than now exists and will produce extreme hardship on the families who have to be relocated."[15]

Many expected that Cobo's administration would at least support public housing development in or near the Gratiot Park project, since that land was located in the inner city. Since Cobo halted construction in White areas, his policy could have provided much-needed housing for inner-city Blacks. The general expectation was that the city would clear the site and then get a private developer to rebuild low-income or mixed-income housing.

But first the site had to be cleared. This, it soon became clear, would not be easy. All the families living on the Gratiot housing site were Black, the very people who had the hardest time finding open housing. The housing commission wrote the Black Detroit Real Estate Brokers Association and asked for a list of vacant rental units open to Blacks. The outraged association replied that they knew of no such vacancies and called for an end to private and public housing segregation, a root cause of the constrained supply.[16] The Detroit Housing Commission, however, was still fighting to keep its own public housing projects segregated and so could hardly criticize segregation in private housing.

The commission proceeded to clear out the first several hundred families at the Gratiot site. Commission staff circulated letters and notices to families implying that tenants should move immediately, but neither offering any other housing nor indicating that the city was responsible for helping in the housing search. By the time the city filed its relocation plan in early 1951, it had "persuaded" almost 400 out of a total of 1900 families to move. When the city signed a U.S. Home and Housing Finance Administration (HHFA) contract for the Title I Gratiot site in April 1952, over 1,000 families had moved. At the time, the waiting list for public housing totaled 5,226 Black families (the list for White families was 2,247 families). Just over 600 of the 1,000 Gratiot families eligible for public housing eventually got into public housing units. Other families crowded into the surrounding slums, taking refuge in doubled or tripled accommodations that were worse than the old slums.[17]

Early on, complaints came from organized tenants' groups. One charged that "The Cobo and Common Council planless so-called 'Detroit Plan' has been exposed during the last few weeks in all its disregard for human misery." People were seeking housing "in a city where there is no housing," said tenant council president J. W. Smith.[18] The Detroit Urban League began to collect case studies documenting human misery. They found that former site residents did not move to safe or sanitary dwellings, as required by federal legislation. Some of the units where the city placed residents were dilapidated and poorly prepared. In one unit, "walls were cracked and dirty, plaster was falling from the ceiling during the interview, and the doors were attached precariously to their hinges." In addition, "the City . . . informed [the relocatee] that it would require too much expense to connect the bathtub and face bowl as the plumbing was beyond repair." Another family found a home for itself because the housing commission "never did at any time offer to place us. In fact, it was only after we moved that we heard the neighbors say that the Urban League said they should have offered us a place if we couldn't find one." In the unit they found, [wear and tear] "has disconnected weather boarding permitting the cold air to enter. Plaster is cracked and falling. There is no water in the bathroom or kitchen. Water is obtained from the basement."[19]

The Detroit Urban League sent its findings of these and similar cases to the federal HHFA. The agency applied some pressure on Detroit, asking for an accounting of relocatees, but it eventually accepted the housing commission's report and proceeded to approve the project.[20]

The intrepid Detroit Urban League continued to monitor relocation. It warned in 1956 that the city's relocation program aggravated racial segregation. Non-White families made up 85 percent of the families living in affected urban renewal locations, yet the city planned to relocate displaced non-Whites only in "traditionally Negro neighborhoods," which were already full. Imminent expressway construction would displace another 9,000 families, many of them Black.[21]

Preparers of the first scholarly study of relocation in Detroit interviewed residents and business owners who moved away from the

Fig. 3.2. President Remus Robinson and Coordinating Secretary William Price, Detroit Urban League, testifying before Detroit Common Council on housing conditions, April 6, 1951. Bentley Historical Library, University of Michigan, Detroit Urban League Collection.

Elmwood I and Medical Center project sites from 1961 to 1963. Given the problems found at that time, the experiences of the original Gratiot relocatees, a decade earlier, could only have been worse. In the early 1960s, Wayne State University researchers found that relocatees experienced great difficulties leaving their homes and finding new ones. They "grieved" over the loss of their former homes and neighborhoods. "About four out of every five reported some negative impact, either short- or long-term, from relocation. For more than half of these people, time seemed to have healed the initial wounds. For [most of the rest], however, two years had passed but had not erased or replaced their sense of loss. . . . A few even felt that relocation marked the end of their lives in any meaningful sense."[22]

The study also found that relocation devastated many small, Black-owned businesses. Harriet Saperstein led the study of businesses which had moved out of Elmwood I. She had asked a simple set of questions of former area business owners, such as: "Did people ever come to you with personal problems, like what to do if a son dropped out of school?" "What would you do if a teen-age fight went on outside your store?" Or "How well did you know the people in the neighborhood?" Using responses to these and similar questions to create a rating scale, Saperstein found that local business owners had provided a strong support system for neighborhood residents before relocation. They had given casual loans when needed, supervised area children and youth, and provided important places for social interaction. Of 64 businesses in the Elmwood I clearance area, perhaps 32 did not survive, 20 of which were owned by Blacks.[23]

The low relocation allowances were partially to blame. Most local failed businesses received under $300 in moving payments from the city, and less than $10,000 in property payments. One pool hall owner and his son had been so important to the community that informants consistently referred to them as "institutions." The pool hall did not survive, in part because of low relocation payments. "I was not paid enough to start over into anything. If you wish to pass any information on you may say I feel very bitter over the way people in general were treated. It will not help to say anymore. I tried for many years and many meetings with people that lived in the area to get a better consideration. We did not get it."[24]

These findings confirmed studies of other cities which suggested that neighborhood businesses suffered especially from urban renewal.[25] The decline of such businesses negatively affected inner-city community life. These business owners were an informal mechanism for community linkage and control. They provided the eyes and ears that helped guide youth, insure public safety, and support the needy.

As a final insult, the city did not build public housing in or near the Gratiot site. In 1953, a private developer explained to Cobo that low-income housing was not marketable. Existing requirements forced developers to build high-rent apartments, because the price of the land, even with incentives, was higher than suburban land. Plans for nearby public housing depreciated the true land value even further.[26] An Urban Land Institute (ULI) panel visited Detroit in 1955 and supported these positions. The city had already planned to reduce nearby public housing units from 3600 to 900. The ULI panel, composed of prominent business leaders from several large cities, urged the city to build even less public housing and instead to focus its attention on attracting "the more productive portion of the population" to the site.[27]

After the ULI visit, the redevelopment corporation asked Cobo not to place public housing in or near the redevelopment site. It feared that "any large concentration of public housing is socially and economically wrong," and that "the proposed construction of nearly 400 dwelling units immediately adjacent to the Gratiot Area is an obvious deterrent to building investors." The group recommended that the city scatter small public housing projects throughout the inner city bounded by Grand Boulevard.[28]

The ULI had suggested that the city rehabilitate existing housing, a cheaper option that would integrate low-income people into the

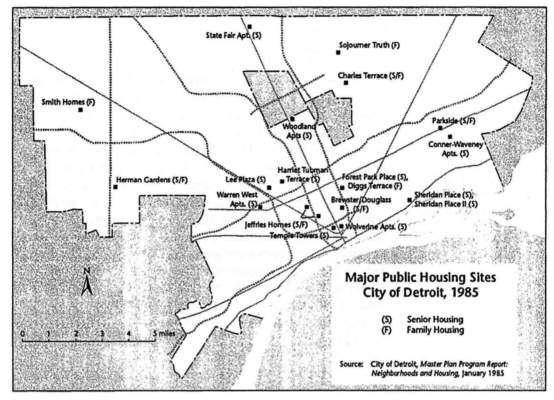

Major Public Housing Sites
City of Detroit, 1985

(S)   Senior Housing
(F)   Family Housing

State Fair Apt. (S)
Sojourner Truth (F)
Charles Terrace (S/F)
Smith Homes (F)
Parkside (S/F)
Woodland Apts. (S)
Conner-Waveney Apts. (S)
Harriet Tubman Terrace (S)
Herman Gardens (S/F)
Lee Plaza (S)
Forest Park Place (S), Diggs Terrace (F)
Warren West Apts. (S)
Brewster/Douglass (S/F)
Sheridan Place (S), Sheridan Place II (S)
Jeffries Homes (S/F)
Wolverine Apts. (S)
Temple Towers (S)

N

0 1 2 3 4 5 miles

Source: City of Detroit, *Master Plan Program Report: Neighborhoods and Housing*, January 1985

Fig. 3.3. Location of major public housing sites, City of Detroit, 1985, shows that the number of major family housing sites did not appreciably expand in forty years. Courtesy Detroit Department of Planning and Development.

general population rather than stigmatize them as public housing residents. Suggestions that the city rehabilitate low-income private housing or scatter public housing made good sense. The only thing wrong was that this countered Cobo's policy of centralizing public housing and protecting White homeowners elsewhere in the city. Even if Cobo had been inclined to carry out the public housing plans, federal legislation made construction of public housing on urban renewal land very expensive. All public housing plans for adjacent sites soon died; the number of sites had not significantly expanded even by the 1980s (see fig. 3.3).

By that time, using new federal housing programs that allowed private nonprofit corporations to sponsor housing, the city developed residential communities in Elmwood Park that boasted an impressive mix of income groups and housing styles. But viewed from the perspective of the 1950s and early 1960s, the failure to build public housing seemed to leave no option for low-income people. Not only did the city cause undue hardship on relocated residents, it also built housing that former residents could not afford.[29]

And so redevelopment grew increasingly unpopular with African Americans. In 1962 a mainstream Detroit newspaper estimated that up until that date perhaps 160,000 Blacks, representing one-third of the city's Black population, had been adversely affected by renewal within the city's core. A Detroit Urban League official claimed that "no single governmental activity has done more to disperse, disorganize, and discourage neighborhood cohesion than has urban redevelopment."[30]

Reconstruction and Race

The effects of racial prejudice did not end with relocation and displacement problems, however; prejudice also hindered reconstruction. In a sign of progressivism, the city tried to develop housing open to the original residents. But it was difficult to find a private developer willing to build in what had been the Black ghetto, and it was difficult to find Whites willing to move into such housing.

At first the city tried to find national firms interested in developing low or moderately priced housing, but several were notably concerned about the race of the tenants. In 1949 James Inglis of the Detroit Housing Commission traveled to New York to interview several major life insurance companies as potential developers. Metropolitan Life was still smarting from the attacks it had drawn for planning New York's racially segregated Stuyvesant Town. It had decided to build future projects without government subsidies, so that it could "maintain complete control over tenant selection." New York Life Insurance Company's O. L. Nelson said that the company would not be interested in Detroit. Its upcoming Chicago redevelopment project might allow "Negro occupancy and his company would not want to throw their program out of balance in favor of Negro occupancy by taking on another such project." Inglis reported to the Detroit Common Council that private enterprise was not prepared to help rebuild and rehouse existing families.[31]

The city decided to try for local sponsorship of racially mixed occupancy, but a marketing study revealed that potential White residents were not ready for racial integration. Only 1.6 percent of the 123 "colored" citizens surveyed objected to mixed housing, but 76.4 percent of 1,244 Whites found mixed occupancy unattractive. The marketing researcher estimated that between 80 and 90 percent of downtown White employees were not potential residents because of their attitude toward interracial living. This meant that the number of "active prospects" for the site fell between 3,000 and 4,000 Whites and between 2,300 and 2,800 Blacks; a realistic construction schedule would target 10 percent of this, or 650 rental or cooperative housing units.[32]

The city formed a development corporation at the instigation of the UAW's Walter Reuther, and it proceeded based on this market survey. It solicited redevelopment plans from noted architectural firms and selected the plans of Ludwig Mies van der Rohe for twin twenty-two-story luxury apartment towers containing just under 600 units. The first tower opened in 1958; soon thereafter, developers built several cooperative apartments and townhouse units.[33]

Gratiot overcame its early setbacks to become a grand experiment in integrated living. Yet it did this by sheltering middle class Whites from lower class Blacks. In 1960, researchers discovered that the new residents of the renamed Lafayette Park were highly educated professionals. They wanted to live close to downtown but also saw their housing choice as "something of a cause," "an experimental area." The project's open commitment to integrated occupancy was laudable, but part of the price for this integration was income homogeneity. High prices allayed "fears about possible Negro inundation. The economic barrier . . . control[led] the proportions of Negro residents. Promotional material stressed the natural selection process created by costs, and in their talks with prospective buyers and renters, salespersons pointed out that anyone who could afford such housing would be of a superior social class."[34]

Even with such protection, Lafayette Park only slowly became acceptable to middle class Whites. In addition to the disincentive of racial integration, delays in constructing schools discouraged unit sales. Some private developers berated the city for clearing an island of land surrounded by poor housing and expecting "people to want to live in this type of area."[35] Although the project won design kudos, it also illustrated the racial pitfalls awaiting an inner-city redevelopment strategy.

This, then, was the mixed record of Detroit's first residential project. Lafayette Park became a model of urban design and community building. In the process, however, the city trampled on the rights of former site residents, and failed to provide comparable low-income housing. To its credit, the city decided to build racially integrated middle-income housing, but it encountered considerable barriers because of Whites' racial prejudice.

An Economic Development Strategy

Lafayette Park marked the beginning of Detroit's housing redevelopment focus. Its economic development strategy, targeted to the central business district and industrial core, built upon the 1947 Detroit Plan. Detroit followed a path similar to other U.S. cities' attempts to survive difficult financial times, although its strategy took a markedly industrial slant.

The drive for economic vitality is particularly strong in U.S. cities because they are dominated by business interests. Cities can neither regulate private assets nor undertake commercial ventures without state authorization. Yet cities face daunting economic conditions. They must raise funds in a private credit market, so they must "please" the givers of credit by demonstrating economic soundness. The federal system does not guarantee fiscal sovereignty for its cities, and they may indeed go bankrupt. Mayors depend on political contributions in order to run for office, which further strengthens the ties between politicians and business interests. Promoting economic growth therefore becomes a natural imperative. Hence, the motivation behind the economic agenda of postwar growth coalitions was deep and systemic.[36]

Given this situation, it is surprising how poorly the political economic agenda performed in Detroit. One would have expected unusual persistence with economic redevelopment projects, since the motivation for success must have been extremely strong. Yet economic redevelopment was one of the least successful initiatives for the city in spite of consistent and robust efforts in that direction. This is evident by examining, first, the city's central business district strategy and, then, its industrial strategy.

Saving the Central Business District

The central business district had been a point of concern in Detroit long before urban renewal. Local businesses supported planning, zoning, and redevelopment because they wanted to protect downtown property values. Yet city leaders could do little to save the downtown.

Detroit's downtown faced unusual disadvantages. The city's heavy dependence upon automobile transportation dispersed workers to suburban homes. Detroit had only a modest trolley system, and no commuter rail system comparable to those in Chicago, New York, and Cleveland. The lack of a commuter rail left downtown stores without a dependable pedestrian population and sentenced the transit-dependent to a slow and unreliable bus system.[37]

The outward spread of the automobile industry did not help. No major automobile company headquarters remained in downtown Detroit after the 1920s. All of the companies now known as the Big Three—Chrysler, Ford, and General Motors—began in central Detroit and then moved outward. Ford Motor Company relocated to Highland Park in 1909 and from there to suburban Dearborn. Chrysler placed its major corporate offices in suburban Highland Park. In 1919 General Motors built its world headquarters in the city but two miles north of the central business district. There General Motors attracted its own cluster of office and commercial establishments; "New Center" became, in effect, a second major business district.[38]

Geography also played a part in dispersion. Even though the Detroit River edged the city, Detroit lacked the major topographical boundaries which forced compression upon peninsular places such as Boston, San Francisco, and New York City's Manhattan. It had no high rent district close to the central business district comparable to Boston's Beacon Hill or Manhattan's Greenwich Village. Even major civic institutions were located away from downtown. Located on Woodward Avenue, the Detroit Public Library and the Detroit Institute of Arts were almost as far from the central business district as General Motors headquarters was. This left major commercial, cultural, and office buildings strung along Woodward Avenue like sparsely placed jewels in a necklace.

By the 1950s, downtown retail trade was declining rapidly. Houston's proportion of area retail sales fell from 42.9 percent to 31.8 percent between 1948 and 1954, while Washington's fell from 28.9 percent to 20.8 percent. Detroit's central business district, which had enjoyed only 15.5 percent of area retail sales in 1948, earned merely 9.9 percent of area retail sales by 1954.[39]

Modern suburban shopping centers aggravated these already anemic tendencies. In 1953 Detroit's J. L. Hudson Company opened Northland, the nation's first regional shopping center of enclosed "hub" design. Northland at one million square feet in size was large enough to draw sales away from Hudson's downtown flagship store. It became a financial success and model for other area malls. Eighteen shopping centers, some rivaling Northland in size, opened in the region between 1954 and 1957.[40] Suburban malls dealt a devastating blow to the already weak downtown.[41]

Building a civic center was an important part of the city's downtown "solution." In the 1940s state and local government offices were so scattered and inadequate that consolidation became an urgent need. Private factories and bulky warehouses blocked the view of the river that central business district patrons and workers might have enjoyed. To promote municipal pride and commercial health, city leaders planned to build a center for public buildings and plazas. This was located at the place where Woodward Avenue, the city's great bisector thoroughfare, met the Detroit River.[42]

To design a suitable center, the city hired Saarinen and Associates in 1947. Eliel Saarinen, an internationally respected Finnish-born architect, had immigrated to the United States and helped establish Cranbrook Institute, a design center in a northern Detroit suburb. Saarinen and his son Eero, also an architect, designed an impressive plaza-oriented plan for Detroit's civic center.[43] A revision of this plan appeared in the 1951 Detroit Master Plan (see fig. 3.4).

The basic structure outlined in the 1951 plan exists today. The first building constructed was the Veterans' Memorial Building, dedicated in 1950. A new city-county office building was completed in 1955. Soon added were Henry and Edsel Ford Auditorium, opened in 1956 as the home of the Detroit Symphony Orchestra, and Cobo Hall and Arena, opened in 1960 to host convention business and trade shows as well as local large-scale public events (see fig. 3.5). Corporate leaders supported these efforts in order to protect downtown investments and encourage spinoff construction. Because of their donations Detroit financed the center entirely with municipal bonds and private donations.[44]

The Civic Center provided Detroit with a beautiful public place, where weekend summer crowds enjoyed festivals, concerts, and simple leisure. It also gave confidence to investors in nearby buildings such as the Pontchartrain Hotel, National Bank of Detroit Building, and Michigan Consolidated Gas Company in the 1950s and 1960s, the Renaissance Center in the 1970s, and nearby Millen-

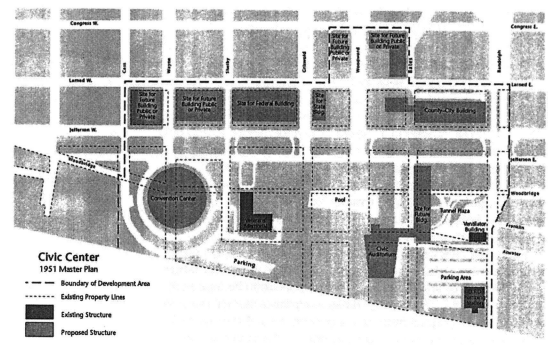

Civic Center
1951 Master Plan

- • ——— —— Boundary of Development Area
- - - - - - - Existing Property Lines

Existing Structure

Proposed Structure

Fig. 3.4. Detroit Civic Center, 1951 Master Plan, shows the outlines of the development plan that the city basically followed, although no "Federal Building" was built. Cobo Hall, the "Convention Center," is the circle on the left. Courtesy Detroit Department of Planning and Development.

der Center in the 1980s. Cobo Hall became the mainstay of the city's convention business and a base for civic improvements. But the Civic Center could not, by itself, salvage the commercial sector.[45]

Neither could expressways, a second part of the city's downtown strategy. At the same time that the city worked to attract people to the central business district with its Civic Center, it helped them leave by constructing expressways. One of the causes of decline was dependence on automobiles, but a solution was to accommodate more automobiles! Viewed from the 1950s, this did not seem illogical. The federal Highway Act of 1956 set up a trust fund that picked up 90 percent of expressway construction costs. This was an irresistible temptation for local and state officials trying to leverage limited tax dollars. The act offered no such incentive for public transit, the most efficient way of moving large groups of people within urban cores. Cities fell into a vicious cycle of seeking relief from traffic by accommodating more and more automobiles. As road systems grew and improved, more people bought more cars, and public transit systems atrophied.

Detroit's expressway focus came not just because of the federal government. The city financed expressway construction well before the 1956 federal highway legislation made it financially easy to do so. Detroit's 1951 master plan devoted much attention to laying out expressways and other streets. The results were a well-thought-out expressway system, linking the central business district with the suburbs, but providing mobility in both directions (see fig. 3.6).

The city did not freely choose its automobile orientation. The au-

Fig. 3.5. Detroit Civic Center, Cobo Hall, and Arena in foreground, looking east (probably early 1960s). The circular building to the right, with the dark dome, is the part of Cobo Hall identified in the 1951 Master Plan as the "Convention Center." Bentley Historical Library, University of Michigan, Michigan Bell Telephone Collection.

tomobile industry pushed it in this direction and actively discouraged rail transit schemes.[46] Local boosterism for expressways reflected a pragmatic adjustment to corporate pressures and federal policy. Yet many city staff seemed to believe that building highways and parking ramps would resolve central city congestion and make downtown competitive with suburban malls. William Sloan, coordinator of the city's industrial and commercial development committee, expected road and parking ramp construction to "make it easier to get downtown and provide parking facilities for the shopper's convenience."[47] Senior planner Richard Ahern argued that the growing network of expressways provided a structure of "well-defined superblocks" that freed the interior from automobile traffic and helped provide "an atmosphere reminiscent of the dignity and beauty of the Greek agora and Roman forum." In his view, the city could improve the central business district's overall organization by channeling the automobile into well-defined corridors.[48]

Ahern's characterization of these benefits was overblown, but Juliet Sabit and Harold Black, the planning staff's "social economists," fell prey to no grand illusions. They noted that the expressways helped city residents get out to outlying suburban malls even though they also eased access to downtown. The city's parking ramps, which charged fees, could never compete with free parking at suburban malls. As the two planners phrased it, "neither the expressway nor the [municipal] parking spaces have changed the simple arithmetic of more cars and fewer people" in downtown De-

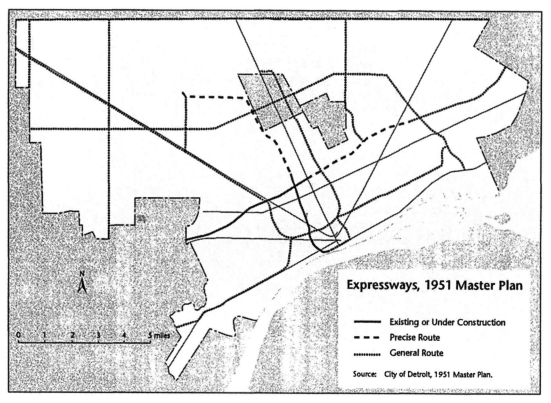

Expressways, 1951 Master Plan

Existing or Under Construction
Precise Route
General Route

Source: City of Detroit, 1951 Master Plan.

Fig. 3.6. Expressways, 1951 Master Plan. Although the city and state eventually revised several of these routes, this shows the extensive network planned, allowing for easy entry to, and exit from, the city's central areas. Courtesy Detroit Department of Planning and Development.

troit. Yet they could suggest few corrective policies other than increasing downtown amenities. This meant that the city sponsored projects which gave downtown streets beautiful landscaping, including brick walks and street sculpture, but often failed to prevent bordering hotels and businesses from going out of business.[49]

The Housing Act of 1949 had reserved Title I redevelopment subsidies for areas that were residential or would become residential after reconstruction. Therefore, cities chose residential project areas that bordered the central business district, such as Gratiot, to help bolster their downtowns. Clearing dilapidated housing thus dovetailed with the economic imperative of downtown improvement. But the Housing Act of 1954 let the federal housing agency use up to 10 percent of its urban renewal funds for nonresidential projects. This opened the door for more direct funding of downtown improvement.

Detroit developed a series of central business district projects, ranging in size from four acres to over fifty. One site cleared out "skid row," which sheltered impoverished alcoholics and other social outcasts.[50] Another site was eventually rebuilt with Blue Cross and other office buildings. In later years, this project area connected with the nearby Greektown, a popular restaurant district.[51]

In spite of several successes, urban renewal did not rebuild Detroit's central business district. Some sites never developed replace-

Fig. 3.7. Aerial photograph of expressway construction near central business district (ca. 1981). Considering the lack of commuter rail transit, Detroit has too many expressways, and thus too many cars, in and near the downtown area. Burton Historical Collection, Detroit Public Library.

Fig. 3.8. Central Business District, looking from Grand Circus Park area at downtown street improvements on Washington Boulevard (probably 1960s). Bentley Historical Library, University of Michigan, Michigan Bell Telephone Collection.

ment uses. Inherent weaknesses in Detroit's downtown meant that all corrective actions fought against market forces. The Civic Center helped, but expressways were counterproductive, helping shoppers and workers become even less tied to the central business district. Those who promoted downtown fought an uphill battle against mall competition.

Battling Industrial Decline

Efforts to support the industrial sector were hardly more effective. It was a particular challenge to recover from losses in the automobile industry.

By 1940 Detroit specialized more in motor vehicle manufacturing than New York City specialized in business, Pittsburgh in steel, or Boston and San Francisco in finance, education, or government. The Detroit metropolitan area was the major American area most committed to manufacturing. In 1940, 48.2 percent of its metropolitan employment was in manufacturing, compared to 35.6 percent in Pittsburgh, and 35.0 percent in Chicago.[52] Even then, the number of service jobs was low compared with that in other cities (see figs. 3.9, 3.10).

In its earliest years, the automobile industry operated huge factories located in the Detroit metropolitan area and other centers in Michigan. When the market changed, Detroit suffered major losses. The rate of growth in the automotive market rose sharply until the 1920s but then leveled off until the early 1950s. Many independent firms combined or went bankrupt during the Great Depression of the 1920s and the lean years thereafter. Eighty firms existed in 1922, but by the early 1950s the number of firms fell to six: General Motors, Chrysler, Ford, American Motors, Studebaker, and Kaiser-Willys.

Automobile firms died because only a few of them met the severe requirements for survival. They had to offer a diversified product line, giving buyers a choice in several price ranges. They had to sell a high enough volume to realize the economies of mass production. They needed to invest massive amounts of money and support research in a rapidly innovating field. These requirements eliminated smaller firms, but competition and diseconomy of size checked the growth of larger firms. Instead of a monopoly, an oligopoly arose, dominated by the Big Three, Chrysler, Ford, and GM.[53] One practical effect was that a neighborhood built under the shadow of several different automobile plants sometimes found itself left with one, or none. The east side Jefferson-Chalmers community, for example, once hosted Hudson Motor Company, Continental Motors, and Chrysler, but the first two companies failed.[54]

Surviving firms sometimes moved out of the central city. Between 1947 and 1955 Chrysler, Ford, and GM built 20 new plants in the Detroit region, employing a total of 72,000 workers. Not a single one of these plants was located within Detroit or within the central

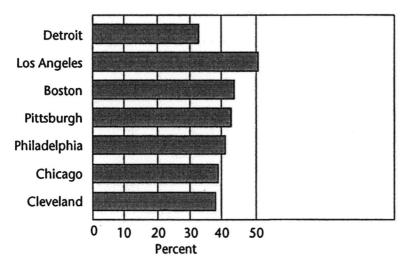

Fig. 3.9. The percent of the labor force employed in services and other secondary activities was relatively small in Detroit in 1940. Courtesy Detroit Department of Planning and Development.

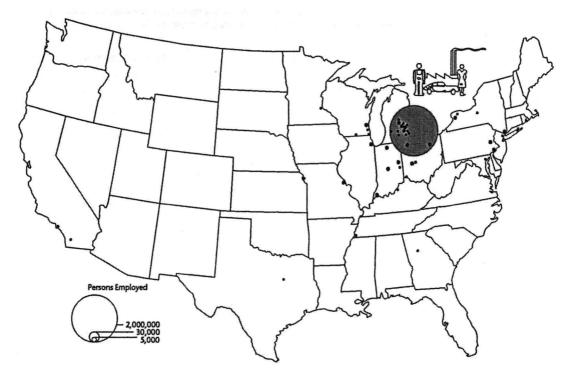

Fig. 3.10. Detroit clearly dominated the nation as a major center of automobile industry employment in 1940. Courtesy Detroit Department of Planning and Development.

suburbs of Highland Park or Hamtramck. The General Motors Technology Center was located in Warren Township; Ford built tractor, transmission, and assembly plants in Birmingham, Livonia, and Ypsilanti; Chrysler opened operations in Sterling Township, Centerline, and Dearborn; and General Motors built assembly plants in Livonia and Romulus Township.[55]

Firms were leaving for practical reasons. As early as the 1930s they cited high city taxes, stringent city building code requirements, and cheap suburban land as motivating factors.[56] In addition, Detroit's planners documented an extreme shortage of sufficiently large in-

TABLE 3.1   MANUFACTURING FIRMS' REASONS FOR LEAVING
DETROIT, 1937 – 1949

Reason	Major Factor	Minor Factor	Does Not Apply
Tax rates	70%	19%	11%
Need for greater space	68	19	13
Zoning restrictions	35	16	49
Lower rent	33	10	56
Labor pay rates	10	25	65
Special inducements	9	17	74
Access to ground water	0	11	89
Other reasons*	76	12	12

Source: Detroit Metropolitan Area Regional Planning Commission, "Movement of Manufacturing Establishments 1937–1949 and Factors influencing Location of Plans" (December 1949), p. 4. Based on survey of 146 exiting manufacturing establishments; 63 responded.
*Ranged from less competition to consolidation of operations.

dustrial parcels within the central city.[57] Paul Reid, a planner for the regional planning commission, surveyed manufacturing establishments that left the city for suburban sites between 1937 and 1949. These firms designated two major reasons for their exodus: the city's tax rates and the need for greater space (see table 3.1). Heavy manufacturing establishments which needed a large amount of land per worker were leaving congested central locations, as might be expected. So too were firms producing light goods, firms which supposedly could operate in multistoried buildings and thus survive in built-up central cities. They were leaving because of the magnetic effect of the larger producers, and because of the lure of cheap industrial land and tax relief.[58]

When Detroit's planners surveyed the city's industrial firms in 1956, over 40 percent of their respondents were dissatisfied with their sites. Visual studies of the industrial corridors revealed that, of 7,109 acres, 840 acres (11.8 percent) were extremely deteriorated and 1700 acres (23.8 percent) exhibited considerable deterioration. Although the city had over 700 acres of vacant land in industrial corridors, the parcels were too small for major industrial development or expansion. Only two of twenty-two vacant industrial sites contained more than twenty acres; most vacant parcels were less than a quarter acre.[59]

Industrial and labor leaders pressured city government for solutions. In the 1940s industrial proponents complained to city council and planning commissioners about unfavorable rezoning decisions and insufficient industrial land set aside within the master plan. They also complained about plans to reclaim the riverfront from industrial use. Labor unions wanted the city to attract industry and save their jobs. In 1945 UAW president R. J. Thomas urged Detroit's council to establish an industrial development authority with

Fig. 3.11. Photograph of houses with Briggs Body plant in background, taken by Works Progress Administration, 1943. A common land use problem in Detroit was the close proximity of housing and heavy industry. Burton Historical Collection, Detroit Public Library.

the power to assemble land for industrial sites. In keeping with the union's other postwar suggestions for housing and for regional planning, Thomas urged that such an authority acquire and develop sites "inside or outside the city."[60]

If development had taken place as outlined in the 1951 master plan, more land would have been available for industry. In that plan the city had placed industrial use in corridors separating protected residential communities, as in figure 3.12. The industrial sectors followed the rough outlines of existing industrial use, supplemented by residential areas located in industrial sectors. These and scattered industrial sites were consolidated into several "fingers" of development. The practical problem was how to get large areas of industrial land, how to relocate existing residents, and how to convince industrial firms to build on designated land. The best that land-use controls could do was to woo new firms and accommodate old ones by approving industrial requests for appropriate zoning, rezoning, or special use permits.[61]

Redevelopment again appeared to be a way out of a dilemma. This would let the city buy existing houses and land, prepare sites, and resell them cheaply to industrial firms. The Lafayette Park project was supposed to remake the eastern flank of the central business district into a residential area attractive to suburban middle and upper class residents. The Corktown industrial project was supposed to do for the west side what Lafayette Park did for the east, plus

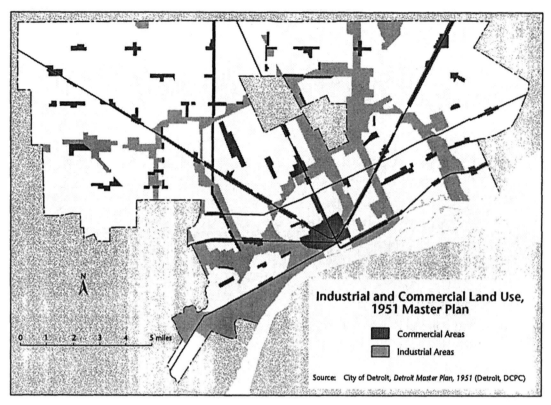

Industrial and Commercial Land Use,
1951 Master Plan

■ Commercial Areas

■ Industrial Areas

Source: City of Detroit, *Detroit Master Plan, 1951* (Detroit, DCPC)

Fig. 3.12. Proposed industrial and commercial land use, as indicated in the 1951 Master Plan. This built upon existing patterns of land use, but suggested a clearer definition of elongated "fingers" of industrial land use, located near rail lines and existing industrial facilities. Courtesy Detroit Department of Planning and Development.

more: clear out unsightly older houses and obsolete industrial buildings and replace them with new warehouses and other tax-generating firms. This was the first of a series of efforts by the city to redevelop land appropriate for industrial use (see fig. 3.13).

Corktown, site of the first Detroit industrial redevelopment project, was located immediately to the west of the central business district. An older section of the city, it was first settled by Irish immigrants from County Cork, Ireland. Mostly residential, Corktown also contained some industrial and commercial users. By 1950 Corktown's residents included Maltese and Mexican immigrants, who made up two-thirds of the population, and other White ethnics and Blacks.[62]

In the early 1940s the city planned to keep Corktown largely residential. But in 1945 the Pennsylvania Railroad and the Detroit Real Estate Board asked the planning commission to rezone sites in Corktown from residential to industrial use. For a time the fate of the area was uncertain, because the housing commission planned public housing for the area. In the early 1950s many local homeowners, opposing the plan to replace their houses with industry, fought a spirited battled against relocation. The 1951 master plan, however, counted Corktown as a nonresidential area (see fig. 3.1), and the city clearly indicated that it would be the site of its second urban renewal site. In the end, the city's first industrial redevelopment project proceeded.[63]

The West Side Industrial Project, still known popularly as Corktown, eventually cleared 75 acres in its first phase, with 92 acres added in 1963. Several light industrial companies moved to the project site, and a major office building and hotel were constructed.[64] An original purpose for the project had been to provide a site for warehouses displaced by construction of the Civic Center, but by the time the project site was ready most of them had already relocated to other areas.[65] Some Corktown sites were still vacant thirty years later. The project was only a drop in the bucket of industrial land needs: It cleared 167 acres, but the planners' 1956 study had shown that 2540 acres of the city's industrial facilities were extremely or considerably deteriorated. Corktown created a west side buffer for downtown, but it led to neither new life for the central business district nor a rebirth of industry.[66]

Corktown was supposed to initiate a major campaign for indus-

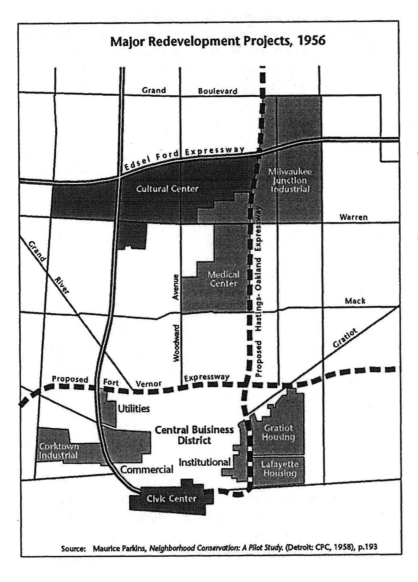

Fig. 3.13. Major redevelopment projects for the City of Detroit, 1956, showing Gratiot–Lafayette Park on the east and Corktown on the west of the central business district. The area here labeled "Cultural Center" included Wayne State University, in a project later separated from the Cultural Center and named "University City." Courtesy Detroit Department of Planning and Development.

trial redevelopment. In 1954 Detroit's planners drafted a tentative list of redevelopment priorities for the next 18 years; their draft list clearly favored industrial redevelopment over commercial and residential.[67] Financing such an industrial agenda was too difficult, however. The city itself was razing the sites of tax-paying firms: Lafayette Park displaced 12 industrial firms, and the Chrysler expressway displaced 28. Furthermore, the federal government would not commit to pay for industrial redevelopment, and Detroit had to figure out how to pay for it itself. While proceeding with the Corktown industrial project, planners helped select a second industrial site, Milwaukee-Junction, 335 acres near the Chrysler Dodge Main assembly plant. Mayor Cobo set aside $300,000 in the 1957–58 budget and planned to issue additional bonds to get the first 17 acres of this project started. In 1958 the planning commission staff made preliminary layout plans for Milwaukee-Junction and three other sites covering 138 acres. But Cobo's death and the next mayor's desire to pay off municipal debt limited the initiative.[68]

By the mid-1960s the only viable industrial redevelopment projects were Corktown, the shrunken Milwaukee-Junction project, and a planned industrial research park project which would cover only 60 acres. The city still lacked large industrial sites, and there was no strategy for coping with onrushing economic decline.[69] Not until 1981 would Detroit attempt another major industrial redevelopment project.

The late 1940s and 1950s offered the best opportunity to provide the land and other amenities industrial firms needed. Industrial location studies suggested that firms were primarily interested in traditional location factors such as access to markets, access to qualified labor, and raw materials, findings that should have made Detroit attractive.[70] But lack of suitable land and obsolescent facilities were real constraints. By the time the city did carry out another major industrial redevelopment project, in the 1980s, factors motivating industrial decisions had changed. By then firms were less bound by the need for favorable urban locations.

Industrial redevelopment turned out to be very difficult. The Corktown project removed older residential and industrial buildings and opened up land for development, but the relatively small project took too long for the city to relocate to Corktown its displaced Civic Center warehouses. The federal government did not supply enough money for Detroit to launch a major industrial sector strategy. With expressway construction and other clearance projects, moreover, the city proceeded to clear out its own economic base.

A number of scholars have overemphasized the supposed relaxation of redevelopment legislation that took place with the Housing Act of 1954. John Mollenkopf and Mark Gelfand have implied that, under the Republican administration of Dwight Eisenhower, business interests gained free rein to exploit the nonresidential exception and launch myriad economic development projects. Mollenkopf suggests that the 1954 urban renewal legislation "allowed downtown business, developers, and their political allies, who had little interest in housing, to use federal power to advance their own ends." Gelfand refers to the "severe distortions" created in the renewal process by the number of office and shopping centers that local officials began to sponsor, ignoring true slum areas if they were not located in places where entrepreneurs could make a dollar.[71]

While in some important cases these charges are true, they are also misleading. The Eisenhower administration hesitated to approve redevelopment projects for anything but housing: nonresidential projects never exceeded 7.7 percent of grant funds, although 10 percent was allowed. Before 1957 the Eisenhower administration had to persuade cities to apply for urban renewal funds. After that time, demand for renewal dollars exceeded supply, making projects more difficult to approve. The federal government funded no massive salvation of either central business districts or industrial sectors.[72]

Detroit's civic and labor leaders pleaded with Congress to finance industrial redevelopment and relief for cyclical unemployment. Yet the federal government actually aggravated problems of industrial flight. It encouraged defense industries to disperse rather than concentrate in easily bombed target areas, and it simultaneously skewed defense industry investment away from the Midwest. In the 1960s federal economic development programs lagged in providing funds to Detroit, claiming that Detroit's unemployment rates indicated little economic distress. The fact is that employment in the Detroit region was extremely volatile, subject to peaks and valleys.[73]

Inherent conflicts also hindered action to save the industrial sector. A basic choice had to be made between industrial and residential land use, as it was impossible to meet industrial expansion needs without radically changing the land-use mix of the city. In the 1960s new industrial developments were using 15 to 20 employees per acre, but Detroit's firms averaged 45 employees per acre. The city had approximately 6,000 acres devoted to industrial use. At modern densities, it would have taken 18,000 acres, half the city's land, just to maintain current employment. The city would have to destroy itself to keep its industrial firms! A planner from that era comments: "Those were just unbelievable conclusions, and we didn't see any way really to do that."[74]

A final dilemma was the fact that industrial leaders did not actively promote business retention. Top automobile executives lived in Detroit's suburbs, where many of their offices could be found. By the 1960s, when asked why they continued to leave the city, industrialists complained more about high wages and high city taxes than about lack of room to expand.[75]

Initial Experiences

With the city's strategies to eliminate "slums" and "blight," the benefits and costs of urban redevelopment became readily apparent.

Lafayette Park became an attractive, well-planned community that exhibited the potential for racial integration. It provided a small but important middle-class presence in an inner city that everyone except the poor had apparently abandoned. It also proved that a market existed for rebuilt residential areas near the central business district. Lafayette Park gave Detroit's urban planners an opportunity to demonstrate their design skills and to promote, in some limited fashion, racial integration.

While these were important benefits, the project caused major hardships for the Black community. It generated significant relocation and rehousing problems for low-income dwellers and devastated local businesses. The perception of racial injustice was inevitable given the hardships suffered because of relocation and rehousing difficulties. Although at first civil rights groups supported "slum clearance," it is little wonder that they came to distrust it.

The social environment of racial prejudice made it difficult to relocate site residents or to find a willing developer. Only by skillful marketing and income selectivity could developers attract White residents. Furthermore, the project was not nearly large enough to attract a significant number of middle class residents back to the inner city. By the mid-1960s, Lafayette/Elmwood Park had 1700 middle and upper income units. People were leaving the central city by the tens of thousands, a process that redevelopment did not slow.[76]

The city's economic redevelopment efforts also faltered. The city successfully built a Civic Center that formed an important focal point for downtown. Other supportive efforts included the residential Lafayette Park project to the east of the downtown area and the industrial Corktown project to the west. But building expressways and parking structures, envisioned as aids for downtown shoppers and workers, only increased the exodus. Central business district projects were only moderately successful, and industrial redevelopment eluded the city.

Federal and local policies were only partially to blame. The central business district had inherent weaknesses long before the 1950s. Many major corporate headquarters and cultural institutions located elsewhere in the city or region. Inadequate public transportation doomed the downtown to simultaneous congestion and dispersal. Surveys of the 1940s and 1950s indicated that plant owners and managers wanted more land, but there is little evidence that they would have stayed if the city had provided it.

However, lack of supportive federal policies certainly did not help. If the most important government policies are those that receive the most funds, the federal government's foremost urban policies during this postwar period were not public housing or urban renewal but, rather, its FHA mortgage interest tax write-off and its highway policies. With the Housing Act of 1949, Congress authorized $1.5 billion for clearance and redevelopment over a five-year period. At the same time Congress authorized $6 billion for the FHA mortgage insurance program, an amount it increased almost yearly. The FHA, income tax policies, and highway programs effectively financed the exodus to the suburbs of the very families and firms that cities, with a fraction of those funds, hoped to hold or attract back.[77]

Racial Flight and the Conservation Experiment

4

One of the most difficult problems facing postwar Detroit was population loss: almost half within a thirty-year period. Some of this loss came as a natural by-product of families moving to the suburbs, a move that the federal government helped finance with highway programs, mortgage insurance subsidies, and income tax policies. Some families moved because of the American love affair with the suburban dream, as symbolized by a single-family house with its own lawn and white picket fence, but others moved because of racial change.

While any individual family's move could have been motivated by a number of innocent reasons, the cumulative effects were vicious and devastating. The almost wholesale middle-class abandonment of the central city was not innocent. It was racially selective, income selective, and motivated, in at least some instances, by intolerance of racial mixing. A White family did not have to be "racist" to participate in a racist process.

Popular mythology holds otherwise. Content in their suburban enclaves, some area residents blame the 1967 riots for driving out Whites, or they suggest that inner-city Blacks prefer isolation. These misconceptions are just that. As this chapter shows, the city's neighborhoods were experiencing the effects of racial turnover long before 1967. African Americans did not move out of the city in comparable numbers because they could not, since discrimination blocked their path. Their residential isolation, largely involuntary, made life in the inner city all the more challenging. Escalating poverty and a declining tax base drove more people out, since neighborhood upkeep faltered, crime increased, and schools declined. But these problems were actually *consequences* of processes that had been taking place for a long time.

Racial flight blocked efforts to maintain stability within residential neighborhoods. Attempts to stabilize neighborhoods continue to this day, but long before today planners were losing the battle against flight. The conservation program of the 1950s offers an early snapshot of the forces of neighborhood decline and the difficulties caused by racial discrimination.

Racial Change

It took some time for analysts to realize that the city's population was declining. In the early 1950s, planners expected the population to reach 2,004,304 by 1980.[1] Detroit's population peaked in the mid-1950s at just over 1.8 million people, and it has declined ever since. The 1960 census was the first to reveal that the city's population had dropped. The city gained only 14 percent in population during the 1940s and fell by 10 percent during the 1950s. Total metropolitan population, however, had increased: Between 1940 and 1950 the population of the three-county standard metropolitan statistical area rose by 27 percent, and between 1950 and 1960 it rose by 25 percent. One suburban county, Macomb, grew by 72 percent during the 1940s and 119 percent during the 1950s.[2]

Between 1940 and 1950, the City of Detroit gained 226,116 Whites and 152,931 non-Whites. Between 1950 and 1960, it gained 183,183 non-Whites and lost 362,877 Whites. By 1960, Blacks constituted only 15 percent of the region, but 29 percent of the central city. Whites were moving out of the city and into racially homogeneous suburban communities. Warren, the largest city in Macomb County, grew from 727 people in 1950 to 89,246 by 1960, but only 19 of its citizens were Black. And Warren was not an exceptional case. Throughout the metropolitan area, municipalities incorporated and developed with little or no racial diversity. Only in isolated communities such as Inkster, a large portion of which Henry Ford developed to house his "colored" River Rouge workers, did Blacks settle in any great numbers outside the city boundaries.[3]

Racial prejudice in the housing market underlay this phenomenon. Whites were leaving the city by the thousands, but Blacks could not leave. Neither public nor private housing was open to Blacks in most suburban communities. Public housing was out of the question: by 1962, only 1,040 public housing units existed in Detroit's suburbs, and 300 of these were in Hamtramck, a suburban enclave embedded within Detroit's city limits. The other 740 public housing units were scattered in four different communities. Inkster and Ecorse, suburbs with substantial Black populations, had 300 and 200 units, respectively, containing a total of fifteen White tenants; Wayne had forty units, with no Blacks; and the River Rouge project divided its Black and White tenants with a time-honored social barrier, a railroad track.[4]

Neither could Blacks buy newly constructed private housing. Builders constructed 178,000 new homes outside the city limits between 1950 and 1956, but only about 750 of these were available to non-Whites. The chief source of dwelling units for Blacks was housing vacated by White families moving out of aged structures within older parts of the central city. The result was a housing market that was artificially restricted for Black families, even as it steadily drew White families outward.[5]

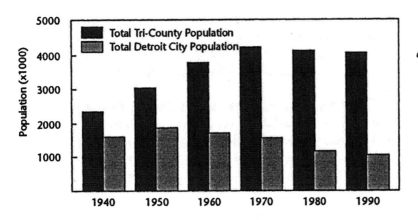

Fig. 4.1. Population change in City of Detroit and three largest metropolitan counties (tri-county area), 1940–90. Population has steadily declined in the City of Detroit, although population in the innermost three counties has remained steady between 1970 and 1990.

Private Market Barriers and White Flight

Two sets of explanations help clarify why Blacks could not move outward at the same rate Whites did, and why inner-city residential neighborhoods tended to change races without stabilizing in a state of racial integration. The first relates to the severely restrained nature of Black mobility and the other to the process of neighborhood change.

Some racial or ethnic groups volunteer to cluster with their own kind. But other groups live in clusters largely because external barriers block free mobility.[6] Voluntary cohesiveness appears to be only a minor factor in the residential pattern of African Americans, since surveys have shown that they prefer racially mixed neighborhoods.[7] The real problem was that Blacks faced major barriers to free mobility. Some of those barriers were institutional, set up by federal mortgage policies.

Beginning in 1933 with the Home Owners Loan Corporation (HOLC), the federal government rated city neighborhoods by placing them in one of four coded categories. These ranged from new and homogeneous, the "A" category, to old and in a state of decline, the "D" category. The uniformly trained appraisers considered any non-White entry into a residential area as a sure sign of decline. They invariably rated Black neighborhoods "D," even if the housing was in excellent condition. The FHA adopted HOLC appraisal techniques and maps. Unlike the HOLC, however, the FHA sometimes refused to make loans to "C" and "D" areas. It also instructed its staff to make sure that properties "continue to be occupied by the same social and racial classes." The FHA *Underwriting Manual* suggested use of subdivision regulations and restrictive covenants to guarantee racial homogeneity. The FHA then refused to insure mortgages that led to racial mixing.[8]

These provisions sometimes led to bizarre behavior, as in Detroit's Eight Mile–Wyoming area. Eight Mile–Wyoming was one of the few Black neighborhoods that was not located near Detroit's older central core. White families began to settle near the Black enclave in the 1930s, and Whites had completely surrounded it by 1940.

But then neither racial group could get FHA mortgage insurance, because a different race lived nearby. To break the impasse, a White developer built a concrete wall between the residential sections in 1941. The FHA then approved the mortgages on the White properties.[9]

Federal dollars financed the development of fringe areas, yet federal policies insured that only Whites lived there. Labor leaders Walter Reuther and James Thimmes wrote President Dwight Eisenhower about the results in 1954. It was inherently unjust, they lamented, for the federal government to exclude non-White families from the vast network of FHA-financed housing and then give "substantial profits to private builders and lenders." Reuther and Thimmes warned that racial segregation would worsen if FHA continued to support exclusionary policies. The Eisenhower administration responded politely to the labor leaders but did nothing.[10]

The federal government was not the only guilty party. Lending institutions refused to give home mortgages either to non-White people seeking financing or to anyone desiring housing in non-White or integrated areas. Blacks were obliged to turn to land contracts, an expensive alternative. The rare White builder who attempted to build housing available to all races was likely to find his efforts blocked by protectionist local officials. Real estate agents routinely encouraged people to buy or rent residences only in "acceptable" areas.[11] Some suburban politicians built their reputations on racial segregation. The most famous of these politicians in the Detroit area was Mayor Orville Hubbard, who publicly bragged about his ability to keep Blacks out of the City of Dearborn. Hubbard and similar politicians provided the public support for private home owner and landlord prejudice.[12]

In the late 1940s, some relief appeared from the courts. One common tool for exclusion had been racially restrictive covenants. These were clauses in private contracts in which buyers agreed not to sell property to people of color. In the 1940s, Detroiter Reginald McGhee, Sr., helped win the legal battle to make racially restrictive covenants impotent. McGhee's family suffered cross burnings and harassment when they moved into a White neighborhood. A neighbor filed suit, citing a restrictive covenant barring anyone not of the Caucasian race. Represented by Thurgood Marshall, NAACP attorney, McGhee eventually took the case to the U.S. Supreme Court, which considered several similar cases simultaneously. A 1948 ruling, *Shelley vs. Kraemer,* stated that racially restrictive covenants could not be legally enforced.[13]

Civil rights and labor leaders celebrated when the U.S. Supreme Court issued its 1948 ruling and extended its applicability in 1953.[14] But the weakening of racially restrictive covenants did not cure the problem. The ruling made such covenants unenforceable but not illegal. It also did not bar racial discrimination. Whites continued to react negatively, sometimes violently, to Blacks moving into their neighborhoods. Newer, more remote sections of the city and metropolitan area did not need covenants to keep Blacks out, because sales and financing policies, and suburban municipal officials, protected them. But at the fringes of Black areas within the central city, the skirmish was real.[15]

The FHA, bankers, builders, real estate agents, local officials, private home owners, and landlords were almost completely unfettered by fair housing laws until 1968 or by antidiscrimination mortgage laws until 1979.[16] Even after that time, enforcement was weak and sporadic. If the Black population size had been stable or shrinking, discrimination in the larger housing market would perhaps have been bearable. But since the number of Blacks in the city continued to grow, they could not remain contained. If residential integration had been an accepted norm, Black families would have simply diffused throughout the metropolitan area, as did Whites. Since integration was not the norm, expansion took place on a block by block basis in a painful process of racial succession, as Blacks put pressures on the margins of their ghetto.[17]

Many scholars have attempted to explain why racial change took place in neighborhoods where only one or two Black families settled. Residential mobility is dependent upon two interrelated factors: how satisfied residents are with their housing and how confident residents are about the future of their neighborhood. The advent of Black families struck at the heart of the confidence Whites had in their neighborhoods.

Often a Black family, searching for good housing, made an individual decision to move into a White neighborhood. This set off a chain reaction. Some Whites felt so strongly about having Black neighbors that they moved away immediately. Others moved after the proportion of Blacks had reached a certain critical percentage or because of the natural course of family life cycle change. Greedy real estate agents descended upon an "invaded" neighborhood and scared other Whites into selling at a lower price than their home was worth. Then other Blacks bought into the newly opened neighborhood, often paying considerably inflated prices. This process was so predictable that sometimes neighborhood groups met together and listened to neighborhood change experts review for them the probable sequence of events. Residents often vowed to fight the flight syndrome, but they seldom succeeded. The result was a great "push" of Whites outward, which joined with the racially selective "pull" of suburbia—easy mortgage money, homogeneity, open space—to create White flight.[18]

As Hirsch discovered in his study of Chicago, this White reaction was more than just blind prejudice. Those who reacted with violence were often working-class Whites with European ethnic backgrounds who feared they were being invaded and forced to move.

Often residents of cohesive ethnic and religious enclaves, they were primarily concerned with protecting the boundaries of community, which meant family, church, and a shared heritage among people of common ancestry. White liberal promoters of racial integration tended to come from the highly educated upper class, and White opponents from lower class origins and circumstances. Although this was partially the situation in Detroit, belief in racial segregation was widespread among several social and economic classes of Whites.[19]

Eleanor Wolf and Charles Lebeaux conducted a study in the early 1960s that explained why racial turnover took place even when the reaction of Whites was relatively mild. In 1962–64, Wolf and Lebeaux interviewed residents of the Bagley neighborhood, a middle-class area located on Detroit's northwest side. The first Blacks had entered the neighborhood in 1959. Over the three-year period of their study the sociologists found that White residents did not "panic sell." What happened, instead, was that Whites steadily lost confidence in the neighborhood.

The reasons for this were complex. Even when new Black residents were middle-class, solid citizens, Whites feared that arrivals in the future would not be. As one respondent predicted, "Like it was in our old neighborhood, mostly professional people at first. Then the others follow."[20] Many Whites were concerned that the neighborhood would become predominantly Black. One White resident stated that "the record of this city in my lifetime has not been good regarding racial stabilization. We've moved four times, not because we wanted to, but because we were forced to. The area was changing, and we didn't want to be the only Whites left." Others feared crime, even if they did not distrust their new neighbors, because Blacks from lower-class areas could enter their neighborhood unnoticed.[21]

The Bagley community council tried to head off racial turnover. It supported a city ordinance for nondiscrimination in the housing market, recognizing the need to relieve the pressure on changing neighborhoods. It organized block clubs to foster neighborhood cohesion and waged a public relations battle to retain neighborhood confidence among old residents. The group even advertised for new White families. But eventually these families stopped buying houses in Bagley. Whenever White families moved out, Black home owners replaced them.[22]

Effects on Planning

The peculiar system of segregation and racial turnover affected many aspects of city life and governance. But it connected with urban planning decisions in three fundamental ways.

The first connection was that urban renewal projects aggravated the housing shortage for Blacks, thus speeding up the turnover process. Redevelopment and expressway construction forced residents from the construction areas into nearby central city residential neighborhoods. The resulting overcrowding placed more pressure on ghetto walls, leading to more rapid racial turnover.[23]

A second relationship between planning and racial instability was that Whites sometimes tried to influence rezoning and other planning decisions to maintain racial homogeneity. Homeowner associations designed to protect White neighborhoods sprang up. These groups tried to get property rezoned or changed to community or recreational use if they knew a developer wanted to construct housing open to all races. They also tried to dissuade the planning commission from approving multiple-family or cooperative housing, options which many felt would allow Blacks "in." By the late 1950s the planning commission had built up a strong political alliance with real estate interests and White homeowner associations in residential areas of northwest Detroit. The mayor appointed several members of these associations to the planning commission, including at least one who was commission president.[24]

Some observers also detected a slackening of planning standards and code enforcement for neighborhoods that had changed racially. A 1960 editorial in the Black *Michigan Chronicle* noted a decided "reluctance or refusal of responsible authorities to continue and enforce land-use restrictions in areas where Negroes have moved in. The net result has been to propel the process of deterioration."[25] Perhaps as important as slackening planning standards was the slackening of housing code enforcement by the building, health, and fire departments. This was a pivotal issue in older areas of the city. Racial discrimination in code enforcement was documented; Black renters could not depend on the city either to enforce the code or to prevent landlords from evicting them once they complained about violations. This led to a protracted war by civil rights organizations against "slum landlords."[26]

Most of this chapter focuses upon the third important effect that racial turnover had upon planning, the weakening of the city's neighborhood improvement programs. Racial flight and housing conservation were diametrically opposed. It was very difficult to persuade White people to improve their homes and develop loyalties to their neighborhoods in the context of current or potential flight. It was also difficult to maintain economic stability in a neighborhood once all Whites left. White refusal to invest in integrated neighborhoods affected neighborhood improvement projects for many years.

The Conservation Program

Conservation was an alternative form of "urban renewal." As practiced in the early 1950s in Chicago, Philadelphia, and Baltimore,

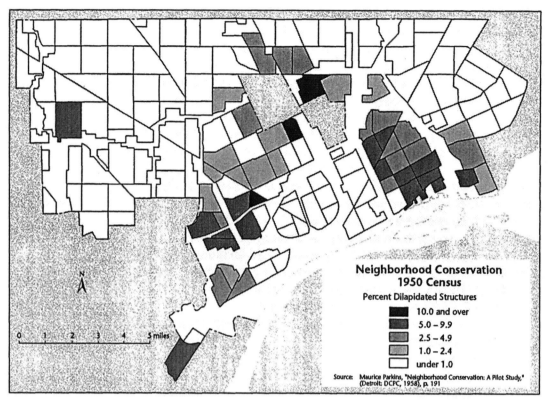

**Neighborhood Conservation
1950 Census**

Percent Dilapidated Structures

■	10.0 and over
■	5.0 – 9.9
■	2.5 – 4.9
■	1.0 – 2.4
□	under 1.0

Source: Maurice Parkins, "Neighborhood Conservation: A Pilot Study," (Detroit: DCPC, 1958), p. 191

0 1 2 3 4 5 miles

Fig. 4.2. Neighborhood conservation: Dilapidated structures, 1950 Census. The extent of deterioration far exceeded the amount of money available to undertake corrective action. Courtesy Detroit Department of Planning and Development.

conservation emphasized strict law enforcement and inspection, housing rehabilitation, and citizen participation. The Housing Act of 1954 provided financial support for the concept.[27]

The attractiveness of conservation as a concept was obvious. By the mid-1950s, cities were already discovering that slum clearance and reconstruction was a slow, frustrating process. Only a few cities had managed to get anything built on their cleared sites, and yet residential decay worsened yearly.[28]

If conservation had succeeded, it might have helped halt the decay creating the slums that cities were trying to clear out. Yet rehabilitating housing stock and upgrading community facilities did not slow the rate of suburban migration. Planner Maurice Parkins, head of DCPC's conservation division, optimistically suggested that conservation could help "make the people belong and be proud of their neighborhood and truly want to stay there and not move to the suburbs."[29] This would have been easier if people were leaving largely because of the physical deterioration of their houses and neighborhoods. Yet many people were leaving because of demographic changes affecting members of their families, upward mobility spurred by the ease of access to suburban housing, or racial change. Federal policies encouraged this exodus outward. Conservation could not make even a dent in these trends.

That the program was needed in a physical sense was undeniable. Detroit planners rated the city's 13,000 residential blocks according

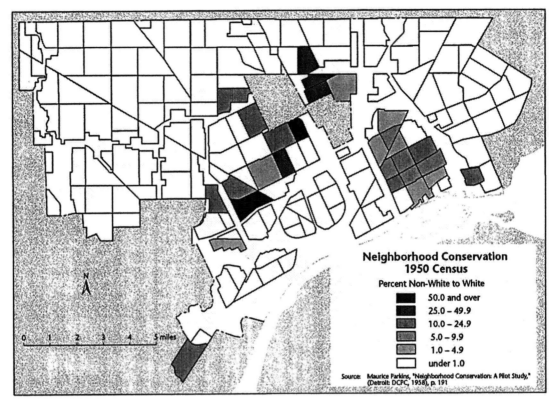

to such variables as overcrowding, dilapidation, income levels, and race (see figs. 4.2, 4.3). They then classified each neighborhood according to whether it required redevelopment (clearance), conservation (rehabilitation), or no action.[30] As a result of this pioneering analysis—a U.S. urban renewal commissioner said that "no city in the United States has developed such neighborhood analyses as has Detroit"[31]—the city planners clearly understood the extent of the problem. The worst of the city's 155 neighborhoods the planners marked for clearance and redevelopment, but they also selected 53 neighborhoods, containing a third of the city's housing supply, for conservation. Planning Director Charles Blessing suggested both a comprehensive program and a pilot program, "to test and perfect conservation planning techniques."[32]

Laying out a ten-year program, the planners designated 35 of 53 target neighborhoods for Title I assistance, under which the federal government would finance public improvements on a two-thirds matching basis. That left 18 neighborhoods, the so-called non–assisted project areas, to receive only FHA home improvement loans. The city estimated that an average yearly investment of approximately eight million dollars in federal and local funds could finance all of the projects.[33]

Detroit applied for federal approval for five Title I conservation neighborhoods in 1954, but the federal government approved only two: Mack-Concord, a "racially changing" area three miles to the

Fig. 4.3. Neighborhood conservation: Percentage of non-White to White, 1950 Census. This map, when compared with the previous one, shows the close connection between Black residence and structure dilapidation. Courtesy Detroit Department of Planning and Development.

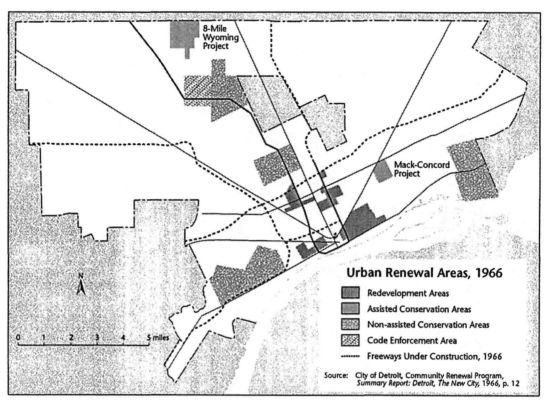

Urban Renewal Areas, 1966

■ Redevelopment Areas

■ Assisted Conservation Areas

▨ Non-assisted Conservation Areas

▨ Code Enforcement Area

···· Freeways Under Construction, 1966

Source: City of Detroit, Community Renewal Program,
          Summary Report: Detroit, The New City, 1966, p. 12

Fig. 4.4. Urban renewal areas, 1966; includes areas for clearance redevelopment projects, as well as for code enforcement and conservation. Note particularly the two conservation neighborhoods of Mack-Concord and Eight Mile–Wyoming. Courtesy Detroit Department of Planning and Development.

east of the central business district, and Eight Mile–Wyoming, the isolated Black enclave next to the northern border of the city (see fig. 4.4). Planners decided to work first with Mack-Concord; the other 34 neighborhoods would have to wait.

Mack-Concord was in need of major improvements, but it was by no means the worst of the conservation neighborhoods. It was instead "broadly characteristic of the middle-aged portion of the city."[34] Even so the problems it faced were substantial. Principal planner Maurice Parkins's description of the Mack-Concord project area gives a picture of some of those problems. According to Parkins, Mack-Concord:

> had been laid out without the benefits of a zoning ordinance and with no thought for outdoor living space and recreation facilities. Although most of the residential structures are still physically sound, they stand too close together, in some instances separated by only three feet. Many of the houses have become obsolete for modern living requirements that new families have come to demand. The streets have become increasingly hazardous for children because of heavy traffic. . . . Overcrowding of structures on the land has caused a parking problem and a sanitation problem in the alleys. When all the disadvantages were weighed against the advantages, such as nearness to downtown, good transportation, and public facilities and services, [the] neighborhood lost out; the young parents moved to the suburbs as soon as they were financially able.

Added to these problems of aged housing, poor lot layout, and inadequate community facilities was racial change. Mack-Concord "was beginning to serve as a haven for many Negro families who were moving outward from the slum-ridden inner core of the city," he noted. However, "with the change in home ownership there also came a social change in the neighborhood which affected its stability."[35]

Planning Director Blessing's conservation strategy included three steps: organizing, to involve citizens in neighborhood upgrading; improving public facilities; and rehabilitating private dwelling units. While physical design solutions could solve layout and community facilities problems, residents themselves would have to rehabilitate their houses.[36]

To help insure citizen participation and cooperation, Blessing assigned one of his newest planners, a sociologist writing his doctoral dissertation. Mel Ravitz, who stayed with the planning commission from 1953 to 1960, viewed the pilot project as a social experiment, a chance to learn how to organize residents effectively in support of neighborhood upgrading. Ravitz proved to be an exceptionally good choice for this position. His sociology graduate work had trained him to look at situations broadly rather than narrowly. He brought new and fresh perceptions to a profession whose members were only beginning to understand the role of neighborhood change and human relations in improving cities. His commitment to social reform was a crucial quality for a neighborhood planner. Ravitz would play a critical role in modern Detroit politics, for later in his career he won a seat on the Common Council.[37]

Ravitz was also an academic, interested in disseminating knowledge. He published a number of observations about neighborhood organizing and the conservation program in nationally distributed journals. At the time he began writing such articles, he was one of the few practicing planners involved in the daily dynamics of neighborhood rehabilitation and change who was willing and able to put observations on paper and get them published.

In one such article, published near the beginning of the program in 1954, he expressed the hope that Detroit's pilot program would encourage residents to stay rather than move. The problem facing planners was not just a technical one of how to propose physical changes to improve the neighborhood, but also "the human or social question of how far at any given time people will go in accepting what is technologically possible."[38]

Ravitz understood the inherent difficulties of the tasks. Soon after his initial efforts, he warned that "many of these [conservation] plans will either not be initiated, will miscarry, or will be so devitalized that they will hardly be worth developing." Why was he so pessimistic? Because resident apathy or inability to afford housing improvement was a widespread problem. Flawed building and zoning

standards and lack of money for public improvements also presented barriers. Yet Ravitz felt that the most difficult obstacles were
social. Could planners successfully fight the tendency of White citizens to run away from the central cities? "Some people who disregard social attitudes as unworthy of 'hard-headed' consideration believe that a program of physical improvements alone can persuade
Whites to remain where they are and to invest to improve their
property," Ravitz warned. "This is a pretty thought but one that is
utterly naive in that it overlooks several points: the strength of the
prevalent anti-Negro prejudice, the opportunities of the first few
Whites to make a good profit on their homes by selling to Negroes,
and the unwillingness of other White families to 'be the only
Whites around.' "[39]

A survey of the Mack-Concord area had shown just how difficult
the task would be. According to a random sample of community
residents, most of the people found little or nothing the matter with
their homes and saw no reason to rehabilitate them. Yet more than
half of those surveyed wanted to leave the area, particularly Whites
who had lived in the neighborhood more than five years. Those aspects of the neighborhood that were the most unsatisfactory were
the lack of parking, traffic on side streets, lack of recreational facilities—all flaws which could be fixed—and the "type of new neighbors moving in," a reference to non-White entry. This, of course,
could not be "fixed."[40]

Official reports on the conservation program reflected dogged optimism. Principal planner Maurice Parkins reported the devastating
survey results, which indicated that White residents had no interest in participating in neighborhood organization or in improving
their homes. He then disputed his own survey results, suggesting
that "the very small sample taken, 3.6 per cent, though scientifically
selected for representativeness, was too small to [analyze] the attitude of the majority of the residents." As evidence for this claim,
Parkins pointed out that Black and White neighborhood residents
did indeed join neighborhood groups organized by Ravitz.[41]

The truth is that neighborhood organizing efforts did succeed,
but in general the conservation program did not, in part because of
the very lack of commitment to the neighborhood revealed by the
opinion survey.

At first the only person assigned to organize 12,000 people into
block clubs, Ravitz mobilized several volunteer social workers and
planners to help him do the job. Ravitz's assignment was to create
the block clubs and then bring in the "physical planners" to explain
fully the potential of conservation. The city had money to build
playgrounds, plant trees, remove dilapidated buildings, or change
streets to improve parking and traffic flow. The block clubs, in return, were supposed to encourage residents to decide which community improvements were most important and to improve their

individual properties. Together these efforts would improve the neighborhood without tearing it down.

There were several benefits of the community organizing process. Informal education of the physical planners helped them understand the social implications of what many had viewed as a design process. As one noted, "Mel [Ravitz] and I sat side by side. He came in as a sociologist concerned about disruption of life, disintegration of urban structure. I came in as an architect concerned about beautiful boulevards, aesthetics, the relationships of buildings and forms. I learned an awful lot from Mel and I've always said that I hoped he learned one-tenth of that from me."[42]

Another major benefit was racial cooperation. Ravitz noted that "at early meetings it was often possible to see a voluntary segregation in the form of the seating arrangements. On some occasions in the beginning, White residents inquired what the city was going to do about returning the neighborhood to its former all-White population." These questions gradually ceased, however, and soon "it was possible to notice a breakdown of the segregated seating pattern as interest in the program and concern with common problems came to the fore."[43] Several people who could not tolerate racial interaction dropped out or moved away, while the others began a slow and steady effort toward building a stable block club. The remaining residents began to develop interracial bonds of cooperation and fellowship. The program brought together "people of diverse racial, religious and nationality backgrounds to concentrate attention on their immediate and most important common problems. Bringing people together under such equal status circumstances seems to help them ignore superficial differences."[44]

Ravitz worked with five full-time planners in what became a formal unit of Community Organization assigned to the Detroit Committee for Neighborhood Conservation and Improved Housing. They created a block club in each one of the thirty-eight blocks in the Mack-Concord conservation area. They then went on to organize block clubs in the next Title I conservation area, Eight Mile –Wyoming, and in areas not assisted by FHA. By 1959, Detroit's program had attained a certain notability among cities for its citizen involvement; it had registered six hundred neighborhood organizations, some of which evolved spontaneously.[45]

In fact, the organizing effort was too successful. The citizens' groups began to take seriously their potential power. They organized petitions, wrote letters, and otherwise pressured the Board of Zoning Appeals, the council, the planning commission, and the mayor's office to provide services to their neighborhoods. When officials realized that it was conservation planners who were organizing these groups, the mayor killed the nuisance at the source. In 1960 he transferred the six community organization planners from the relatively benign environment of the planning commission, which supported their organizing efforts with encouragement and flexible work hours, to the oppressive, bureaucratic environment of the housing commission. Discouraged by the desk-bound, time-clock mentality of the housing commission, all but one of the planners soon resigned from the city, including Ravitz.[46]

Of the three steps that Blessing had laid out as a strategy for conservation—organizing area citizens, improving public facilities, and encouraging private citizens to rehabilitate their houses—the city had brought about success in at least two. The citizens were organized to degrees far exceeding expectations. The planners had also designed creative public facilities improvements, informed by citizen input.

But in the third area, private rehabilitation, they were not successful. Individual families did not rehabilitate their homes. The older, White population did not remain long enough to rehabilitate. Of 72 Black and 58 White homeowners interviewed, none of the Blacks had lived in the neighborhood for more than fourteen years, but only three of the Whites had moved in within the previous three years. Blacks, the new arrivals, were still "buying" their property with expensive land contracts and so had less money or credit to pay for rehabilitation. Whites were more likely to own their property "free and clear," but displayed such negative attitudes toward racially and economically different groups that their turnover was high. Especially hostile were Whites who were older or had low incomes, the very people who were least able to flee. Both Blacks and Whites complained about the behavior and housing upkeep standards of lower-class newcomers, many of them renters.[47]

The University of Detroit published a study of the program in 1965 that revealed even more ominous results. Although the city had made several solid improvements in community facilities, residential decline was still evident. Code enforcement was unsystematic, "visible" deterioration extensive, community organization ineffective, and health department complaints on the rise. The researchers concluded that conservation was a failure. An August 1964 survey showed that the average annual mobility was 16.3 percent, compared to a mobility rate of 1.9 percent between 1940 and 1953, and 7.2 percent in the three years prior to conservation treatment. Even so, 26.5 percent of the sampled population indicated they intended to move out in the near future. Both Whites and Blacks reported a mutual dislike for each other. Between the 1950 and 1960 census, the area had lost over 7,000 Whites, for a drop of 75 percent, and gained over 5,000 non-Whites, for a gain of 74 percent (see figs. 4.5, 4.6). Unemployment had increased, median family income had fallen below city average for the first time, and crime was rising rapidly.[48]

What had happened? Rampant racial change was an important factor. As Ravitz had warned in 1955, "many White families living now in neighborhoods that are beginning to be . . . occupied by

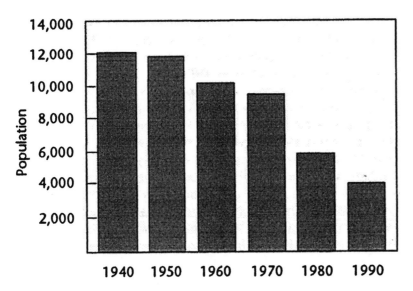

Fig. 4.5. Population change in Mack-Concord conservation neighborhood tracts, #5162 and #5151, 1940–90. Population continued to drop during each decade, as it did in the city at large.

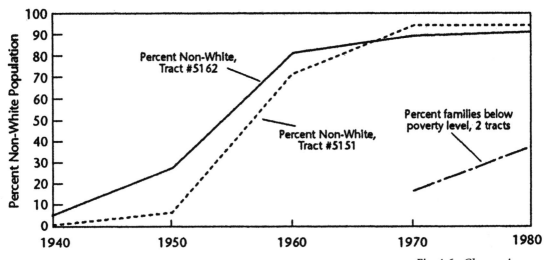

Fig. 4.6. Changes in percent of non-White and in families below poverty level in Mack-Concord neighborhood tracts, #5162 and 5151, 1940–80. First the area "changed" by race, and then by income.

Negroes will not invest any sizable sum of money in home improvement." This was, he noted, "a patterned behavior of Whites that must be reckoned with by those who plan and execute conservation programs."[49] In 1991 Ravitz reflected yet again on the experience and concluded, "We couldn't stop the racial and social-economic tides."[50] The well-organized block clubs had facilitated race relations, but they did not stop racial flight. Federal legislation also hindered the program. Public improvements were not enough to encourage people to spend their own money to rehabilitate their homes. The federal government required cities to choose target areas that were at least 20 percent dilapidated, but such neighborhoods were hard to revive, particularly as income levels dropped.[51] The conservation program provided only loans, not grants, and these never materialized for most. Detroit's Mack-Concord project area contained over 1,000 substandard dwelling units (36 percent of total units) before conservation began, but only 40 families applied for rehabilitation loans. Banks approved only 27 of those applicants. Local bankers complained about lack of publicity, burdensome paperwork, and labyrinthine forms.[52]

Insufficient financing stymied conservation efforts in several cities, including Philadelphia, Cincinnati, and Chicago, whose planners all cited major difficulties with FHA loans. Of all the cities that the University of Detroit researchers studied—Philadelphia, Cincinnati, Chicago, New Haven, and Detroit—they discovered only one partially "successful" conservation program, New Haven's.[53]

In essence, the federal government was not putting enough money into its conservation effort to make a difference, and it did not create a program that made what money it did invest easy to use. Simultaneously, it continued to sponsor new home construction with its regular FHA programs. Tax policies, highway construction programs, and mortgage loan insurance programs far outweighed puny efforts to support conservation and other urban renewal programs.

Ravitz had suggested in 1955 that one solution to neighborhood flight was to choose neighborhoods that were fairly stable, perhaps because they had already "changed." Even as the University of Detroit study concluded the entire Detroit conservation program was a failure, they noted that rehabilitation efforts had been a success in the predominantly Black Eight Mile–Wyoming project area. Without the tumultuous turnover that took place in the multiracial Mack-Concord project, perhaps it too could have been more successful.[54]

Experience with the housing code suggested that the issue was far more complicated. Areas that became African American were more likely to increase the percentage of renters because of the pressure for housing. Yet the city health, building, and fire departments were notoriously lax in their enforcement of the city's weak housing code. Thus, middle-class Black homeowners had to deal not only with the loss of White neighbors and the likely advent of lower income renters, but also with failure to enforce the housing code, leading to even more deterioration.[55]

Open Housing

Beginning in the early 1960s, the federal government took steps to insure that housing was "open" to all races. Local civil rights leaders and other social activists worked to promote open housing in Detroit and its suburbs. This movement made important gains, but it by no means resolved the problem of chronic neighborhood turnover.

On November 20, 1962, President John F. Kennedy signed Executive Order 11063, which prohibited federal agencies from discriminating in the sale, lease, or occupancy of federally owned property, or of property assisted by federal grants or insured loans. It also prohibited discrimination in housing funded with federal urban renewal or slum clearance support.[56] The order came too late and left too much territory uncovered. Projects or transactions completed before November 20, 1962, were exempt. The order hardly affected public housing, which in many inner cities was already predominantly Black, and it barely touched the private housing market.[57]

In 1963 the State of Michigan prohibited discrimination in housing built with urban renewal subsidy. Unlike other states, such as Massachusetts, Minnesota, New Jersey, and New York, Michigan did not prohibit discrimination in such key areas as public housing, privately transacted housing, actions of real estate agents and lenders, or advertising. Obviously, local action was still necessary, since federal laws were weak and state laws uneven.[58]

Many people worked throughout the mid-1960s to persuade Detroit's city council to take action. In 1961 Detroit's voters had elected to city council Mel Ravitz, former planner/organizer for Mack-Concord and other city neighborhoods. Ravitz had organized so many neighborhoods for the conservation program that he had gained a strong grassroots reputation. He was elected to city council in 1961, 1965, and 1969, ran unsuccessfully for mayor in 1973, and was again elected to council in 1981, and serves still. At various times he was president of the council, chairman of the county board of supervisors, and chairman of the Southeast Michigan Council of Governments. This he managed while he maintained, before retiring, a two-thirds faculty position with the sociology department of Wayne State University.[59]

Soon after his first election, Ravitz tried to resolve some of the problems he saw as a conservation planner. Together with the city's first Black council member, William Patrick, Jr., he proposed a strong fair housing ordinance for council adoption. The public hearing was so big it had to be moved to Ford Auditorium. Ravitz also needed personal police protection, because "the prevailing attitude in Detroit was that Black people should stay bottled up where Black people had been."[60] Although the council defeated the proposed ordinance, in November 1962 it passed a weak Fair Neighborhood Practices Ordinance. The ordinance did little more than state that equal access to housing was the right of all citizens.[61]

In the meantime, 40 White homeowners' groups organized themselves into the Greater Detroit Homeowners Council. One representative of this council said that "the Negro is not suitable for the place in society which he is trying to push into." The homeowners circulated petitions for a rival ordinance that prohibited any restrictions on the sale or rental of homes. This blatant attempt to justify racial discrimination was actually placed on the ballot in September 1964 and approved by the electorate 136,671 to 111,994. Only when outlawed by the county circuit court did the discriminatory ordinance die.[62]

In January 1966, the housing committee of the Detroit Commission on Community Relations—descendant of Mayor Jeffries's interracial committee—found that realty agents were still actively soliciting residents in racially changing neighborhoods, sometimes contacting one family two or three times a week. Realtors actively discouraged prospective White buyers from looking at housing in integrated areas and did not show homes to Blacks in any areas beyond changing neighborhoods. The committee lamented the degree and depth of hardship endured by citizens of Detroit in seeking shelter. "Negroes suffer physically, psychologically, and financially. . . . Whites suffer too, from the pressures on them to leave."[63]

A few months after the 1967 civil disturbances, the council approved a stronger citywide Fair Housing Ordinance.[64] One year later the federal government passed the Civil Rights Act of 1968. This prohibited a wide range of discriminatory actions in housing, albeit with weak guarantees for enforcement.

Voluntary efforts were joined with these attempts to strengthen the law. Eight northwestern Detroit community councils formed "to support the right to purchase and live in property of [one's] own choosing, and to promote a harmonious and democratic community without regard to race, religion, or national origin." Churches established some of these groups, as did the Jewish Community Council.[65] Such groups contributed to a more receptive atmosphere for Black families who dared to move out of the ghetto, but they were not able to prevent racial turnover.[66]

In 1971, the Detroit Commission on Community Relations reported to Mayor Roman Gribbs that at least 7,000 to 9,000 houses within the city were changing every year from Caucasian to African-American occupancy, a rate that had continued undiminished for the previous 20 years. Some census tracts contained fewer than one percent Blacks, including 53 contiguous tracts on the city's northeast side. Black newcomers continued to suffer firebombs and other forms of harassment. At least 27 tracts had changed from less than 10 percent to 66 percent Black during the 1960s. Simultaneously, 200,000 new dwelling units were constructed in Detroit's suburbs, but only 6,000 "were made available to Black families."[67]

Clearly, open housing efforts would work best on a metropolitan scale. By the late 1960s the Detroit Commission on Community Relations was helping suburban municipalities establish human relations councils. These efforts expanded throughout the 1970s and 1980s. In the several suburban municipalities to which Blacks began to move, such as Oak Park and Southfield, local councils facilitated stability.[68] Although the rate of Black suburban growth began to increase gradually in the 1970s and 1980s, the Detroit metropolitan area remained severely segregated racially.

Open housing laws did not solve the problem within the city, either. By the time these laws passed, city segregation and White flight patterns were firmly entrenched. Many people had long worried about the need "to eliminate housing discrimination without driving out so many Whites that Detroit becomes an all-Negro city."[69] The new demography gave Blacks decided advantages in the political realm, but generated spinoff problems that were difficult to solve. Racial change severely affected the demand for houses, since it limited the number of home-seekers interested in a neighborhood. With this smaller number of home-seekers, few were willing to buy when residents were ready to sell. All-Black neighborhoods became vulnerable to falling prices and abandonment.

Neighborhood Change and Development

As this chapter has shown, racial change strongly affected the city's neighborhoods. Blacks could not leave the central city at the same rate as Whites because of barriers to their free mobility, and unnatural constraints set up volatile instability on the fringes of the ghetto. Contemporary racial segregation is the legacy. This chapter described the 1950s and 1960s, but the patterns of racial change affected neighborhoods before and after that period.

Federal policy facilitated this process. The discriminatory actions of the HOLC and FHA encouraged racial segregation and therefore racial instability. Lack of strong antidiscriminatory policies and weak enforcement of open housing laws caused the same problems. But local policies and private initiatives were to blame as well. City and suburban politicians supported racial segregation and fought actively against open housing or mixed-income housing. Lending institutions, real estate agents, and private citizens practiced exclusionary "gatekeeper" behavior.

Detroit's urban planners played some part in perpetuating discrimination. White homeowners gained appointments to the citizen-based planning commission, skewing decisions against racial integration and causing neglect of Black neighborhoods. But with the conservation program, the planners made a noble effort. They promoted innovative solutions to neighborhood decline and laid out a reasonable agenda for a physical support system in the pilot neighborhood. Led by Ravitz, they set in motion a process of interracial cooperation for neighborhood improvement. Unfortunately, they could not counter the lure of the suburbs. The insidious process of racial and income turnover was unrelenting. The pressure on city hall generated when Detroit's planners organized neighborhoods reduced the planners' political support and cost some of them their jobs.

The federal conservation program had significant flaws. Detroit could not halt decline in one pilot conservation neighborhood, much less in the one-third of the city needing rehabilitation assistance. Successful conservation required much more than was available. A federal government that would finance central city conservation rather than suburban exodus was required. More constraints on White mobility and fewer on Black mobility were required. Widespread adoption of a means to promote interracial harmony and cooperation was required. None of these requirements was met.[70]

Countering neighborhood decline is still an important planning task for central cities. Many cities have used the conservation approach to make visible, positive changes in their inner-city neighborhoods.[71] The current Community Development Block Grant program is a more effective offspring of the conservation program but still relies upon resident faith and willingness to upgrade property, which is difficult to insure in the midst of racial or income change. Contemporary urban researchers and decision-makers do not fully understand how to halt neighborhood decline. They are just beginning to discover tactics for stabilizing and upgrading neighborhoods in such situations, and these tactics are not foolproof. Thus, we find modern versions of old problems.[72]

One example is the continuing dilemma of all-Black neighborhoods. Once Whites did move out of neighborhoods such as Bagley and Mack-Concord, poorer Blacks were likely to join or replace middle-class Blacks. These areas therefore underwent income shifts as well as racial shifts. Socioeconomic changes often led to problems of housing upkeep or crime.[73] As the numbers of renters increased, the city reduced attempts to enforce the housing code. Lending institutions withheld mortgages or loans for home improvement, and real estate agents steered young White families away. All of this led to a self-fulfilling prophecy: Black entry into neighborhoods did lead to deterioration—a classic case of blaming the victim.

Revisioning
Urban Renewal

5

The conservation program, for all of its innovations, was too small and ineffective to make a major difference in city redevelopment. This chapter returns to the better known urban renewal program, which involved clearance and reconstruction. As the years passed in the 1960s, the single-minded pursuit of the clearance agenda came under increasing attack. Protests erupted from African-American groups, which awoke to the threat of urban renewal and demanded more just treatment. Citizen resistance forced more inclusionary decision-making and put a halt to the design-based improvement of the city concept. Activism compelled the city to include low-income housing and churches in projects planned to exclude them.

Planners suffered the repercussions of failing to acknowledge the needs of the Black community. Detroit's once-favored urban professionals fell into increasing disfavor, even as they gained a national reputation for their redevelopment work. Some of the planners drew particular fire for focusing on aesthetics without acknowledging the concerns for neighborhood self-preservation. A new planning professional arose, more dedicated to meeting the needs of inner-city neighborhoods. Planners Charles Blessing and Hilanius Phillips represented the old and the new.

In spite of notable successes, Detroit's redevelopment strategy faltered during the urban renewal era. Problems included not only citizen protest and the design orientation of professionals but also the city's redevelopment operation, which lacked both leadership and organization.

Comprehensive Plan Successes

By the 1960s, Detroit had implemented many of its postwar improvement projects. The city's planners felt sufficiently self-assured about these successes to apply for the 1964 American Institute of Planners (AIP) Honors Award in Comprehensive Planning.[1]

Their application listed impressive accomplishments. Many goals of the 1944 postwar improvements plan and the 1951 master plan had been met, particularly those related to municipal facilities. By 1964 the city had implemented the facilities plans for schools and recreational resources. It had demolished, rehabilitated, or built schools and other public service facilities; acquired over 1400 acres of park and recreational land; and coordinated placement of schools and new playgrounds. The master plan had guided construction of the expressway system and of several Civic Center buildings, including the City-County Building, which housed most municipal offices.

With Gratiot–Lafayette Park to the east and industrial Corktown to the west, the city had sheltered the commercial core from blight and, with Lafayette Park, diversified the inner city's residential income mix. Important institutional development projects formed a tight nucleus of development on either side of Woodward Avenue. The Detroit Medical Center project created a core of hospitals surrounded by a supportive ring of housing, schools, churches, and professional buildings. The University City project allowed Wayne State University to expand from its formerly cramped site, and provided land for closely affiliated residential development. The Detroit Cultural Center redevelopment plan expanded the influence of key cultural institutions and linked the Detroit Medical Center and the University Center projects. If successfully implemented and expanded, these three institutional projects—the Medical Center, University City, and the Cultural Center—would have merged and redeveloped a significant portion of the inner city. None of these projects was complete in 1964, but basic plans were in place and construction begun.

The Detroit City Plan Commission won the 1964 AIP award for which it applied. This confirmed that Detroit had successfully implemented much of its 1951 comprehensive plan and had significantly improved the city's municipal services. It had started admirable efforts to redevelop deteriorated inner-city areas. What the application and award did not note was that the city had simultaneously weathered increasing opposition to its redevelopment agenda.

Citizens Protest

Citizen protest against redevelopment projects grew in intensity throughout the 1960s. Much of the protest came from Black citizens, as opposition to clearance projects became a civil rights issue. First seen as a minor matter, and then a major annoyance, such protest slowed down the redevelopment process and forced changes in the growth agenda.

The biggest source of protest was dissatisfaction over relocation and displacement. Cities all over the country razed residential project sites by forcing thousands of people to move without adequate relocation assistance. By 1963, Detroit had demolished or was scheduled to demolish 10,000 structures. This required displacing 43,096 people, 70 percent of them Black.[2]

Over time, neighborhood groups became more vocal, more sophisticated, and more influential in protesting this situation. Because the burdens of redevelopment injustices fell to a disproportionate degree upon Blacks, civil rights groups led defensive actions. Each subsequent project found citizens better and more effectively organized to resist. With each escalation, pressure on the city and its development agencies, the housing and planning commissions, grew more heated. By the mid-1960s, citizen groups were reshaping redevelopment.

The first two redevelopment projects, Gratiot and Corktown, generated early, fairly crude forms of citizen protest. Although the largely Black residents of the Gratiot project did not organize to protest their removal, the Detroit Urban League offered an important service as abuse watchdog. Its input may have made the city more careful, and the experience alerted other neighborhood residents to potential abuses. Residents of the industrial Corktown project, more mixed racially and with vocal White residents, were able to launch a stronger protest campaign than had Gratiot residents. Citizen activists there gained little ground because many residents were renters, thus diluting opposition, and the city's economic needs made it hard to argue against clearance. In addition, it was much easier to relocate the Corktown residents, because most of them were White.[3]

By the 1960s, social protest forced changes in several major redevelopment projects. With the Detroit Medical Center, civil rights groups forced concessions from the city and hospitals. With another project, Wayne State University's University City, protesters pressured city leaders to make permanent changes in the way they made decisions about redevelopment.

Medical Center

Protests against the Detroit Medical Center complex were the first effective response by the city's Black community to redevelopment abuses.

In the mid-1950s the hospitals near Wayne State University organized to address their mutual problem of deteriorated physical facilities surrounded by deteriorated neighborhoods. The hospitals had three choices. One, they could move to the suburbs, which would require expensive new facilities. A second alternative, "far more distasteful," was "to become slum hospitals caring for slum patients, practicing perforce slum medicine." The last choice, which they preferred, was to rehabilitate their surrounding areas. They asked the city to condemn the land, relocate existing residents, and prepare the site.[4]

The planning and housing commissions hastened to facilitate this request. Director Blessing recruited an architect/planner to

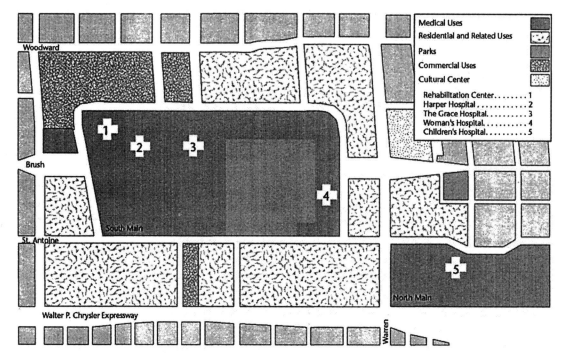

Legend:
- Medical Uses
- Residential and Related Uses
- Parks
- Commercial Uses
- Cultural Center

Rehabilitation Center........1
Harper Hospital............2
The Grace Hospital.........3
Woman's Hospital..........4
Children's Hospital........5

Woodward
Brush
South Main
St. Antoine
North Main
Walter P. Chrysler Expressway
Warren

Fig. 5.1. Sketch of proposed land use, as presented in the 1958 Medical Center Plan, shows the broad contours of the plan's combination of hospital, institutional, park, and housing facilities. Courtesy Detroit Department of Planning and Development.

draw up a master plan for the Detroit Medical Center project. The 1954 proposal for the Medical Center foresaw a multiuse complex containing medical buildings, middle-income housing, community facilities, and commercial development, all woven around existing churches of architectural significance. The project master plan, issued in 1958, was a model of institutional area planning. Project architect Gerald Crane, experienced with hospital projects, produced superior design work for the center (see fig. 5.1). Blessing's introduction to the published plan congratulated the supervisory committee for "what should prove to be the finest conceived and designed Medical Center in America."[5]

But displacement was a major issue. In 1958, 3400 families lived on the project site, and 3,000 of them were non-White.[6] Proponents of the center wanted to clear out existing residents from the vicinity in order to insure the safety and comfort of hospital employees. Hospital administrators were concerned that hospital staff did not feel safe traveling to work. The plan included a residential section with apartments only for "professional people and others of the comfortable income groups," so that more staff would live nearby.[7]

The problem with this agenda was not only displacement. These health institutions, which wanted public support to clear out the predominantly Black community that surrounded them, blatantly discriminated against Black patients and health care professionals. Furthermore, early project proposals excluded Black residents from the site by excluding their churches and by failing to provide low-income housing.

The health care discrimination problem was well documented. As early as 1948 the Detroit Urban League had uncovered chronic segregation of hospital facilities. Black professional personnel were denied access, and admissions for Black patients were limited. In one hospital, White medical students were allowed to deliver only Black babies until they became more competent. All but one of the four hospitals seeking city and federal funds for a medical center carried out such practices.[8]

Civil rights groups supported the new medical center in concept, recognizing the physical dilapidation of the area and the need for the hospitals to expand. But they were understandably determined to insure equality of access and opportunity. The Detroit Urban League spoke against the relocation hardships imposed upon the thousands of Black families and hundreds of Black businesses that the city would move from the area. It was even more concerned about whether or not these people would be able to live within the new project and whether or not they could use the hospital, as could any White person. The Urban League argued that subjecting former residents to racial bias from the very medical facilities that physically replaced their houses, churches, and neighborhood businesses was inherently unjust.[9]

With the hospital discrimination issue, neighborhood proponents had leverage. Since the federal government could disqualify projects where discriminatory practices were evident, the protesters could have killed the project. In 1962 and 1963 the Common Council resolved that no property would be released to hospitals that discriminated. Pressure on the hospitals also came from individual Black physicians, who reported problems to civil rights groups and congressional representatives. The combined efforts forced the hospitals to reform.[10]

A group formed in 1961 to insure that community churches were included in or near the project. The Detroit Fellowship of Urban Renewal Churches was a ministers' alliance of those churches slated for clearance. No sites had been reserved for them to rebuild in the project plan, which included only the more expensive and architecturally significant churches, all with White congregations. At first city representatives asked why the Black churches wanted project sites, since former residents were not going to be able to live in the Medical Center. Rev. Louis Johnson of Friendship Baptist Church responded: "Well, if we can't afford to live there, at least we can afford to worship there."[11] The ministerial group organized local residents to attend public hearings and protest the lack of affordable housing and the exclusion of existing Black churches. Some churches successfully filed suit over low property appraisals and negotiated with the city to buy sites in the clearance area. Three Black churches won this right: Friendship, Plymouth Congregational, and Bethel AME.

Fig. 5.2. Plymouth Congregational United Church of Christ, African-American church which fought for right to build in Detroit Medical Center and later built subsidized housing as well, 1996 photo. J. Thomas, photographer.

After the battle was over and the churches were built, they tapped federal programs to finance low- and moderate-income housing on or near the Medical Center site. For the first time, Black leaders had forced the city to redefine a redevelopment project to fit their needs. In the process, they fought a mentality that assumed that neither the houses nor the churches of the original residents belonged in the new project and that it was all right for medical institutions to discriminate racially.[12]

University City

The debate over the University City project was even more acrimonious. This site near Wayne State University was more racially diverse than was the Medical Center site, although it too contained a high number of Black residents. Protest came from the West Central Organization (WCO), perhaps the most vocal protest group to arise before 1980. The project's five phases were to involve 1500 residents. The first two phases, University City 1 and 2, would clear land for the university, the third would expand Murray-Wright High School, and the fourth and fifth would be sold to private developers for housing.[13]

WCO spurred a major reexamination of redevelopment and centralized planning. A 1966 resolution bemoaned the lack of "self-determination" in urban renewal areas and strongly protested the

Fig. 5.3. Forest Park Village, subsidized housing located very close to the Detroit Medical Center and sponsored by African-American church (Friendship Baptist Church) located in Medical Center, 1995 photo. The grandparents of Tracey Thomas, who is holding her child, moved into Brewster Homes public housing in 1940. J. Thomas, photographer.

city's lack of "a long range low income housing program for all Detroit residents." It called for an end to "planning of [our] neighborhood by politicians downtown," since such planning was "against the interests and desires of neighborhood people." WCO opposed any further demolition of occupied houses in their area for urban renewal, expressway, or school construction unless the city provided an equal amount of new or rehabilitated housing beforehand.[14]

Before the organization was one year old it hired Chicago community activist Saul Alinsky as a short-term consultant on effective tactics. Inspired by Alinsky's experiences, the group expanded the typical route of lawsuits and began to picket absentee landlords, occupy abandoned buildings, and form angry crowds to demand justice from the mayor.[15] They directed most of their anger toward Mayor Cavanagh and Bob Knox of the housing commission, although they also held long, agitated meetings with the planning commission and Blessing. Cavanagh, who did not wish to spoil his image as a liberal, directed the city's community relations commission to meet with WCO. These meetings led to promises from Cavanagh for more affordable housing and a more open development process.[16]

A further step came with an important 1966 Common Council resolution to deny any future applications for urban renewal projects unless the city could provide housing for relocatees at prices they could afford. Council further promised to study all phases of University City and to provide a reasonable supply of low- and moderate-income housing. The city resolved to undertake "a program of full citizen organization and participation" in planning University City and all other urban renewal projects. State Senator Coleman Young introduced a complementary bill in 1966, which eventually passed the state legislature in 1968, that required citizens' district councils in all areas slated for redevelopment.[17]

These were remarkable developments. The rise of sophisticated citizen activism had forced procedural changes in Detroit's postwar agenda several years before similar changes were required by federal legislation. The redevelopment process was no longer completely controlled by city government and by the growth coalitions. Neighborhood redevelopment plans were subject to the input, if not approval, of ordinary citizens.

Unfortunately, greater resident input did not guarantee that residents benefited. The University City project is a prime example of this. WCO won the battle for more openness but lost the war for the neighborhood. The university built a new physical education center in the first of the five phases, University City 1. Other phases retained existing rehabilitated housing, but WCO did not survive the process. Project delays caused massive neighborhood deterioration. Property owners stopped making repairs, and lending institutions stopped making loans. By 1970, the area looked like "a disaster area. On every block are boarded-up homes or apartment buildings, looking blind and gagged. Here and there homes are burnt, charred, gutted, dotted with broken windows." Many residents moved out as the transition phase proved unbearable. By the 1980s, other community-based groups built new subsidized housing, but many of the original residents were long gone.[18]

WCO was a multiracial effort that built on the experiences of African-American neighbors in the medical center. It also tapped into Black political influence with its connection with Senator Coleman Young. WCO's calls for more participation by local residents had lasting effects on local policy decisions. However, the price its own neighborhood paid for these contributions was high, since resistance prolonged the agony of clearance.

Although the Detroit Medical Center and University City protesters successfully pushed for more equitable decisions, their efforts did not appreciably change the record. Between 1960 and 1967, the city demolished a grand total of 25,927 dwellings because of urban renewal, highway construction, school and recreational building, or abandonment. During the same time period, only 15,494 new housing units were built, most of them middle- or upper-class in price. Of the more than 36,000 substandard housing units in 1966, 29,600 were occupied by Blacks. Thus the city had cleared out neighborhoods, many of them predominantly Black; rebuilt an insufficient number of replacement housing units for upper-income groups; and, for all this, barely attacked the problem of substandard housing.[19]

The Fall of the Growth Agenda

As the credibility of the city's urban renewal program declined among civil rights and community-based groups, so too did the credibility of the city's urban planners. The resulting confrontation came just as Detroit's planners gained national kudos for their professional work.

Detroit's planning director Charles Blessing, a national leader in urban design, was a magnet of influence and praise. Blessing and his counterpart, Philadelphia's Edmund Bacon, exemplified the best of the architecturally trained urban planners. The African-American community produced extraordinary planners as well. We present one example: Detroit's Hilanius Phillips actively fought the tendency to sacrifice neighborhoods for the sake of aesthetically pleasing schemes.

Planning Director Blessing led the quest for what was literally "a finer city." His perspective stamped an indelible mark on planning in the city. A talented planner with impeccable credentials, including an undergraduate degree in engineering from the University of Colorado and master's degrees in planning and architecture from Massachusetts Institute of Technology, he came to Detroit in 1953, having already worked as state plan engineer for New Hampshire, regional plan director for the Greater Boston Development Committee, a naval officer in charge of collecting data about European cities during World War II, and head of the master plan division for the City of Chicago. When, in 1952, he and forty-five applicants took a civil service examination for the planning directorship of Detroit, Blessing's score was the highest.[20]

According to Blessing, before his tenure the staff of twenty-seven "presided over a good collection of statistics and demographic data" but knew little about urban planning. Blessing sought to upgrade the quality and variety of staff planners. He hired a few planners trained in economics and sociology, but particularly attracted urban designers, architects, and landscape architects. At that time, a large number of urban planners had architectural backgrounds. It was also Blessing's natural inclination to bring in urban designers.[21]

Blessing's professional linkages depended heavily on urban design, a topic which dominated the bulk of his correspondence from 1953 to the early 1970s. These letters went to or came from such notables as Baltimore's James Rouse, asking for advice on Baltimore's riverfront; Norman Williams, seeking advice on planning Venezuela's Ciudad Guayana; Kevin Lynch, famed observer of urban design and human response, whom Blessing asked to help recruit student designer/planners to Detroit; and Robert Weaver of the federal HHFA, appointing Blessing to a community design awards committee. He also received numerous invitations to speak on urban design, from Harvard Graduate School of Design, Princeton and Notre Dame universities, and the Kansas City Conference on Design.[22] Small wonder that in 1963 the American Institute of Architects recognized his distinguished service by naming him a Fellow. His planning colleagues had selected him president of AIP in 1959.[23]

Blessing, passionate about city design, used even vacations to photograph and sketch the world's cities. He was a gifted sketcher and a keen observer of ancient and modern cities. Only a fraction of his voluminous personal drawings of cities around the world were published. The February 1964 issue of the *Journal of the American Institute of Architects* published sketches made during a two-month journey through Greece, Crete, and the Middle East. During this trip Blessing took over 3,000 photographs and visited famed urbanist Constantinos Doxiadis, but the most important results of the trip were his drawings. His beautiful renderings of buildings, plazas, and urban forms, such as the Acropolis in Athens, the palace city of Phaestos in Crete, and the temples of Egypt, clearly reflect the heart of a man enamored of city design.[24]

Designing Detroit

Blessing tried to apply to Detroit the design principles he learned through his travels and professional associations. He carefully monitored projects such as Gratiot–Lafayette Park, the Medical Center, and neighborhood plans for conservation areas such as Mack-Concord.[25] Blessing also initiated an urban design agenda for the city.

A 1956 *Detroit News* series, appropriately entitled "Detroit's 'City of Tomorrow,'" presented Blessing's goal: to reconstruct 30 square miles of Detroit's inner city according to good planning and design concepts. The series included Blessing's pen-and-ink sketch of a redesigned inner city and offered the Civic Center, Detroit Medical Center, and Lafayette Park projects as patterns for new development. Blessing hoped to restore the inner city "to the beauty and dignity it had fifty years ago." The eventual goal, for a broader geographic area, was to "make our city beautiful, healthful and safe from one [city] limit to the other."[26]

Blessing hoped to finance a new "pilot city" by supplementing federal funds with local corporate donations. He proposed that Detroit's automobile manufacturers finance an urban design center as a way of protecting the city's tax base. Designers at such a center could research building and redevelopment concepts just as manufacturers researched automobile design concepts. "Detroit can lead the world in city design and planning," he proclaimed.[27] This idea for a privately funded laboratory soon died. To expect automobile manufacturers to finance a technical center for improving urban design and redevelopment was wishful thinking. While in the 1950s

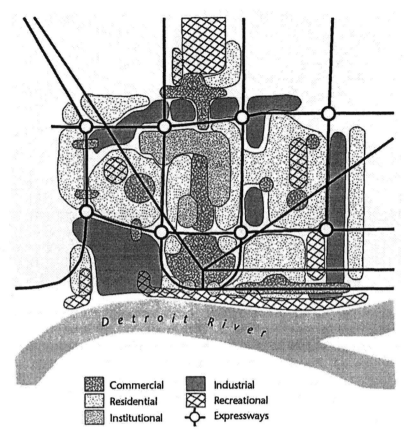

Fig. 5.4. Schematic drawing and redesign of central city (n.d.) shows an example of the visionary plans of Planning Director Blessing's designers for reordering the central business district and surrounding areas. Courtesy Detroit Department of Planning and Development.

D e t r o i t   R i v e r

Commercial	Industrial
Residential	Recreational
Institutional	Expressways

Blessing used his staff to design redevelopment projects, in the 1960s he became more focused. He would, if necessary, create his own laboratory.

Blessing proceeded to carry out what was, he said in 1963, a "simple task": "recording everything of design worth in the city." In 1965 he estimated that the planning staff was undertaking "very possibly the most extensive center city redesign assignment currently under study in the nation. We are projecting what we call a new city of a third of a million people in the thirty square miles of contiguous blight, generally identified as the area within the Grand Boulevard in Detroit."[28]

The most visible result of the surveys is a series of impressive pamphlets and brochures that show the design potential of the city. Some of these focus on projects such as the Cultural Center, others on existing features such as architecturally significant churches, and another laid out a design agenda for the city (see fig. 5.4). While these publications reflect careful design standards, their practical results are apparent largely in the redevelopment projects the designers helped supervise.

Upholding such design standards, however, sometimes cost valuable political support. During Mayor Albert Cobo's administration (1950–57), constituents called the mayor to complain about Bles-

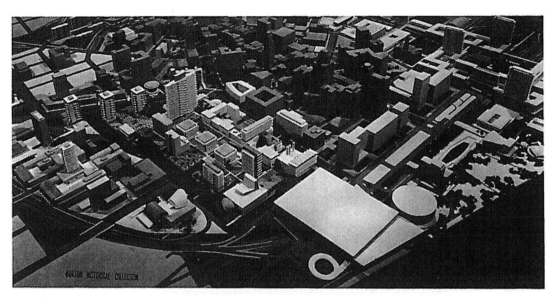

Fig. 5.5. Three-dimensional model of the central business district developed under Planning Director Blessing's direction. Burton Historical Collection, Detroit Public Library.

sing's three-dimensional model, which replaced existing houses or churches in the central area of Detroit with multistory cardboard buildings. Louis Miriani's administration (1957–61) brought conflicts when downtown business interests persuaded the mayor to tear down historic city hall, in spite of Blessing's opposition. And the planners waged a prolonged confrontation in the 1960s over the Civic Center. For this last case, during Jerome Cavanagh's administration (1962–70), Blessing fought powerful city agencies over their plans to change the Civic Center plan.[29]

As described previously, the Civic Center designed by Eliel Saarinen and later supplemented by his son Eero dated back to the 1940s. After Eero died in 1961, changes to the Saarinen plan were needed because the Dodge family donated $2 million for a new fountain and parking facilities. Planning commission staff preferred the original plan, however, and objected to new proposals by the local architectural firm of Smith, Hinchman & Grylls. The voluminous letters and memos planners wrote on this issue called the new plans inferior and advocated the Saarinen plan. Blessing and his staff, in numerous meetings, tried in vain to tutor other departmental representatives and the mayor in the superiority of the Saarinen plan. In the end the planners failed, as the city ignored their counsel and retained Smith, Hinchman & Grylls.[30]

Yet another major conflict came over Blessing's plans for the Cultural Center. This conflict vividly showed that the planning commission's design preoccupation could cause opposition in the community as well as in city hall.

The Battle of the Reflecting Pools

The Cultural Center, two miles north of the Civic Center, contains the main building of the Detroit Public Library and the Detroit Institute of Arts.

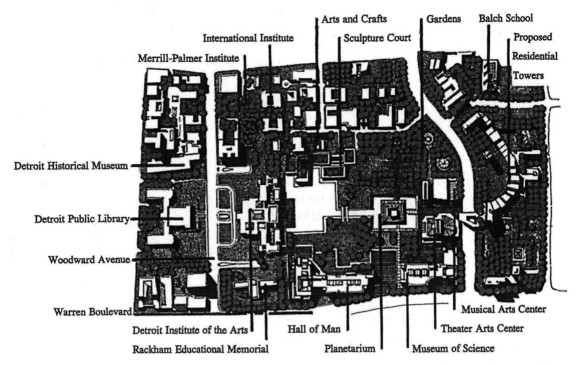

Arts and Crafts   Gardens   Balch School

International Institute   Sculpture Court   Proposed

Merrill-Palmer Institute   Residential

Towers

Detroit Historical Museum

Detroit Public Library

Woodward Avenue

Warren Boulevard   Musical Arts Center

Detroit Institute of the Arts   Hall of Man   Theater Arts Center

Rackham Educational Memorial   Planetarium   Museum of Science

In late 1964 Mayor Cavanagh negotiated an agreement to expand the art institute and library and to encourage allied development within a larger project area. Cavanagh needed an updated area plan to work within and ordered Blessing to produce one within a month. Blessing turned to his urban design section, which had already developed preliminary ideas for the area. The designers' resulting plan was a marvel in urban design, but it would have meant demolishing the neighborhood.[31] (See fig. 5.6.)

The concept of an expanded Cultural Center was not new. The city had long planned to enlarge existing facilities and add museums and other cultural buildings. The 1951 master plan included sketches of an expanded art institute, public library, historical museum, several new buildings for a planetarium, a "hall of man," and a natural history museum. An even larger project area appeared in a 1962 document. But the new Cultural Center brochure, issued around 1965, graphically dramatized how large the project area would be. Few existing houses and other buildings remained. In their place were clustered apartment towers and townhouses, a beautifully sketched park with gardens, two huge connected reflecting pools, bricked plazas, and sculpture courts.[32]

The text of the new Cultural Center brochure was certainly ambitious. "This brochure," it began, "is a graphic presentation of a complete cultural center . . . which, if developed according to this plan, will be comparable to the great cultural centers of the world, such as St. Mark's Square in Venice, with its panorama of life with-

Fig. 5.6. Segment of Detroit Cultural Center plan (ca. 1965). The Detroit Institute of Arts was expanded as intended, and a museum, science center, housing, and other buildings were constructed. The extensive outdoor reflective pools, plazas, gardens, planetarium, and several other "cultural" facilities indicated in the plan do not exist. Courtesy Detroit Department of Planning and Development.

in a magnificently unified architectural composition, and Salzburg and Edinburgh, with their world famous music festivals." The Institute of Arts would anchor "the grand composition, with the reflecting pool lying at its base, merging into the sweeps of lawn, mirroring the shadowed trees." Equally flowery language described the park, gardens, and each major proposed building, with appropriate references to European antecedents.[33]

If this had been developed as envisioned it would have gone a long way toward creating the totally redeveloped, beautifully designed inner city that Blessing dreamed of. The Cultural Center could make the city the focal point of art, drama, music, history, and science in the region and help bring "the best of the world into Detroit." It would have linked with University Park and Wayne State University to the west, the Detroit Medical Center to the southeast, and the central business district farther south. In a cover letter, Blessing called the Cultural Center "a central feature in the new inner city."[34]

But politically the mid-1960s were not the time to replace neighborhood buildings and housing with gardens and reflecting pools. With the exception of Corktown and the central business district, every major urban renewal project had torn down Black neighborhoods. Dissatisfaction with urban renewal caused serious problems in the relationship between the Black community and the larger city. Detroit was, almost literally, a tinderbox. Race relations had deteriorated, and Black political activism was escalating. The Cultural Center plan would have uprooted over 2,900 Black families at a time when 29,600 of the 36,000 city households living in substandard housing were Black.[35] Cultural Center public hearings in late 1967 revealed sharp battle lines. On one side were the mayor, planning director, and cultural institutions, including the president of the Detroit Science Museum Society and vice-president of Wayne State University. Also speaking in favor of the project was Willis Hall, former planning commissioner and chair of the progrowth group of 36 "civic leaders" that Cavanagh had appointed as the Mayor's Committee for a Cultural Center.[36]

The mayor stated the city's position best. He noted that "often we become so involved in the very serious and great problems of housing and jobs that we forget the kind of city we want for all citizens." That city should be known as more than an "industrial city"; it should also be one that uplifted the human spirit.

On the other side were a state representative, the assistant director of the Model Cities program, several church leaders and residents, and a group of Black architecture and planning professionals. State Representative David Holmes, Jr., criticized the lack of citizen participation in the new plans and claimed the need to develop low-cost housing rather than cultural centers. Why had the city not called meetings in the Model Cities area to consider the proposal, he asked. Expecting residents to move was especially unjust, he charged, since Black city residents were surrounded by areas "that have previously denied homes" to them.

Hank Rogers represented a group of African-American architects, engineers, and planners. The center area already had "culture," he noted, and that culture was "soul": African-American presence and heritage. He charged that DCPC in advocating the plan would cause further deterioration of the area, since landlords would cease repairs because of project announcements. Area residents attending the public hearing opposed the project, he noted, because it would simply displace them.[37]

In previous years it would not have been a contest; the institutional powers would have won handily. By this time, however, redevelopment protests had made political leaders wary. The Black community had gained creditable, professionally trained champions who argued as forcefully against the project as their White comrades argued for it. The city retreated; council did not formally approve Blessing's project plan and, instead, began to reconsider and adjust the project. The president of the Art Center Community Development Corporation, a resident group based just east of the Cultural Center's Detroit Institute of Arts, contacted an outside group of designers to develop a new plan, with a strong emphasis on residential development. In 1971 the planning commission approved the Art Center plan.[38]

Opposition to the redevelopment agenda did not come simply from outside city government. Planners, traditionally White, had expanded their numbers to include racial minorities. These planners often had a perspective entirely different from that of their White colleagues.

Hilanius Phillips, the planner assigned to the Cultural Center in the early 1970s, is an example. Outspoken and forthright, Phillips identified strongly with historical African-American neighborhoods. Phillips began work for the planning commission in 1969 as a junior clerk. Like Black planner Harold Smith, who began as a draftsman, Phillips attended planning school while a city employee and upgraded his status to staff planner. Phillips was not the only planner assigned to neighborhoods: another notable example was Quintus Green, who worked with the Forest Park neighborhood, as well as Phillips's supervisor in the community planning division. All such planners were expected to serve as advocates for "their" neighborhoods in the world of city government, but Phillips was among the most vocal of their number.[39]

Phillips and Green agreed to move to the new Community Development Department in 1972 or 1973 to deflect community complaints that the department had no Black planners assigned to urban renewal sites.[40] Phillips was assigned to the Cultural Center. He soon discovered that the project as planned would raze a building where his grandmother, Bertha Hansbury, founded an important music school in the 1920s. The area also included other buildings of historical significance to the African-American community. These included old Bethel AME Church; Peck Park, named after a Bethel minister who promoted community development; Curtis Laboratory, an independent company headed by a former assistant to George Washington Carver; the first site of Dunbar Hospital, constructed in 1918 to serve Blacks refused access to White hospitals; and the offices of the NAACP. Also directly in the path of a reflecting pool was Barat House, a residential facility for teenaged girls built in the early 1960s.[41]

Phillips represented the new breed of planners coming into the profession. His roots were in sociology and social protest rather than architecture. Phillips honed his perspective in classes at Wayne State University for which he wrote papers sharply critical of the city's planning record. Amazingly, Phillips seemed to lack the average bureaucrat's timidity, and he was willing to speak out where others might be silent. A commentary he wrote, while he worked for the city, gives some indication of his blunt style:

Blessing's grand proposal [for a museum site plan] encompasses three city blocks. I guess City Plan didn't know the work Reverend Peck of Bethel AME did to uplift Detroit blacks. They had no second thoughts about destroying his name sake. I guess City did not know that the community and Detroit Renaissance were in the process of relandscaping the park. . . . Destroy Peck Park, destroy the church Reverend Peck built. Move out those who participated in a Black Renaissance that took place in the Cultural Center area. Mimic the vulture that devours a kill to nourish his own.[42]

Phillips saw in the Cultural Center plan a gross example of insensitivity to inner-city residents and obeisance to dominant economic interests. As he put it:

it was basically who are the big shots and what do the big shots want, what do the big institutions want. Let's accommodate their needs, who cares about the adjacent property owners. And what really incensed me was the fact that in the Cultural Center I'd answer to the big wheels, the Founders' Society of the Art Institute, the Center for Creative Study, and the proposed science museum people. All of those were [suburban] Farmington Hill folk, people with money.[43]

The planning commission's elevation of urban design only made matters worse, putting a beautiful facade upon what was, to this planner and his neighborhood charges, oppression. The designers themselves, chosen because of "how well they could render," tended to seek little input from users. Phillips notes that "it was easy to see why the orientation was that way simply by talking with those people. They had very introverted personalities and, yes, they were talented in drawing, but you could see that their designs didn't take into account how other people might view them and use them."[44]

Phillips became what one pair of authors have called a "guerrilla in the bureaucracy," fighting for neighborhoods from within the planning commission and then from within the community development department. He constantly reminded his superiors of the historic significance of the Cultural Center area and of the need to consider residents' concerns. He helped the Barat House seek permission to improve its facilities. He fought for neighborhood proposals for new, affordable housing. In 1977 he won historic designation for one block of the neighborhood, now listed in the State Register of Historic Sites.[45]

By that time the area had deteriorated significantly. The mayor and Common Council had relented and changed the master plan designation of the Cultural Center to a smaller area, but for several years the city refused to give residents permits to rehabilitate their homes. This helped bring the area down so badly that some residents filed suit, charging that the planners' actions devalued their property. Throughout his tenure Blessing continued to defend the Cultural Center plan; this did not help his credibility.[46]

The Cultural Center was never developed as Blessing envisioned it. Blessing was trying to push a higher level of urban design than citizens were willing to support. During the 1960s and early 1970s, Detroit faced many more difficult problems than poor design. Poverty, racism, depopulation, and economic decline all clamored for attention. Physical survival became a real issue as housing and jobs deteriorated and unfair treatment of Blacks by police escalated. In this context, people could not be expected to become enthusiastic about design agendas, especially those that cleared out viable neighborhoods.

Detroit's Redevelopment Flaws

The experience with the Cultural Center was just one symptom of a larger redevelopment problem for the City of Detroit. Blessing's efforts were almost certainly doomed to fail, and not just because of inherent contradictions between residents' needs and aesthetics. The truth is that the Detroit redevelopment agenda, for all of its accolades, had serious shortcomings compared to that of several other U.S. cities, even after citizens succeeded in forcing a more inclusionary process.

The experience of Philadelphia, whose planners tried to do many of the things Blessing did, offers instructive insight into the ingredients of redevelopment "success." The 1947 Better Philadelphia Exhibition, based on Planning Director Edmund Bacon's architectural model of a renewed central business district, captured public imagination. First presented in a department store and later in a museum, this multimedia exhibit attracted 400,000 Philadelphians in the first year alone. It was a show in the true sense of the word, offering viewers a graphic, mobile model of the city's future. The three-dimensional model displayed both the present state of the downtown and a new plan for each section of that downtown. Local citizens found this present/future perspective fascinating, and the exhibit bolstered popular enthusiasm for planning.

Bacon urged other planners to follow his lead. Hire staff with strong design credentials, he urged, select developers with good design plans, and promote a well-designed city. Blessing had of course already undertaken these steps in Detroit.[47]

It was Bacon's program that got more attention, however. A special issue of the *Journal of the American Institute of Planners* highlighted the great achievements of Philadelphia's urban renewal program. A 1964 edition of *Architectural Forum* stated that "Philadelphia has what is generally accepted as the most rounded, well-coordinated renewal program in the U.S." In a 1964 cover story on urban renewal, *Time* magazine featured cities that appeared to be "succeeding" in reshaping their central core areas, and included Philadelphia among its top three, with New York City and San Francisco. In 1966 Robert Weaver, secretary of the new U.S. Department of Housing and Urban Development, called Philadelphia "a trailblazer in planning, in renewal, and, indeed, in most of our federal urban aid programs," a place "where planning has worked."[48]

Gaining particular attention in Philadelphia were several visible project successes built on Bacon's design strategy. These included beautiful garden concourses, located next to subway stations; Penn Center, a nine-building complex on Kennedy Boulevard; and the Market East project, which creatively combined retail operations with train, subway, and bus stations. Philadelphia constructed major new apartment buildings and townhouses designed by architect I. M. Pei, and renewed the University City district, which contained several educational institutions and hospitals. Much of the credit for these successes went to Bacon.

The reason Bacon was in some senses more visible and apparently more successful than Blessing in promulgating his model for Philadelphia had something to do with the two planning directors and something to do with the cities and their redevelopment organizations.

Both Charles Blessing and Edmund Bacon were widely respected as competent planning directors. A 1961 survey of thirty-one prominent U.S. planners showed that Detroit's comprehensive planning program was the most widely respected. Twenty-nine of the respondents mentioned Detroit, and twenty-five mentioned Philadelphia. Bacon and Blessing received almost equal numbers of votes as the best individual planning director, with Bacon getting nineteen votes and Blessing eighteen.[49]

But the two men were very different. Bacon had a much more dominant personality than Blessing and a particular flair for publicity and promotion. One former Detroit planner, who watched what he called a "friendly rivalry" between Blessing and Bacon, calls Bacon "more of a showman than Blessing." He was also more influential with the public. In 1988, long after his retirement, Bacon caused a maelstrom in Philadelphia by publicly attacking a new comprehensive plan that he saw as too vague, insufficiently visual, and too divergent from his 1963 plan. Very soon the public debate centered not on the new 1988 plan but on Bacon's perception of it. This is the kind of influence Bacon wielded throughout his tenure. Blessing, on the other hand, valued professionalism above political skills. He was less aggressive than Bacon about using the press to air his opinions. While Blessing was publishing short commentaries and sketches of Greece, Bacon was publishing promotional journal articles on Philadelphia, and, eventually, a textbook on urban design.[50]

Bacon also had the considerable advantage of operating in a city with a stronger renewal program than Detroit's. Philadelphia had aggressive entrepreneurial leaders, a good administrative structure, and a strong growth coalition. Detroit had none of these, even though it had one of the strongest planning directors in the country.

The matter of "success" is a debatable one. With a process so fraught with conflicts, one could question which was more important: implementing visible redevelopment projects or promoting social improvement and social justice. But, certainly, making the judgment based on strength of implementation, certain factors appeared to be important.

American cities with strong postwar redevelopment efforts almost always had at least one strong *entrepreneurial leader.* New Haven, New York, Boston, San Francisco, and Philadelphia had highly visible, dominant, construction-oriented mayors and redevelopment leaders. The urban renewal program required the courtship and cooperation of economically motivated developers. "Urban entrepreneurs" were municipal promoters who made urban redevelopment successes happen. Their lives involved continual rounds of negotiations with politicians, developers, and federal officials, and they served as linchpins between the political order and the economic order.[51]

Of the Detroit mayors who held office from 1950 to 1973, including Cobo, Miriani, Cavanagh, and Gribbs, not one can be singled out as a powerful moving force in redevelopment. Cobo had the personality and the drive necessary for such a role, but, when he died in 1957, several projects were just beginning. His successor, Mayor Miriani, had to cope with a hostile state legislature, a severe loss in state aid, a pre-existing budget deficit, and a two-year recession during his term of office (1957–61). Cavanagh (1962–70) supported redevelopment but also spent a great deal of effort overseeing antipoverty programs in the city, trying to quell racial conflict, and promoting himself as a national leader in urban affairs. Roman Gribbs (1970–73) was largely a law-and-order caretaker elected by White voters to counter the potential threat of a Black mayor and to strengthen police action against rebellious Blacks. After 1974, Coleman Young arose as a major entrepreneurial leader, but his extensive story will take time to tell so we will describe Detroit's "messiah mayor" in chapter 7.[52]

Philadelphia's redevelopment authority gained considerable unity of purpose with the 1956 selection of promoter William Rafsky as urban development coordinator. No staff member in Detroit arose as a major urban entrepreneur. Strong candidates would have been the housing commission directors, particularly Robert Knox. But Knox's commission shared power with Blessing's planning commission. Blessing had many strengths, but he could hardly be called a redevelopment entrepreneur, confronting as he did bureaucrats and citizens alike over design issues concerning the Civic Center and Cultural Center. Besides, as Bellush and Hausknecht conclude in their study, "the renewal entrepreneur owes at least part of his success to a career line other than planning." Blessing's interests and skills focused on planning and urban design.[53]

Good *administrative structures* worked in combination with strong entrepreneurial leaders. Philadelphia's redevelopment authority was a good example, but so was the Boston Redevelopment Authority, headed by Edward Logue. Logue first made his mark by launching a nationally acclaimed downtown redevelopment effort in New Haven. He then moved on to work with Mayor John Collins in Boston, organizing an aggressive redevelopment agenda. San Francisco's M. Justin Herman transformed the central core of his city. Robert Moses used the Mayor's Slum Clearance Committee to supplement his already considerable influence over development in New York City. Moses, Logue, Herman, and Rafsky each demanded the organizational format necessary to back them up.[54]

In Detroit, however, no single organization was powerful enough to lead the urban redevelopment campaign, in part because no entrepreneurial leader demanded such an organization. Twenty governmental and nongovernmental offices and groups participated in the redevelopment process. The shared arrangement for the housing and planning commission staff sometimes led to gridlock. The mayor could control neither the planning commission, whose director was a civil servant protected from political pressure, nor the housing commission, where the mayor appointed only five of nine citizen commission members.[55]

Strong *growth coalitions* were also key. As Mollenkopf showed for Boston and San Francisco, significant institutions, business leaders, and politicians wanted to protect the central business district and other important institutions, and so they arranged for central city redevelopment according to their own interests. As long as redevelopment activity represented a coherent political or economic agenda, these coalitions were able to steer activities as they liked.[56]

In San Francisco, Philadelphia, and Boston, such important people and institutions remained actively involved for long periods of time. In Detroit, however, growth coalitions were not as unified as they were in other cities. These groups helped boost Lafayette Park, the central business district, Corktown, the Detroit Medical Center, the Cultural Center, and other project areas. The coalitions were almost always different, however, and no one exercised consistent power over more than his or her small area of concern. None truly represented the automobile industry, the Atlas that held up the economic base of the City of Detroit. This did not halt activity but may have slowed it and reduced its potency.

Linda Ewen's work on Detroit's interlocking directorates shows that the city's economic interests were organized, formally and informally. The range of organizations to which several wealthy families and executives of major companies belonged is extensive. But the connection between these organizations and redevelopment is not clear. Very few of the formal organizations Ewen lists had any ongoing relationship with redevelopment, with the exception of the Central Business District Association. Even though many of the economic elite had ties to this particular group, their power did not translate into a strong redevelopment policy for the central business district.[57]

Each of the other redevelopment projects relied upon a limited, promotional coalition. In Lafayette Park the Citizen Redevelopment Committee, an amalgamation of business, labor, and citizen leaders, played a strong role at first and then faded in importance. The central business district coalition was weak and fluid, and the major automobile companies distanced themselves from an industrial redevelopment strategy. The Detroit Medical Center and Wayne State University coalitions themselves were separate and highly project-specific.

A unified growth coalition with a strong, consistent vision and collective promotion of what Detroit should become, backed by the support of major economic interests in the city, simply did not exist in the formative years for redevelopment. Blessing had an extraordinary vision, but he had neither citizen support nor the necessary redevelopment organization to support him.

Postwar Agenda Reconsidered

Here was the contradiction: In spite of organizational handicaps, by the mid-1960s the City of Detroit had done much of what its postwar planners had set out to do. In the opinion of the national community of planners, the planning commission had successfully promulgated the city's landmark 1951 master plan. It had protected the central business district with the Lafayette Park and Corktown projects. It had improved the city's infrastructure and helped several major institutions to expand. Yet, at the same time, the city's postwar agenda was losing popular support.

With the Detroit Medical Center, civil rights organizations and church leaders put the city on notice. They would not tolerate racial discrimination in services from the very agencies that proposed to clear Blacks out of their homes. They forced inclusion of Black institutions into a project plan that had conveniently left them out. University City escalated citizen protest and forced the city to include citizens in the planning process for their neighborhoods.

Gradually, it became obvious that an urban design initiative could hinder as well as assist. Blessing's staff lost political support within city government over such issues as changing the Civic Center plans. Conflicts over the Cultural Center reduced the credibility of the design agenda among neighborhood residents and some neighborhood planners.

Blessing had a magnificent vision for the city during years when many people found it difficult to be optimistic. His consummate professional skills led some to call him "a planner's planner." But design solutions were not sufficient to rebuild the city. As Blessing's star waned, a new breed of urban planner came to the fore, represented here by Hilanius Phillips. From outside the planning commission staff, Phillips and his colleagues waged guerilla warfare on behalf of Black neighborhoods from within the bureaucracy.

A visitor to the Detroit Medical Center, Cultural Center, and Wayne State University areas in the 1990s would find hospitals, university facilities, a new science center, museums, office buildings, and housing built for professionals. All of these projects show the signs of good community design. In addition, within or close to these project borders are located subsidized housing for people of low- and moderate-income, commercial and service buildings of importance to all area residents and employees, and several churches and their ancillary service institutions. These were the fruits of years of effort by city staff but also years of struggle by civil rights and community-based groups and by guerilla planners who worked for social equity.

One would also find, within or just outside of project boundaries, pockets of vacant land or deterioration. Private investment was not matching public investment in the synergistic relationship that would have taken place if private capital were not disengaging so thoroughly from central city Detroit. Only a strongly pro–central city set of federal policies—which did not exist—and a particularly effective local redevelopment operation could have countered this situation. Yet for many years Detroit struggled not only with insufficient federal support but also with no strong entrepreneurial leader, no strongly unified redevelopment administration, and no cohesive growth coalition. Simultaneously, it had to reshape redevelopment so as to rectify the grievous lack of consideration for African-American citizens that characterized the traditional redevelopment agenda. Given these circumstances, it is a wonder Detroit accomplished as much as it did.

Progress amidst Decline   III

Rising from the Fire

6

The 1967 civil disorders were symbolic of all that had gone wrong with the old order. They were a dramatic statement that the city's African-American community would not remain quiet and confined, that everything was not improving, that racial injustice would not be tolerated. Sadly, however, the disorders caused further decay and abandonment. It was as if, in frustration and self-loathing, the city burned itself down.

Every major central city in the United States with a sizable Black population experienced civil disorder in the 1960s. These pivotal events had a marked effect on central cities and their regions. They burned out inner-city residential and commercial areas and spurred greater exodus by the middle class. Official investigations concluded that the riots were cries for help, protests against the cumulative effects of discrimination, and demands for greater assistance. But they were also statements of frustration with the existing social order, expressions of community pride and assertiveness. Hence, the insistence of many that these were urban rebellions or civil disorders rather than riots. Even their label is volatile.[1]

This chapter will describe the origins of Detroit's civil disturbances and why the War on Poverty and other social planning initiatives could not prevent them. The nation had developed social planning tools, but these were hardly more effective than physical planning in improving the city. Soon the nation abandoned all but the appearance of its social planning initiatives. In the City of Detroit, an ensuing effect of the civil rebellion and the failure of social planning was the demise of urban planning.

The Fire

Although the immediate event that set off the 1967 Detroit disturbances was a police raid on an illegal social club, racial conflict was long standing. The 1943 race riots had introduced post-Depression era Detroit to racial street fights. The process of neighborhood succession caused sporadic attacks against "intruders" for years. The 1967 incidents were simply a spectacular variation of a theme.

In the 1960s, police-community conflict heated up when the police force, largely White, became noticeably hostile toward inner-city African Americans. This hostility—due in part to the fact that police officers were interacting with people of another race rather than their White friends and neighbors, who were leaving the city—bred numerous civil rights violations. Yet the police department was unwilling to diversify its ranks. Mayor Cavanagh considered police department reform a top priority but was "remarkably unsuccessful" in getting the department to hire more Black officers. Vicious harassment by fellow officers drove Blacks out of the police force. Sessions in human relations training did little more than reveal the deep bigotry and racial hatred White police officers felt toward Blacks.[2]

Social and economic crises added to the discontent. Employment discrimination was rampant in spite of federal civil rights laws, since employers could easily select workers on the basis of residence. Resentment lingered over the legacy of urban renewal. Segregation and unequal racial treatment of Blacks in the city's school system caused widespread outrage. The city had a national reputation for good race relations, but it was undeserved.[3]

The 1960s were volatile times for other reasons as well. On television, Northern Blacks saw Southern Blacks suffer from police dogs and fire hoses. A revolutionary fervor arose, with nationalists urging armed self-defense or civil rebellion. Detroit was the center of such small but vocal groups as the Revolutionary Action Movement, founded by Robert F. Williams, advocate of "organized violence"; UHURU, formed by students at Wayne State University; Reverend Albert Cleage's Black Christian Nationalist Movement, a separatist church group; and the multiracial WCO, which used Alinsky methods to protest redevelopment abuses in the Wayne State University area. These groups raised the pitch of political resistance. Their rhetoric was mostly that, but it contrasted greatly with the pacific perspective of the civil rights movement leaders. More conservative organizations, such as the NAACP, Urban League, and Trade Union Leadership Council, had larger memberships, but they were losing touch with young people.[4]

City after city erupted in the mid-1960s. Detroit's first major disorders occurred in 1966. Afterward, community leaders urged the city to recruit 1,000 Black police officers, open more recreation facilities, and promote equal access to employment. They also suggested "a crash program to deal with the issues of ghetto housing and slum living conditions." Mayor Cavanagh responded with only half-hearted solutions. To remedy housing conditions, he promised to purchase a mere 30 to 50 existing homes for large families displaced by urban renewal.[5]

Detroit "blew" on July 22, 1967. In the wee hours of the morning, the police raided yet another illegal drinking establishment—known as a "blind pig"—but were unprepared for the large number

Fig. 6.1. Aerial photograph taken during 1967 civil rebellions of a burned-out commercial corner, with a fire engine, at Warren and Grand River Avenue. Burton Historical Collection, Detroit Public Library.

Fig. 6.2. Press conference during 1967 civil disturbances; seated are Gov. George Romney, Cyrus Vance, Mayor Jerome Cavanagh. Burton Historical Collection, Detroit Public Library.

of patrons they found. A crowd gathered in the street and objected to police officers' methods of arrest. Soon the crowd raged out of control, touching off days of looting, arson, and shooting. Forty-three people, thirty-three of them Black, lost their lives in the next few days. Law enforcement officers killed thirty, including several innocent bystanders.[6]

President Lyndon Johnson established a national commission to study the string of urban civil disorders. In its March 1968 report, this commission documented a wide variety of social and economic grievances which preceded the disturbances. It warned that the nation was moving toward two societies, one White and one Black, and it blamed White racism for the problems leading to riots. These findings had little noticeable effect on national policy. In the same month that the commission issued its report, Lyndon Johnson announced he would not run for reelection. The national response to urban disorder was to buttress police units and elect conservative politicians, including Richard Nixon as president.[7]

The effects of the civil disorders were far reaching. The most immediate effect was physical, as entire blocks of commercial and residential buildings were damaged, some never to be rebuilt. Commercial owners hesitated to reinvest in areas where the residents were likely to burn down their buildings. Residents who could move out received a strong push in that direction. White flight had been taking place for years before the civil disturbances, so those who blame the exodus largely on the disorders are overstating their case.[8] But many remaining Whites did leave more quickly than they would have otherwise. An average of 22,000 Whites left the city each year from 1964 through 1966. In 1967, however, 47,000 Whites left, 80,000 left in 1968, and 46,000 in 1969. Suburban Whites bought guns, hired private police guards, and steadily cut ties with the city.[9]

The national advisory commission noted that the Twelfth Street area, where Detroit's violence began, housed perhaps 21,000 persons per square mile, double the city's average density, because urban renewal clearance of nearby project sites had caused an influx of Blacks into the area. As a result almost all White residents left, leaving only a few merchants. Surveys conducted before the riot showed that 25 percent of the housing units in the area were so deteriorated that they required clearance, and another 19 percent suffered from major deficiencies.[10]

But poor urban renewal practices were not the sole conditions leading to the disorders. In fact, open-ended surveys of citizens hardly mentioned them directly. When the *Detroit Free Press* surveyed Black residents in 1968 about conditions leading to the disorders, they discovered the following top ten complaints, ranked according to importance:

1. Police brutality
2. Poor housing

3. Poverty
4. Lack of jobs
5. Overcrowded living conditions
6. Failure of parents to control children
7. Dirty neighborhoods
8. Teenagers
9. Too much drinking
10. Broken political promises[11]

Fig. 6.3. Photograph of two dapper young men and burned out buildings, on Pingree near 12th Street, July 25, 1967. Burton Historical Collection, Detroit Public Library.

Housing could be considered a redevelopment issue, and police brutality was in a class by itself. Lack of parental control and alcohol were also to blame, according to this survey. But other top conditions—poverty, lack of jobs, overcrowding, dirty neighborhoods and, in a sense, housing—related strongly to poverty. Ironically, just before this period, the nation had begun a major campaign to improve the lives of poor people; this had obviously failed to prevent civil disorder.

The Social Planning Agenda

Just before the 1960s eruptions, President Johnson had initiated the War on Poverty and then a much-lauded Model Cities program.

While the first aimed at rural and urban poverty, Model Cities was specifically targeted at urban distress. Since each of these efforts ended in disappointment, however, it was a time of deepening disillusionment.

President Johnson's "unconditional war on poverty in America," financed by the U.S. Economic Opportunity Act of 1964, was part of a blitz of legislation that Johnson moved through Congress. With it Johnson attacked what had always been accepted as a fact of life: poverty. The government funded Medicaid and Medicare to provide health services for the indigent and elderly, job training and educational programs for youth, legal assistance for the poor, and Head Start for preschoolers. Many of these programs provided real benefits and survived into future decades. Some programs, however, were essentially blind efforts, since few antipoverty ideas had stood the test of trial and error.

When OEO designers tackled poverty by providing assorted social services to rural and urban poor people, they assumed that reforming the poor in their locality was better than dispersing them to more prosperous communities. Without firm evidence, they assumed that the poor lived in a "cycle of poverty" that could be broken with age-specific programs. OEO set up local community action agencies to give the poor "maximum feasible participation" in program design, believing that helping the poor to demand more just treatment from local city halls would improve their lives. Yet the federal policy designers hardly understood "maximum feasible participation," much less how to help people end their poverty. Community action caused a political maelstrom when poor citizens pressured city halls to provide services.

Perhaps these problems could have been worked out with enough time and federal commitment, but antipoverty did not get the time it needed. Lyndon Johnson, at first a popular and powerful president, became enmeshed in the Vietnam War. When he turned his attention to Vietnam, he left his urban and antipoverty initiatives defenseless. Liberal politics fell before a growing conservatism, symbolized by the 1968 election of Richard Nixon as president.[12]

Detroit made a noble effort. As its community action agency, Detroit created Total Action Against Poverty (TAP, later TAAP). TAP's 1964 allocation of $2.8 million was the nation's largest per capita grant and the second largest total grant in the country. The next year it received $5.5 million, the next $10.8 million, and $15.7 million in 1967, amounts that consistently gave Detroit more than its share of national allocations based on population size. But after the first year ongoing programs such as Head Start absorbed most funds, leaving other programs underfunded. The diversity of programs—Head Start, Neighborhood Youth Corps and Upward Bound, Medicare Alert, a credit union, an intramural physical education program, and others—became hard to sustain.[13]

Killing poverty was much more difficult than anyone had imagined. Detroit's low-income families experienced chronic physical and mental health problems. Many had major problems disciplining teenage children, especially in single-parent households. Unemployment suggested the need for strong vocational training and job counseling. TAP had neither a strong system of supportive services and follow up nor staff experienced in dealing with these issues. Community aides tallied up astonishingly high numbers of "contacts" with residents, but many of these were single meetings with people beset by complex difficulties.[14]

The War on Poverty was only a skirmish, with a number of conceptual and organizational flaws. These flaws were inherent within the federal legislation governing the program, but at the local level citizens did not see federal legislators, they saw the mayor and local civil servants who represented, it was beginning to appear, an oppressive city hall.

Social Renewal

Detroit tried again with "social renewal," another federal idea that foundered in the hinterland. The city had created the Community Renewal Program (CRP) to bring more cohesion to urban renewal programs and to forge a closer bond between physical and social planning. The federal government encouraged social renewal as a direct response to the ills caused by physical redevelopment.[15]

Detroit's CRP accomplished modest results. It sponsored several important studies, including analyses of poverty and relocation abuses in the city. CRP proposed a network of sixteen family centers to provide comprehensive social and cultural services for Detroit's families. This evolved into a series of neighborhood family health centers. CRP also collected physical and social data on the city and its neighborhoods.[16]

The organization was an important source of expertise for Cavanagh, helping him write proposals for the antipoverty program and Model Cities. A few key planners were actively involved in this work. Planning Director Blessing served on its supervisory committee, as did other major department directors. Harold Black, CRP's first assistant director and second director, was a former "social economist" within the planning commission, and other planners joined the CRP staff.

CRP, however, had no clear mandate or road map for how to proceed. It tackled a daunting array of concerns, ranging from job training to health care. CRP placed strong emphasis upon citizen participation but, almost in contradiction, it promoted scientific management techniques via project planning, monitoring, and budgeting.[17]

When Cavanagh addressed the 1965 National League of Cities convention, he called the city's social renewal program "one step beyond" the War on Poverty. It would, he said, let cities coordinate attacks on both physical and social blight. Its physical data bank would give within seconds a profile of the physical characteristics of any city neighborhood. CRP's social data bank, with its storehouse of over 25 different social indicators, was an important supplement. "Using these two [data] banks, we can take the pulse of any section of the city at any given time. We can measure the impact of our programs on human lives. We can also take a close, objective look at each neighborhood and its problems and design exact programs to fit them. It will flash danger signals when neighborhoods are beginning to have problems. We will not have to wait until the problem is a crisis before dealing with it."[18]

This is a 1960s version of utopia. In an earlier era the physical environment was key. The mid-1960s brought a leap of faith into the realm of improving the total human being within the urban community, using scientific management techniques. The mayor and CRP planners reflected the confidence in urban scholarship and social indicators common at that time. The whirring, buzzing world of computers, it seemed, would help solve all urban problems. These problems only needed to be quantified so that programs could be properly targeted. This mechanistic faith in physical and social data banks joined with the political optimism that came with good economic times.

The CRP effort soon foundered. It was a gimmick, an attempt to patch up the old urban renewal programs, append social planning to them, cover all with the gloss of scientific data collection, and thereby create something new. Soon the federal government stopped pushing social renewal and moved to a new omnibus program that promised to do much the same, only better.

Model Cities

Model Cities differed from CRP in that it focused on a targeted area of the city. Model Cities also supported strong methods of citizen participation to resolve urban problems, as did OEO's community action component. Backers of the federal legislation promised that it would target a wide variety of federal programs into focused areas, showing the world how to fight urban distress successfully.

The fear that policy-makers were creating yet another poorly conceived solution to urban problems worried some. Lewis Mumford warned Congress to "go slow" and experiment with small measures. He urged, "do not hastily pour tens of billions into any national program until the mistakes that have been made during the last quarter century have been analyzed and corrected," or "until new agencies on a regional basis are created."[19] Urban planner Paul Davidoff suggested it would be better to break open suburban walls and encourage residential mobility than to rebuild the ghetto.[20] But Congress chose to launch the program without the forethought that Mumford counseled, and with a strong emphasis upon improving the ghetto rather than, as Davidoff urged, integrating the suburbs. For such an effort to remain small and experimental, as Mumford counseled, was not possible. The civil disorders of the mid-1960s appeared to confirm the urgent need to do something, even if Congress was not sure what.

Detroit's Mayor Cavanagh had helped develop the original idea for Model Cities. Elected in a surprise 1961 win over Louis Miriani, Cavanagh was at age thirty-three the second youngest man elected as Detroit's mayor. The charismatic leader easily gained national prominence and served as the only elected official on Johnson's Task Force on Urban and Metropolitan Development. Simultaneously president of the U.S. Conference of Mayors and the National League of Cities, Cavanagh captivated the press as surely as he had the mayors and won praise from *Life, Time,* and *Look* magazines. He and his attractive wife, Mary, appeared to be living the Detroit version of John and Jackie Kennedy's Camelot. "On a clear day," said one close associate, alluding to presidential prospects, "Cavanagh can see the White House."[21]

Cavanagh urged President Johnson's Task Force on Urban and Metropolitan Development to pick Detroit to demonstrate the effects of massive injections of federal resources. In January 1965, he confidently declared that "we stand on the threshold of being Demonstration City, U.S.A." Cavanagh held on to his dream that Detroit would be the major beneficiary even after Walter Reuther suggested that the program target six cities, and then ten. Cavanagh submitted a proposal asking for $982 million over ten years for Detroit. However, in January 1966, Johnson announced his plans to fund a demonstration city program for $2.4 billion over six years, benefiting sixty or seventy cities rather than one or six or ten. Later the number was expanded to 150, as the administration added cities in order to get congressional support.[22] The number of target cities grew even as the potential money remained the same, and so in the field Model Cities—the term still used in the national literature—turned into Model Neighborhoods, a more modest description of the target areas actually chosen (see fig. 6.4).

The program's designers expected that the new U.S. Department of Housing and Urban Development (HUD) could encourage other federal agencies to target their resources to the designated neighborhoods. But coordinating federal agencies proved almost impossible for the weak new department. Somewhat more effective were plans for citizen participation: The program provided for popularly elected local governing boards to design programs based on local community needs. Model Cities gave unprecedented power to local residents to guide physical redevelopment in their community and to link that redevelopment with social improvement.

The concept may have been progressive, but insufficient resources hindered success. Most local programs struggled mightily, with little guidance from the federal government, to use a teacup of

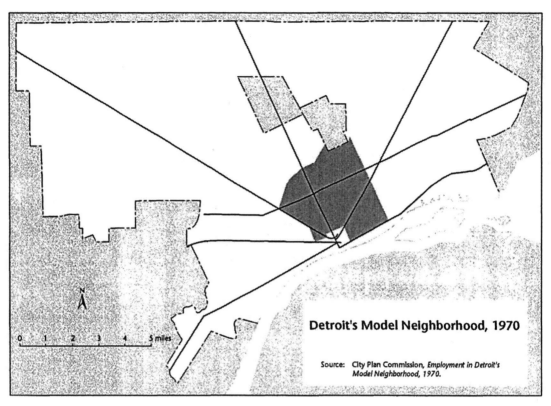

Detroit's Model Neighborhood, 1970

Source: City Plan Commission, *Employment in Detroit's Model Neighborhood, 1970.*

Fig. 6.4. Detroit's Model Neighborhood, 1970, included the area surrounding the central business district, and a high proportion of African-American residents. Courtesy Detroit Department of Planning and Development.

money to attack an ocean of problems. Essentially, local agencies were left on their own to resolve problems that had taken decades to develop.[23]

Detroit's Model Neighborhood Program

Detroit's community renewal planners proposed a wide variety of program initiatives, including housing, health, crime reduction, social services, private enterprise, public facilities, education, recreation, and employment, in a massive orchestration of social reform and physical renewal. After hiring staff, including professional planners, the agency administered an impressive mix of physical, social, and economic programs in its target Model Neighborhood area.[24]

But Detroit's program started at a bad time. The city applied for its planning grant just a few months before the civil disorders in 1967, and so the Model Neighborhood Agency had to help rebuild a still smoldering inner city. Even if the rebellions had not taken place, the agenda was too much to tackle. As one planner commented, "It seemed to me like getting dressed up for Saturday night with no place to go. You're the planner, you keep seeing all of these plans upon plans upon plans and [you say], my God, how are we ever going to get all these things done? And that's the problem I had with [Model Cities]."[25]

Even more than the War on Poverty had, Model Cities suffered from a lack of consistent federal support. At the end of Detroit's first planning year in 1968, the nation elected Richard Nixon as president. The Nixon administration continued to support the program but systematically searched for an urban policy more friendly to Republican constituencies. When the program formally ended in 1974 it was roundly, and somewhat unfairly, condemned.

Detroit agency staff put together a final evaluation in 1975, during the closing months of their program. The report listed accomplishments but acknowledged that many problems remained unsolved. As they noted, "the extensive physical, social, and economic problems of the City have [not] been resolved, or even substantially affected. Many multiples of the amount granted to Detroit would have been needed to eliminate only some of the City's least difficult problems." Moreover, "Detroit's remaining problems are so complex as to defy resolution simply by [infusing] categorical or otherwise restricted grants. Their resolution depends on the elimination of social and racial inequalities, the changing of ingrained attitudes, and the massive shifting of economic resources."

No amount of money could have changed "ingrained attitudes" leading to racial conflicts or eliminated the "social and racial inequalities" that the staff referred to. Society continued to invest in suburban development and away from inner cities, and Detroit's Model Neighborhood Agency did nothing to change that. If the federal government had channeled hundreds of millions of dollars into Detroit, perhaps success would have been possible; but the problem was one of knowing what to do, as well as having the money to do it. Knowing what to do necessitated a long-term commitment to learning from the program's successes and failures and then making necessary adjustments. Model Cities did not have a long-term commitment.

Detroit spent close to $75 million in just under six years. This was about $140 each year for every resident of the Model Neighborhood area, a "ludicrous" sum, the staff evaluation noted. Housing efforts were doomed from the start because of market trends, and small business assistance programs failed miserably. Many other initiatives confronted problems ranging from staff or subcontractor incompetence to bureaucratic inertia.

Yet the benefits were noteworthy. The program provided at least temporary employment for 8,000 target area residents, opening up new career ladders for many. It also helped improve achievement levels in local elementary schools and put in place a public health care delivery system.[26] The agency improved evaluation capacity within city government through its encouragement of professional policy analysis. An effective social planning unit lobbied for positive changes for city residents in bus fares and utility rates and actively promoted affirmative action in city government.[27]

Perhaps the most notable benefit was the support for neighborhood power. Model Cities funding let citizens design and administer community-based programs, giving citizens a sense of self-determination and confidence. The Citizens Governing Board had 140 members, 108 of them elected. The board maintained a full-time professional staff of 23 and hired its own legal, planning, and auditing consultants. This board had considerable authority over the Model Neighborhood Agency, guiding planning, implementation, monitoring, and evaluation.[28]

Finally, the Model Neighborhood Agency educated city planners. Several planners went to work directly with the agency or with subcommittees of the governing board. In a fine turnabout of power, these planners became employees of the low-income citizens whose neighborhoods they served. Loyalties changed as did sources of salaries; planners became more attuned to the desires and needs of ordinary citizens.

Given these changes, it is misleading to call Model Cities a failure. If nothing else it provided supportive social and community service programs for distressed inner-city residents. It also helped democratize decision-making in inner-city neighborhoods, finance social planning initiatives, and improve the planning process. It provided genuine citizen involvement in urban redevelopment, a privilege many appreciated all the more when the nation turned to less participatory urban policies. Yet, in spite of all of these positive influences, Model Cities did not make of Detroit a model city; neither did it create a model neighborhood.

The Alternative

When Model Cities died, the federal government did not replace it with another program of coordinated physical and social improvement. It did not support an urban policy that encouraged citizen participation. In hindsight, neighborhood activists yearned for the good old days of Model Cities, as its replacement was, in some ways, a setback.

Community Development Block Grants consolidated a number of special grant programs, including Model Cities and urban renewal, into a single block grant. Although CDBG allowed a wide range of expenditures to improve housing, neighborhoods, and (after 1978) economic development, it severely limited social services. Thus, its agenda was much more physically oriented than that of Model Cities. This led some citizens to complain that CDBG was a "bricks and mortar program," whereas the true needs of inner-city residents were more complex.[29] Even the "bricks and mortar" programs were underfunded, however. After a three-year transition phase, many large cities received less under CDBG formulas than they did under the old programs, and cities with high poverty populations did not receive significantly higher CDBG allocations than did other cities.[30]

Another major change with CDBG was a sharp reduction in citizen power. Model Cities residents heavily influenced expenditure patterns and made meaningful decisions. In Detroit, the governing

TABLE 6.1 MODEL NEIGHBORHOOD AGENCY PRIORITIES
DETROIT EXPENDITURES, 1968 – 1975

Ranked Expenditures	Amount (000s)
1. Education	$13,949
2. Health	15,136
3. Housing	5,121
4. Social services	5,060
5. Manpower and job development	4,842
6. Recreation/culture	4,578
7. Transportation/communication	4,386
8. Relocation	3,283
9. Citizen participation	3,190
10. Environmental protection	2,109
11. Crime/delinquency	1,968
12. Evaluation and information	1,081
13. Economic and business development	822
14. Office building	937
15. Program administration	9,217
Total	$73,335

Source: Michigan Advisory Committee to the U.S. Commission on Civil Rights, "Civil Rights and the Housing and Community Development Act of 1974," vol. 2, A Comparison with Model Cities, June, 1976, p. 86.

board and its agency had "dual veto power," and council could not approve any contract or program without their approval. With CDBG, citizens became strictly advisory. At first, cities needed only to hold public hearings describing their plans.[31]

As table 6.1 shows, the Model Neighborhood Agency selected a mix of physical and social programs, with heavy emphasis upon public services. Topping the list were education and health programs, with housing a somewhat distant third. Even then the agency chose to spend almost as much on social services and on job development as on housing. In contrast, the CDBG program focused once again upon physical development. Table 6.2 shows that the main expenditure item for Detroit's first year was completion of urban renewal projects. Future years brought expenditures largely on housing and physical aspects of community development.

Detroit was left with no way to coordinate social and physical renewal. As poverty rates climbed, Detroit could not focus social and economic development programs on the residents of specific low-income inner-city neighborhoods. Federal poverty programs were under attack as well. Even the bedrock of welfare programs, Aid to Families with Dependent Children, steadily lost funding in real dollars.[32]

After the 1967 rebellions, Detroit became a smoldering fire. The city did not break out into spectacular looting and street battles, but

TABLE 6.2 DETROIT'S FIRST-YEAR EXPENDITURES ON
COMMUNITY DEVELOPMENT BLOCK GRANT PRIORITIES,
1974 – 1975

Ranked Expenditures	Amount (000s)
1. Completion of urban renewal projects	$13,170
2. Public service	2,883
3. Property acquisition	2,471
4. Public works, facilities, site improvements	1,223
5. Clearance, demolition, rehabilitation	1,724
6. Relocation	1,550
7. Other (loans & grants, expenses)	1,604
8. Administrative	3,224
9. Contingencies	2,848
10. Planning and management development	614
Total	$31,331

Source: Michigan Advisory Committee to the U.S. Commission on Civil Rights, "Civil Rights and the Housing and Community Development Act of 1974," vol. 2, A Comparison with Model Cities, June, 1976, p. 88.

in many areas the murder rate grew, the drug trade flourished, and public school quality dropped. The injustices its children and inner-city poor suffered every day of their lives became, in effect, a dramatic continuing story of urban riots.

Disintegration of Planning

In one additional manner did public policy respond to the devastating effects of the civil rebellions of 1967, although this time at the local policy level: In reaction to the rebellions, Detroit's leaders reordered the redevelopment apparatus and emasculated the city's planning process. Planners became, in effect, scapegoats for the destruction of the city. Their experience offers a case study in how a bureaucratic agency can lose power in a political environment and confirms the now accepted notion that urban planners must be able to function effectively in a political environment in order to survive.

Many problems had led to the civil rebellions, including poor housing, housing segregation, limited employment opportunity, contentious police-community relations, inadequate community services, and racial conflict. But the city's political leaders lacked control over these problems. They could not force police to be civil. They could not immediately produce subsidized housing. They could not mandate open housing even within the city, and they had absolutely no power to force the suburbs to accept Blacks. Poverty and unemployment were even more intractable, as Detroit had learned from its War on Poverty and Model Neighborhood Agency programs. The only thing the city had certain power over was its own bureaucratic structure.

The incentive to produce change was strong. Before the 1967 disorders, the national press had treated Cavanagh as a great liberal savior. A disastrous 1966 Senate race considerably dimmed his luster. The 1967 disorders were the final blow to a promising career. Anxious to appear in charge, Cavanagh reacted by changing what he could control. He convened the Mayor's Development Team to explore the implications of the civil disturbances for city government. The executive order establishing the team directed it to coordinate "a blueprint for the social and physical redevelopment of the city." With the team Cavanagh attempted to redress the wrongs which led to the civil disturbances by reorganizing city government, a response which made perfect sense politically.[33]

The team recommended that the mayor create a single development agency that would absorb the functions and staffs of the planning and housing commissions. The city could merge those two citizen commissions into one unified city development commission and transfer all development agencies to the new superagency. This was not a new concept. Community Renewal's Harold Black had made a similar suggestion as he tried to streamline the city's redevelopment programs. Several nationally recognized authors had also suggested that development superagencies were the most effective.[34]

Planning staff tried to defend itself from the development team report. They explained reasons for delays in redevelopment and argued that a single planning and development agency would not be more effective than separate commissions. The planners offered their commission's services "in every social program for recommendations as to its physical planning and programming aspects." From Cavanagh's perspective, however, the most direct course of action was to reorganize city government. The city charter limited his options, so the next logical step was to change the city charter. Cavanagh appointed a charter study commission, which not surprisingly confirmed that indeed the 1918 charter was out of date. It set up an election allowing city voters to choose a charter revision commission from a preselected slate, heavily stacked with Cavanagh appointees.[35]

Many citizens had begun to see planners as villains, lackeys of an oppressive political system, perpetrators of wrongs against central city residents. Grievances against redevelopment and other related activities caused planning to lose legitimacy and status. The Detroit City Plan Commission tried, with limited success, to respond to the new environment. After the disorders of the summer of 1967 the planners set up numerous night meetings in the affected neighborhoods, greatly expanding their workload, to the point of nervous exhaustion for many. Staff trooped into the field to tally the physical damage and revised area plans to provide corrective action. In spite of these efforts, their attempts to accommodate citizens did not dissolve long-standing distrust. The relationship was particularly rocky with Model Cities citizen leaders. Governing board members charged that "the planning commission did not know how to communicate with citizen groups" and that "the sins of the past have been so great that completely new methods of doing things should be explored."[36]

The enmity ran deep. Some of it came about because of perceived racial exclusion in planning commission hiring practices. One of the early Model Neighborhood Agency directors, a former member of the Detroit Housing Commission staff, viewed DCPC as an elitist organization. Planning commission staff, he felt, saw themselves as "the professionals, the prima donnas. They looked down on the people in housing as quasi-professionals. [The Detroit] Housing [Commission] was the place for Blacks. 'We won't let them in planning because, after all, White people would get excited if you had Black planners in there.' Because remember, Detroit was still controlled by Whites, and it still had exclusive White neighborhoods with [exclusionary] neighborhood associations."[37]

Spurred by demands from the Model Neighborhood Agency, the planning commission tried to implement affirmative hiring. When its own social planning unit pressured city departments to adopt affirmative action plans, the planning commission led the way. Its plan frankly acknowledged previous problems attracting and retaining qualified women and racial minorities and promised to make a renewed effort.[38]

Such promises did little to stop citizens from attacking the symbol of centralized planning: the master plan. In the early 1970s, in neighborhood after neighborhood, residents organized to combat the effects of urban renewal and then to plan for their neighborhoods from the grassroots. The planners began a massive process of revising the formal master plan to accommodate neighborhood wishes. This happened in the Cultural Center area, where acreage for the planned (and never built) plaza and reflecting pool complex was cut back; in the Hubbard-Richard and Corktown areas, where citizens halted further expansion of industrial parks; and in the Wayne State University area, where citizens forced the city to change part of a planned redevelopment project, Research Park, from industrial to residential.[39]

Citizens testifying before the charter revision commission urged it to decentralize planning to the neighborhood level. They complained about "large-scale, centrally planned and controlled 'development'; a 'bulldoze first and worry about consequences later' attitude; physical solutions to social, economic, and political problems; and 'citizen participation' as a tack-on, peripheral process in bureaucratic decision-making." The protesting citizens warned that Detroit residents should not "turn over what little control of development we presently have to the Mayor and his cronies—the large corporate interests," since "what's good for Burroughs, Holiday Inn, Detroit Edison, Ford Motor, Blue Cross–Blue Shield, and other corporate giants is [not necessarily] good for us."[40]

Cavanagh declined to run for another term, and voters selected Roman Gribbs mayor in 1969. Gribbs continued to support the efforts of Cavanagh's charter commission. A former Wayne County sheriff who had defeated Richard Austin, the city's first Black candidate for mayor, Gribbs had a "law and order" perspective very different from Cavanagh's liberal reputation. Yet defining the city's problems as organizational was as attractive for Gribbs as it had been for Cavanagh. An aide in the Gribbs administration during that period identified two forces that propelled their efforts: the need for new ideas such as neighborhood city halls and the need for reconstruction after the riot. For the latter, the mayor's "inner team" relied on Cavanagh's development team report.

Planners lost the support of even that member of council most closely identified with them: former planner Mel Ravitz. Councilman Ravitz created a minor furor when he spoke to the 1972 American Society of Planning Officials (ASPO) convention, which met in Detroit. In that speech Ravitz criticized not only the Detroit City Plan Commission but planning in general. In fact, he suggested that planning mattered little, if at all. His words were hard for planners to accept, but they had a devastating ring of truth about them:

America's urban regions, both central cities and urban fringes alike, have been shaped far more by basic cultural and social forces than by the skills and perceptions of their planners. . . . The unfortunate truth is that planners have counted for little in the development of our cities and suburbs compared with giant technological, political, economic, and social forces. Most of what has happened in and to our urban areas would probably have happened even if there had been no planners or planning agencies.

To make sure his national audience understood his point, he drove it home:

If we would make our urban regions more rational, more efficient, and more comfortable, we must understand that what has hitherto passed as planning is passé. The colorful charts, the exotic sketches, even zoning restrictions and master plans, are no longer effective tools to reshape the region. Although they worked in minor ways in the smaller, less crowded, more manageable society of the past, they are no longer useful in dealing with the massive technological and institutional elements relevant today.

Such tools, he argued, were particularly irrelevant to solving the problems of the central cities and their regions, which were "in deep trouble" because of "social, economic, and political factors that run deep in the nature of our society."

Foremost among these factors, Ravitz argued, were: the automobile; the inequitable tax system, which punished low-income people trapped in central cities; and attitudes toward race and poverty. As recent civil disturbances had proven, he noted, attitudes toward race and poverty were particularly important, since they determined where people lived, attended school, and socialized. "These attitudes of the White, middle-class majority about race and poverty—not the concepts of the planners—decide how the American urban region grows and changes." Ravitz told his audience it was necessary not just to upgrade the central city but also to end racism and classism; otherwise, central city residents would gain only "an improved environment in an apartheid society."[41]

To an audience of urban scholars his words would have been unremarkable. To members of ASPO—a group of professional planners and planning officials dedicated to the idea that planning was not passé, that it was indeed a path to the future—it was a devastating speech. Urban planning had grown, it had become more diverse, it had weathered the urban renewal storm and become more socially oriented: but its effectiveness was still questioned, as were its traditional tools. And here was a prominent city politician, former planner himself, stating publicly that planning did not count, that its tools were ineffective in the face of racism and poverty, which actually shaped urban regions.

One of the most wounded responses to the speech came from Walter Blucher, Detroit's planning director until 1934, who had returned to the city after he retired from ASPO. He wrote the *Detroit News* complaining about Ravitz's speech and counting off a litany of planning successes in Detroit, including "the best highway-street system of any major city in the country." The editors responded by agreeing that Detroit's planners had made great contributions to the city, but noted that "it's not the fault of planners that the rush of urban events has dropped them behind."[42]

Ravitz and the newspaper reporter might have added that it was not simply contemporary urban problems that hindered planning in Detroit. Also important were citizens angered by negative experiences with urban renewal and emboldened by OEO and Model Cities. Heightening the resentment in Detroit was a series of conflicts over the design agenda. This was true in projects such as the Civic Center, which caused conflicts with Cavanagh's administration, and the Cultural Center, which caused conflicts with Black citizens. Those conflicts put Director Blessing on the firing line.

The conflict that may have been the last straw took place over the Renaissance Center. During the period from 1971 to 1973, Henry Ford II was preparing to construct a large, privately financed downtown building. According to one planner assigned to the central business district, Ford expected the city to do whatever was necessary to facilitate the project, and indeed much of the city did respond just as Ford expected. Director Blessing, however, said that the proposed building did not fit the plans for the Civic Center, which the Renaissance Center would border. It would be, he said, too isolated from downtown, unlike the other surrounding buildings. Furthermore, he charged, its setback (amount of buffer zone

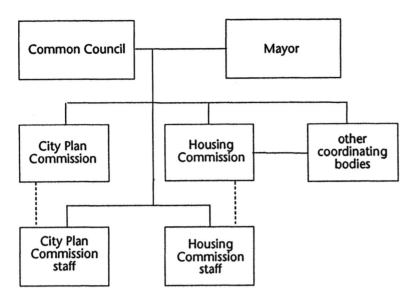

Fig. 6.5. A simplified schematic of the organization of major planning and development functions before the 1974 Charter.

between the building's walls and the street) and orientation toward the river were out of synchronization with other nearby buildings, which all surrounded the Civic Center like a graceful horseshoe, all with proper setbacks and harmonious design.[43]

The new city charter, which voters approved in 1973, either deliberately or incidentally curbed the power of a planning director to halt such a project. The charter revision commission had spent a great deal of time discussing planning and development, which one internal report called "the most involved and complicated problem" facing the commission. The revision commission staff carefully researched the status of planning thought at that time, but the literature appeared to offer contradictory advice on the organization of planning and development in city government. Some authorities suggested keeping them separate, while others advocated setting up large development agencies that included all related fields.[44]

The revision commission, significantly, did not set up a neighborhood planning structure. Instead, it fragmented planning and development into three bureaucratic components (see figs. 6.5, 6.6). It established a nine-member planning commission separate from the planning department. Placed in the legislative branch, the planning commission advised the city council, but the charter gave it no specific implementation powers (except as delegated by the council). The assignment of the planning department, located in the executive branch, was to prepare the mayor's master plan and carry out other liaison and information-processing functions. The charge of the Community and Economic Development Department (CEDD), also housed in the executive branch, was to carry out projects for conserving stable areas and eliminating blight.

Staff who once served the city plan commission either left city

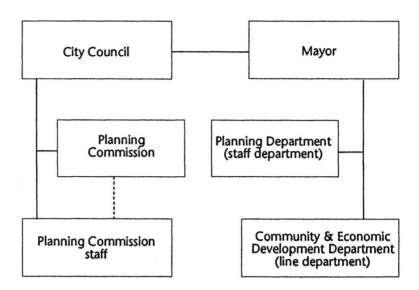

Fig. 6.6. A simplified schematic of the organization of major planning and development functions after the 1974 Charter. Changes in July 1994 merged the executive branch's Planning Department and Community and Economic Development Department.

government or went to one of the three agencies that the new charter created. Hilanius Phillips, project planner for the Cultural Center and lover of African-American historic sites, had already left planning to work with Gribb's community development department, and he stayed with it during the transition to CEDD. Phillips later applied unsuccessfully for the directorship of the planning commission's staff and eventually became head of the CEDD zoning office.

Under the old charter, no one could fire Blessing, who was protected under civil service. Just before the new charter was implemented, this planner, architect, engineer, and extraordinary city designer received an office, a telephone, and no job duties. He retired gracefully shortly thereafter. Blessing had placed first in the city's civil service examination. His successors, under the terms of the revised charter, were political appointees who needed to demonstrate no objective job qualifications. After charter revision the planning department went through at least six directors. Some lasted only a year.

Aftermath

The civil disturbances of 1967 severely affected attempts to improve the lives of urban residents. Originating in legitimate grievances about housing, urban renewal, and police brutality, these events nevertheless set in motion a further cycle of decline from which the city never fully recovered.

The disturbances came as a result of failed attempts to soothe racial conflict and to find more human-centered tools for urban improvement. High expectations for Lyndon Johnson's War on Poverty fell as the practical difficulties of antipoverty programs became apparent. Assorted efforts at social renewal through educational, health, and community service programs fell short. Model Cities did not funnel a billion dollars into Detroit, as Cavanagh originally hoped; instead urban problems easily outstripped the resources available. Community Development Block Grants spelled the end of even modest efforts to coordinate social and physical planning.

The atmosphere in the city after the civil rebellions led to major changes in redevelopment and planning. The frustration that Cavanagh felt because he could not solve major problems within Detroit, and his consequent drive for power in city government, helped bring about major organizational change. Detroit's newly revised city charter formalized what had already become obvious: the declining influence of urban planners. Indeed, as Ravitz forcefully noted, poverty and race relations were stronger forces than urban planning, and the tools that planners used were simply not sufficient for the tasks at hand.

Coleman Young and Redevelopment

7

After 1973, redevelopment in Detroit became inextricably tied to the leadership of Mayor Coleman Young. The single most influential person in Detroit's modern history, Young came into office on a wave of votes cast by citizens tired of racial inequality and injustice. Like ethnic groups throughout American history, African Americans elected one of their own as a symbol of their right to control their city.

By the time Young grasped political power, however, conditions had grown steadily worse. As Joseph Hudson, corporate leader of New Detroit, Inc., warned: "The black man has the feeling he is about to take power in the city, but he is going to be left with an empty bag." [1] Suffering from increasing poverty, deteriorating physical facilities, and a stagnant tax base, Detroit had to depend on unreliable federal, state, and corporate funds for its support. [2] In addition, it faced additional burdens brought by the civil disorders of the mid-1960s.

Mayor Young, like mayors of several other large cities, used aggressive and highly visible development projects to attack economic decline. He built a new sports arena, downtown apartment buildings, and industrial plants, giving Detroit the appearance of comeback. Yet this supposed comeback was an illusion; persistent problems prevailed in the very sectors with the most visible project successes. The voters nevertheless continued to support Young, electing him to an unprecedented five terms. This chapter focuses on what it was about Mayor Young that made the city's voters so loyal and what difference his leadership made to redevelopment in Detroit.

Messiah Mayor

Young wielded strong mayoral power largely because of his talents as racial champion, contemporary urban politician, and successful promoter of redevelopment. These talents joined with changes in city government to create a mayor of unusual influence and longevity.

From a Black politician's perspective, population change had tangible benefits, since White flight allowed mayors like Coleman Young to come to power. Between 1969 and 1974 the number of Black elected officials in the United States increased by 120 percent, to include 16 congressional representatives and 104 mayors. By 1974 Blacks were mayors of Los Angeles, Atlanta, Newark, Raleigh, Gary, and Detroit, which together contained 5.5 million people.[3]

African-American voters were impressed with candidate Young's labor background and his forthright willingness to stand up to the power structure. A former UAW labor organizer, Young helped organize the National Negro Labor Council in 1951. In 1952 Senator Joseph McCarthy called Young to Washington to testify before the House Committee on Un-American Activities, a witch-hunting group determined to seek out Communist infiltrators. Young startled the congressional representatives when he refused to cow before them and fearlessly lectured them for mispronouncing the word "Negro." Phonograph copies of Young's remarks soon circulated throughout Detroit's Black community, turning him into a minor folk hero. Young entered political life in a series of elections starting in 1959 and won a seat in the state senate in 1964, where he served until 1973.[4]

Young was also an attractive candidate because he had worked to counter the injustices of urban renewal. When Young was five years old, his family had moved from Alabama to Detroit's historic ghetto, known as Black Bottom. The city and state cleared out that area for the Gratiot project and the Chrysler Expressway (I-75). When he reached the state senate, Young introduced legislation that improved relocation benefits for residents and required citizen advisory committees in project areas.[5]

In 1973, White mayoral candidate John Nichols, the city's police chief, promised to restore "law and order" to Detroit's streets, a pledge that played to White fears of riots and street crime. Candidate Young promised to reform the city's police department, by abolishing STRESS (Stop the Robberies, Enjoy Safe Streets), an undercover police operation that killed 17 African Americans under controversial circumstances, and by diversifying the police force. Thus, African-American voters saw in Coleman Young a man tied to the liberal labor movement who would speak forthrightly, improve the benefit patterns of redevelopment, and defend the community against an oppressive police force. Turning out in large numbers, they gave Young 92 percent of their votes; Nichols won 91 percent of the White votes.[6]

Young came into office in 1974, a few months before the new charter went into effect. This remarkable confluence of events—the election of a race-oriented, outspoken mayor and the implementation of a strong-mayor charter—offered a unique opportunity. Young had the background, the personality, and the official powers necessary to remake Detroit's city government.

Young took full advantage of that opportunity. He carried out most of what his constituents expected of him. He immediately abolished STRESS and diversified the police force. He vocally confronted the White power structure, even though he also developed a comfortable working relationship with several corporate leaders. He tried to protect the central business district, still important for Black shoppers, and vital automobile industry jobs, crucial for Black workers. Thus, he kept his constituency loyal, and they reelected him in 1977, 1981, 1985, and 1989.

Young's skill as a racial leader was an important reason he was able to stay in office so long. But Young was more than an adept Black mayor. He also exemplified many of the characteristics of similar big city mayors, men that author Jon Teaford has labeled "urban messiahs."[7]

The "messiah mayors" were specialists who found new ways to govern their distressed big cities. They were very different from their predecessors, such as Detroit's Jerome Cavanagh, New York's John Lindsay, and Cleveland's Carl Stokes. Those men were popular but could not cope with the modern challenges of governing their cities. The new breed of mayors—Ed Koch in New York City, William Schaefer in Baltimore, George Voinovich in Cleveland, and Coleman Young—were less charismatic but more able to fashion pragmatic policies. They particularly excelled at what Teaford calls "urban hype": use of visible redevelopment projects to cover up deep-seated social and economic decline.[8]

Handling fiscal crises well was one of the characteristics of messiah mayors. During Young's tenure, Detroit suffered several such crises. For the first, in 1975, Young used layoffs, attrition, and service delays to weather the slump and convinced the state to increase subsidies for city cultural and educational institutions. In 1981, Young increased income taxes and won wage concessions from city unions. With almost every fiscal crisis, Young found a new way out.[9] Thus he saved the city from the humiliation of New York, which lost control of its municipal finances to a special state-appointed board, or of Cleveland, which defaulted on its municipal loans. In contrast, one Detroit newspaper called Young's leadership in resolving the 1981 fiscal crisis "little short of genius."[10]

Young also displayed a political savvy typical of other messiah mayors. Many cities had experienced political instability because of municipal reforms. Although the old political machines were corrupt, they were predictable, and they kept municipal employees in line. When modern municipal unions replaced political machines, labor costs escalated, and mayors lost valuable mechanisms for insuring their reelection. Adept politicians invented new ways to carry out the machines' functions. Boston's Kevin White established a permanent campaign organization that tied precinct captains into a city service delivery network, awarding municipal jobs to those who turned out the vote. St. Louis's mayor revived machine politics by gaining control of the civil service bureaucracy.[11]

Young could not turn back the clock to the time before civil service requirements and unions. He could not remake city departments into hiring halls for his racial group—an action quite common among certain European Americans in the days before reform.[12] But he did appoint Blacks to several key positions, and he expanded the city's use of minority contractors. He also appointed women to several prominent positions.[13]

Young then cemented his political position. He specialized in massive fund raisers, for which he expected municipal employees to buy and sell tickets. He based appointments on strict expectations of loyalty and maintained strong connections with African-American churches and union members. Using blunt street talk, which resonated extremely well among working-class Blacks, he lashed out at his critics in White suburbia and in the city's media and invoked racial pride to defend his policies. In these ways he combined his strengths as racial leader and as politician. The results were something vaguely approaching an old-fashioned political organization, if not a machine.[14]

The last characteristic of the new messiah mayors was their civic boosterism. Frozen out by erratic and then declining federal dollars, hemmed in by growing suburbs, and buffeted by continual population and economic decline, these mayors turned to visible if shallow symbols of progress. They promoted new office buildings and riverfront developments as effective antidotes to urban decline.

Young was a master at this strategy of urban improvement. This may have seemed incongruous given Young's background as radical labor leader, rebel against power structures, defender of neighborhoods from urban renewal. Yet Young was focused in his determination to wrest Detroit from the jaws of decline, and he stepped easily into the role of "entrepreneurial leader," activist promoter of redevelopment.[15]

The messiah mayor concept is not the only theory that helps explain Young's action. Earlier, we noted that a mixture of both economic and political influences determine urban decision-making and that cities are political entities dominated by economic interests. Revisiting that issue will offer a stronger framework for understanding the Coleman Young era.

Several models of elitism suggest that economic leaders control the actions of political leaders, either overtly or covertly. They share common interests, in part because of local political leaders' dependency on economic interests for tax revenue and political support. As John Logan and Harvey Molotch have explained, the city becomes a "growth machine" when economic and institutional leaders, referred to by author John Mollenkopf as the "growth" or "pro-growth" coalition, successfully persuade politicians to increase economic vitality and land values.[16] From that perspective, the economic interests have the greater power. The growth machine model explains much of the activity described thus far in Detroit, beginning with the early Gratiot project and continuing with the medical center and central business district.

But the manner of interaction and cooperation between political and economic interests is important as well. The pattern of interaction that the two sets of actors use to make decisions, termed the "urban regime" by Clarence Stone, can vary from city to city.[17] The quality of previous interactions is important, as are the personality and nature of contemporary leaders. Bryan Jones and Lynn Bachelor emphasize that innovative political leaders can change the course of events that economic powers would normally control.[18]

Politicians have become more important in the process of shaping patterns of interaction, or regimes, because of modern circumstances. Firms in central business districts have become less interested in increasing the value of their properties, because they are more mobile. Large export-based industrial firms have become almost completely uncoupled from place and have little incentive to invest in older central cities. Therefore, an innovative political leader, such as Young, can excel in specific situations and reshape the urban regime to meet his or her will. This is what happened in Detroit.

The Young Redevelopment Agenda

When he first entered office, Young expected significant federal assistance. His administration wrote an audacious document, "Moving Detroit Forward: A Plan for Urban Economic Revitalization," which asked the federal and state governments to finance almost $3 billion in improvements. Soon it became clear that the city would have to find support elsewhere.

In "Moving Detroit Forward," the city asked for $555 million in federal funds to retrain the unemployed and finance public service jobs. For industrial redevelopment, it sought $526 million to develop the riverfront, improve industrial corridors, construct industrial parks and business incubators, refurbish existing industrial plants, and update municipal services. Plans for commercial revitalization in the downtown and in neighborhood shopping centers would cost $300 million; a construction, rehabilitation, and demolition program for housing would cost $735 million. Finally came requests for $120 million to build new police facilities and hire a more diverse police force and $730 million to assist public transit, construct a downtown "people mover," and launch a regional rail transit system.[19]

From the prevailing perspective in 1975, the document must have seemed outrageous. The entire body of CDBG "entitlement" communities in the United States—including all municipalities with more than 50,000 people and all urban counties—received only $2.2 billion in 1975. Detroit asked for $2.5 billion in federal funding and $328 million in state funds, over five years. "Moving Detroit Forward" read almost like a call for a Model City, as originally defined: a city into which the federal government infused an extraordinary amount of funds, in order to generate a model of success.[20]

Federal urban policy had changed drastically from the 1960s. The 1974 CDBG program dispersed funds to a wider variety of municipalities than did Model Cities, because entitlement communities almost automatically received money allocated by formula. While Model Cities assisted about 150 localities, for the first year the number of entitlement CDBG communities totaled 581. Another 740 metropolitan and nonmetropolitan communities received money through a combination of formulas and phasing-in provisions. An additional 1,536 nonmetropolitan communities received about 20 percent of the total funds.[21] For older distressed cities, the message was clear. Favored status was ended; they had to share CDBG with other cities and suburbs, using a CDBG formula that gave only slight advantage to distressed cities.[22]

Although the federal government did not "move Detroit forward" as envisioned, the city eventually carried out many of its projects. Mayor Young stayed in office 20 years, long enough to pursue his agenda. The 1976–80 tenure of President James E. Carter helped; Young had strong political ties with Carter's administration, which channeled several discretionary grants to the city. During the same period, Coleman Young enjoyed good relations with Governor William Milliken, a moderate Republican with his own urban policy for Michigan's distressed cities.[23]

Another asset the newly elected Young inherited was the corporate support which arose after the 1967 disorders. New Detroit, Inc., headed at first by department store magnate Joseph L. Hudson, Jr., funded a diversity of community, government, and organizational projects.[24] New Detroit's annual budget for programs, however, totaled only $2 to $3 million, too little to make a major impact on social and economic problems.[25] A larger group was Detroit Renaissance, Inc., the coalition that Henry Ford II put together. Ford personally persuaded each chief executive of major corporations located in Detroit or linked with the automobile industry to invest in construction of Renaissance Center, the mixed-use complex located next to the Civic Center. The resulting 51-member partnership was then the largest private investment group ever assembled for an American urban real estate venture. Financing came from a $200 million construction loan advanced by a consortium of 28 banks, mortgage loans from major insurance companies, and investments from the corporate partners, including at least $300 million from Ford Motor Company. The partnership broke ground for the building on May 22, 1973, just before Young's election.[26]

Fig. 7.1. Photograph (triple exposure) of Phase I of Detroit's Renaissance Center (ca. 1977); center tower is the Westin Hotel, and surrounding towers hold offices. Burton Historical Collection, Detroit Public Library, Harold Wolf Collection.

The resulting complex became an instant Detroit landmark. Five high towers made up the original phase, with a hotel offering 1400 rooms occupying the innermost, 73-story cylinder. Four outer towers were 39 stories each and accommodated offices. Base floors included a literal maze of conference rooms, restaurants, retail shops, theaters, and other commercial facilities. Designed by architect John Portman, the Renaissance Center was three times larger than Portman's similar Peachtree Center in Atlanta.

The Renaissance Center, popularly known as RenCen, experienced a number of problems which were not unrelated to Planning Director Blessing's criticisms concerning its lack of connection with the Civic Center plan. Designed as a protected sanctuary, RenCen was cut off from the downtown by huge two-story berms facing Jefferson Avenue, ten lanes wide. Pedestrians found it difficult to enter, and navigating its complex corridors was a frightening experience. Many expensive shops closed after a few years for lack of customers. Ford transferred several company offices from downtown and Dearborn to help fill the space and built two new office towers, but older downtown office buildings lost tenants as leasers moved upward in a soft market already struggling with over-capacity. RenCen suffered major financial losses, forcing the original investors to sell it.[27]

In spite of these difficulties, the complex symbolized the potential of the riverfront and the central business district. Young used the privately financed RenCen as a centerpiece for allied development.

Fig. 7.2. Pedestrians approaching southern entrance to Renaissance Center. Poor pedestrian access, heavy traffic, and huge plant-covered berms (seen here—these house some of the buildings' mechanical systems), help give the complex the air of a forbidding "fortress." J. Thomas, photographer.

He turned to the business elite as co-sponsors of a central business district redevelopment strategy, for which some faulted him.[28] Yet, given the limited contributions of the federal government, corporate support undoubtedly seemed essential. Young lost little support from his constituency by working with development magnates, and his approach was only a local variation of the process many other cities followed. Taking the RenCen model one step further, mayors matched private investment with publicly funded incentives, courting the private sector into "public-private partnerships."

Superficially these mayors were saving the central city, but these successes sometimes surrendered public funds for the sake of private development. For tax increment financing—allowed in Michigan after 1975—Detroit issued bonds to finance improvements in approved target areas and dedicated future tax revenues to bond repayment. For property tax abatement, the city reduced an approved firm's property taxes by as much as 50 percent for up to 12 years. Such incentives favored some firms but raised taxes for others. These seemingly self-defeating policies actually followed an iron-clad logic. Federal resources were limited, and competing localities were offering incentives. Not to offer such incentives appeared suicidal.

Some federal programs helped. From 1977 to 1989, Urban Development Action Grants (UDAG) provided distressed cities and urban counties with an average of $2 million per approved project as a match for private dollars. But total U.S. allocations ranged from only $400 million during the early years, to a peak of $675 million in 1980, and $275 million in 1988.[29] Although Detroit won over $114 million from 1978 to 1984, it competed for each of its project grants, making planning ahead difficult.[30]

Typically a new hotel, apartment building, or industrial plant required subsidies from many different sources, such as tax abatements, tax increment financing, CDBG funds (current and future), UDAG, and other money from municipal bonds, other federal and state programs, and private financing. Each project became a financing "deal," subject to bargaining between public officials and private entrepreneurs. But Young provided the focused and aggressive leadership that had often been missing before. Soon he accumulated an impressive list of completed projects, particularly in the central business district, riverfront, and industrial sectors.

The Central Business District and Riverfront

Young's most visible efforts were on the riverfront and in the central business district. Like other messiah mayors, Young considered the waterfront a tempting canvas for city redevelopment. During the 1973 election, he anticipated this focus: "Revitalize the riverfront," he said, "and I guarantee you'll revitalize the whole city."[31]

One of the earliest downtown development projects was Joe Louis Arena. The city had already lost one of its four major sports teams, the Detroit Lions football club, when the Pistons basketball team and Red Wings hockey team also threatened to leave. Young resolved to build a new arena for them. Finding no buyers for municipal bonds, he convinced the Carter administration to lend the city $38 million. This was, up to that time, the largest loan of its kind and the only one given for a sports facility.[32] Most of the money for repaying the loan came from the city's parking revenues. Detroit pledged its future CDBG allocations as security for the loan, meaning that if the city failed to issue a successful bond sale five years later, it would use its CDBG monies to pay for the stadium. This borrowing provision later became formalized as Section 108 of CDBG legislation.

The city provided a $38 million building; in exchange, the hockey team owners received a yearly rent bill for $450,000, a ceiling on property taxes of $242,000 a year, and the right to earn revenues from arena events and concessions. Rent and property tax returns did not provide nearly enough to pay off the bonds, but the deal got the project built. Since Young arranged financing and started construction before the Red Wings agreed to be tenants, he risked his political career in the process. A municipal bond expert stated: "The guy broke everybody's arm to get it through. It is . . . an incredible show of power. And there aren't too many people who could do that."[33]

Another demonstration of Young's style came with riverfront apartments. Developer Max Fisher wanted to build an apartment complex that would become, for the western end of the central riverfront area, what Henry Ford's Renaissance Center had become for the eastern end. As one observer commented, "Riverfront and RenCen were to be Max and Henry's bookends. It went all the way back to the riots and their vision of a new Detroit. You could look at Detroit from [Canada] and see Henry's RenCen and Coleman's Joe Louis Arena and Max and Al's [Taubman] two apartment towers and understand Detroit pretty much at a glance."[34]

Again Young used his considerable influence to get the project financed. The head of HUD's Detroit office recommended rejecting a proposed federally insured mortgage. This man lost his job when Young complained to Carter's HUD secretary, Patricia Harris, who transferred him to another city. Young and Detroit legislators then pushed the bill through the state legislature which enabled a 12-year property tax abatement for the project.

In case after case, Young and his administration found a project, coordinated private and public funds, worked with prominent developers and corporate leaders, and pushed through opposition to get the project built. Once it became clear that Young excelled in this process, the tendency was to repeat the formula. The result was a string of projects along the riverfront and within the central business district.

By 1990, a scan of Detroit's east riverfront revealed the results. Within the "bookends"—Riverfront Apartments to the west and RenCen to the east—sat a series of new buildings and public places. The Riverfront Apartments themselves contained two 29-story towers and a 77-boat marina; next came the Joe Louis Arena; Cobo Hall, expanded in 1988 to more than 700,000 square feet at a cost of $180 million; Hart Plaza, a series of improvements to the Civic Center completed in 1978; and RenCen.

Development had extended beyond the "bookends" as well. West of the Joe Louis Arena, the city helped the *Detroit Free Press* build a riverfront plant, completed in 1979 and expanded in 1985. To the east of RenCen lay three linked riverfront parks: St. Aubin Park and Marina, Chene Park, and the site of the planned Mt. Elliot Park. In 1985 Stroh Brewery Company's Peter Stroh opened River Place,

Fig. 7.3. Chene Park, a beautifully landscaped complex, lies to the east of the central business district and helps fulfil part of the city's east riverfront plan. Pictured here is a pavilion which serves as a popular amphitheater for musical entertainment during the summer months. J. Thomas, photographer.

which contained an office-retail center, apartment complex, hotel, and a prestigious restaurant. Harbortown, completed in 1987, included townhouse condominiums, an apartment tower, and 88,000 square feet of shops. Farther to the east lay Grayhaven Estates, a residential/marina complex.[35]

Across the street from the RenCen stood the Millender Center, completed in 1985 as a mixed-use project with a hotel, retail shops and restaurants, a parking garage, and 32-story apartment tower. Other downtown buildings included Trappers Alley, a festival marketplace mall in Greektown; Trolley Plaza, an apartment building; and a new district court building. The Detroit People Mover, a light rail system, pulled together many of these downtown buildings.[36] The Civic Center—modest central business district strategy

Fig. 7.4. Trolley Plaza, white building to the right of center, is a successful although somewhat isolated downtown apartment building. It overlooks streetscape changes made to Washington Boulevard, the same street shown in figure 3.8. J. Thomas, photographer.

of the 1950s—had become the centerpiece of a string of riverfront and downtown projects, and downtown showed signs of new construction.

The bright new shiny buildings failed to hide persistent problems and aborted initiatives. The city had trouble marketing parcels west of the *Detroit Free Press* building. On the east riverfront, a huge Uniroyal plant was abandoned and then demolished, leaving an unsightly, contaminated vacant lot bordering the bridge entrance to Detroit's Belle Isle Park. Several anticipated projects, such as the reconstruction of the landmark Book Cadillac Hotel, never came to fruition. Plans to rehabilitate the massive Hudson's Department Store, closed in 1983, did not materialize. Owners of the River Place and other showcase projects sustained financial losses for years.[37]

The downtown Detroit People Mover symbolized successes and

missed opportunities. This elevated monorail was meant to termi-
nate an extensive light rail network that extended to the suburbs.
But debilitating technical and financial difficulties slowed down
construction. Young took over responsibility from the regional transit authority and completed the project, but only after costs had
swollen to $202 million. This sum bought an impressive system,
with commissioned art gracing each station, that transported
people along a 2.9 mile circular route *within* the central business
district, but linked with no rail service bringing them *to* the district.
The people mover therefore became an expensive, glorified downtown trolley.[38]

Young had accomplished stunning successes in the central business district, but problems lingered. It was much the same story for
industrial redevelopment.

Industrial Redevelopment

Young laid the foundation for industrial redevelopment in the 1975
"Moving Detroit Forward" document. Throughout the 1970s the
city remained ready to start a major project but was unable to do
so.[39] Then in 1979 a crisis loomed: Chrysler teetered on the brink of
failure.

Chrysler was the city's second largest employer with 28,185 workers, and it supported another 51,000 workers in supplier firms. The
city's second largest taxpayer, with $135 million in assessed prop-
erty value, Chrysler owned 15 facilities in Detroit, out of 21 in the
metropolitan area. Nationwide, one-third of its blue collar workers
and one-tenth of its white collar workers were Black; half of these
lived and worked in the Detroit area.[40]

And yet the entire U.S. domestic automobile industry, saddled
with big cars in an era of fuel shortage, suffered from the growing competition from successful Japanese firms. By the end of the
1970s, it was clear that the U.S. industry could no longer assume
they would have market dominance and that marginal firms could
fail. It appeared that Chrysler could be one of those firms.

Corporate and political leaders convinced the U.S. Congress to
grant unprecedented loan guarantees to keep Chrysler afloat. Even
so, the company closed several plants, shutting down the old Dodge
Main in January 1980.[41] At its peak in the 1950s, Dodge Main employed 35,000 workers in 4.1 million square feet of floor space.[42] By
1979, fewer than 5,000 workers remained.[43] Within a span of two
years, 1978 to 1980, metropolitan area Chrysler jobs fell by 42 percent, from 81,700 to 47,200.[44]

The city was ripe for a deal with an automobile manufacturer. Negotiations began with General Motors because of an incident during
a meeting; Young challenged GM Chairman Thomas A. Murphy
while the executive was issuing yet another perfunctory offer for
the city to provide a plant site. Startled into a response by Young's
strong reaction, Murphy promised that the company would soon

Fig. 7.5. Aerial photograph of the Dodge Main assembly plant, 1954; its multistoried construction and outdated facilities made it a liability by 1980, when Chrysler shut it down. Burton Historical Collection, Detroit Public Library.

give Detroit a real chance to compete for a plant. In June 1980, GM and the city announced a joint venture to build a new assembly plant. After a selection process, they chose a project area—just northeast of the old Milwaukee Junction industrial redevelopment site—that included the grounds of the former Dodge Main plant.[45] Central Industrial Park and its Detroit-Hamtramck Assembly Center—the project popularly known as Poletown—is one of the most closely scrutinized redevelopment efforts in modern American cities. At the time, it was the largest urban land assemblage and clearance project in American history, 465 acres. In all 1,176 buildings were cleared for the project and 3,438 residents relocated.[46] It required a new state law that speeded up property acquisition under eminent domain and set a precedent for public clearance of land identified as intended for one corporation's private use.[47] Poletown also provoked a strong opposition movement, an ultimately unsuccessful neighborhood-based campaign that gained national headlines with photos of police dragging elderly Polish women out of a church slated for demolition.[48]

This project offers many important lessons about industrial redevelopment in the nation as well as in Detroit. Three issues seem most important to review here. The first is the role of Young and his bureaucracy in carrying out the project. The second is the relationship of Poletown to racial politics in Detroit. The third is Poletown's success, or lack of it, in revitalizing the city's economy.

Concerning the role of Young and his bureaucracy: We have already described how effectively the mayor put together redevelopment "deals" for the downtown and riverfront. Young used much the same approach with Poletown, an incredibly complex project which depended absolutely upon the unusual talents of the mayor and his redevelopment staff.

This was no ordinary site. People, houses, businesses, churches, manufacturing firms, and a hospital occupied much of it. The city and state had to acquire properties, demolish buildings, reroute roads, work around rail lines, install utilities, create unprecedented financing, and fight off court challenges. All took place within a tightly constrained time frame: GM refused to relax its requirement that the city complete all phases of site preparation within two years, by June 1, 1982, and so the leisurely pace of urban renewal would not do. The city could afford no missteps, lest the company withdraw, and it had to proceed quickly in spite of citizen opposition and the city's lack of experience in large-scale industrial redevelopment.

According to Jones and Bachelor, Poletown offers a stunning case study of the true nature of the "urban regime." They suggest that the performance of Young and his staff forces a reconsideration of traditional concepts about how the urban regime functions. Some theoretical models may have overemphasized the role of the economic elite in determining the course of redevelopment action by politicians. One would think that GM's most rational step would have been to build elsewhere. Market forces seemed to dictate that the company build elsewhere, since it could easily move its Detroit assembly operations to other places, following modern industrial trends of decentralizing operations.

That Young and his talented staff, particularly CEDD Director Emmett Moten, were able to carry out this project without missing a step is testimony to both technical and political skills. Detroit received important technical assistance from State of Michigan personnel, particularly from the commerce and transportation departments. But leadership for the work effort came largely from Moten and his staff. These city workers mastered the details of the process so well that ordinary judges and lawyers working with a lawsuit against the project could barely follow their testimony. Similarly, the city council in large part deferred to the city's economic development "experts," expressing reservations only about some aspects of the financing and about citizen opposition.[49]

Coleman Young's political skills were essential to the success of the project in several ways. His popularity, as measured by an overall approval rating of 72 percent (1980)—which included 93 percent of the city's Black citizens and 47 percent of White—allowed him to act as strong spokesman for the project and effectively silence opponents.[50] His extensive connections with the national and state capitals helped, and his support in the unions and the Black community gave him an effective base of legitimacy.

Fig. 7.6. Photograph of a small church and a commercial building in the Poletown neighborhood, before demolition made way for General Motors' Poletown plant. The plant's huge parking lot supplanted most of the neighborhood's demolished buildings. Burton Historical Collection, Detroit Public Library.

This leads to a second issue: Racial factors played an important role in Young's ability to proceed. The project in no way jeopardized the support of Young's loyal constituency. Many African Americans stayed on his side because auto industry decline had been particularly devastating for Black workers. Horace L. Sheffield, president of the Detroit Coalition of Black Trade Unionists (CBTU), wrote consumer crusader Ralph Nader and asked him to stop supporting the opposition movement. Sheffield explained that the closing of Chrysler Dodge Main plant caused major despair among automobile workers. "In CBTU's view, the new facility is a giant step forward . . . we will not see it hobbled by an emotional dispute that threatens to hide the critical need for more industrial jobs."[51]

Significantly, most Poletown Blacks supported Young instead of the major opposition group, the Poletown Neighborhood Council (PNC). In spite of its nickname, the Poletown plant did not displace mostly Polish residents. In fact, about half of the project area residents were African American. The other half included largely Polish Whites, but also Albanians, Arabs, and others. A large proportion of the Black residents were young and middle-aged families, many of them fairly recent residents. The Polish residents, in contrast, were older; their children had grown and moved away, but their connections to the neighborhood were lifelong.

Because of the differences among the population, PNC never built a broad-based, multiracial opposition movement. Its members were largely long-term Polish homeowners. Blacks in the Poletown area tended either to support the city's official citizens' district council or to be apathetic. The city's generous relocation offers also undercut opposition, as many Blacks had moved from other urban renewal project areas and realized the relocation benefits this time around were generous. It is even possible that Young could not have acceded to PNC demands without alienating his political base, who could have asked why this neighborhood was more precious than their all-Black neighborhoods had been.[52]

PNC was never able to stop or alter the project. Although it attracted favorable media attention and enlisted Nader's able assistance, and although it argued a compelling case before the state supreme court, the project's combined support, from the federal government, state, city, and citizenry, was too much to overcome.

A third important point: Poletown illustrated the relative helplessness of Detroit in the face of industrial decline. The city tried to buy its way out of economic decline, but its concessions cost it dearly. Poletown required over $200 million in government funds for land clearance and relocation alone, plus $60 million for a twelve-year tax abatement to match the company's $600 million investment. Of the government funds, $100 million was a loan against future CDBG funds (Section 108), $30 million came from UDAG, and at least $18 million came from current CDBG allocations.[53] The city gave so many concessions to GM, particularly abatements and tax increment financing, that even after abatements end in 1997, the city and other taxing jurisdictions will receive virtually no revenues from the project.[54]

At enormous cost, Coleman Young helped build a plant that promised to provide over 6,000 direct jobs and generate other spin-off developments. The job estimate, however, was based upon two shifts of workers at the assembly plant. Once built, the plant almost always used only one shift, at 3400 workers. Even with the full two shifts, the city could not have recouped the money it invested into the deal. The city had anticipated that the project would produce many spin-off supplier plants, but these did not appear.[55]

Nevertheless, Detroit repeated the Poletown strategy. By 1985 Chrysler was considering closing its landmark Jefferson Avenue plant, but the city and the company agreed to seek federal funds for replacing it. Unlike Poletown, the neighborhood did not protest; abandonment had already cleared much of the property. But Detroit again paid a small fortune to retain dwindling numbers of jobs. The city had granted Chrysler six tax abatements between 1974 and 1988 for various construction and rehabilitation projects. In return, the company promised to retain 15,000 jobs but fell far short of its promises. When it opened in 1992, the new plant's employee count was 2,500.[56]

Furthermore, the Poletown strategy did not repeat well. The Poletown project was a tour de force, an illustration of the power of an innovative leader and his staff to break the mold of traditional regime processes. But the Chrysler project was plagued with costly mistakes, including the purchase of expensive industrial properties later determined to be unnecessary. Unscrupulous business owners inflated the value of their properties and took advantage of the city. The Young administration lost its reputation as efficient, and Young lost the services of industrial redevelopment wizard Moten, who resigned under pressure because of the financial losses.

Jones and Bachelor suggest that this situation also offers important lessons concerning the urban regime. Detroit tried to apply the Poletown model, but the growing familiarity with the process held unforeseen dangers. Young had developed a spectacular "solution-set" for his urban regime but tended to apply the same formula to almost all situations. The solution for Young was to push through the mega-project, whether for commercial or industrial development. This solution, at first creative and responsive to the real environment, eventually calcified into ineffectiveness.[57]

Poletown and Jefferson Avenue were bold but futile efforts to fight the tide of waning industrial jobs. In late 1987 GM closed its two sister Cadillac Fleetwood plants, devastating their west side neighborhoods and throwing 3,250 workers on the streets. One year before, the assembly operation had housed more than 6,500 hourly and salaried employees.[58]

In 1979 Chrysler was the city's largest employer, with over 28,000 workers.[59] By 1990, its workers in the city totaled 8,636. As table 7.1 shows, this number climbed to 15,000 for the three cities of Detroit, Hamtramck, and Highland Park by January 1993. During that period, the number of Detroit Medical Center employees had remained close to 12,000. By 1990, only four of Detroit's thirteen largest employers were for-profit operations; the rest were government units or nonprofit corporations.[60]

Neighborhood Redevelopment

Year after year, the city council fought with Mayor Young about whether the city should spend its resources on big ticket items in the central business district, riverfront, or industrial sector, or spread funding around to benefit smaller neighborhood projects. The tradeoff was real, because Young frequently used funds designated for neighborhoods to pay for projects such as the Detroit People Mover and Poletown. Mel Ravitz was one of the city council opponents of such policies.[61] In many years, funding for neighborhood organizations survived only because of protracted battles between the mayor and the council.

TABLE 7.1   DETROIT'S TEN LARGEST PRIVATE
EMPLOYERS, 1993

Employer	Number of Employees
1. Chrysler	15,000
2. General Motors Corporation	14,427
3. Detroit Medical Center	11,952
4. Henry Ford Health System	7,218
5. Wayne State University	4,326
6. Blue Cross–Blue Shield of Michigan	3,537
7. Detroit Edison	3,388
8. St. John Health Corporation	3,120
9. Ameritech	3,014
10. Comerica	2,974

Source: Crain's Detroit Business, December 27, 1993, p. 73. Based on data as of January 1993,
and includes Hamtramck and Highland Park. Data for General Motors is from 1992.

Detroit did support neighborhood redevelopment under CDBG. Its citizens' district councils received at least $100,000 a year each in CDBG funds. Among the nineteen councils that existed in the mid-1980s were Elmwood Park, Medical Center, and Woodbridge, all located in or near old urban renewal projects.[62] Working in part through such groups, Detroit helped rehabilitate over 6,000 housing units between 1982 and 1991.[63] By the late 1980s several former urban renewal sites, supported by CDBG, had begun to show the positive effects of years of planning efforts.

Jefferson-Chalmers, located on the far east side, was one such area. By the early 1990s, it gained multifamily housing developments, a vocational education facility, and a single-family housing development, Victoria Park. The city's first new subdivision in thirty years, Victoria Park amazed city detractors when its developers easily sold more than 150 units, priced at over $100,000, in two years. Another revived area was Virginia Park, the epicenter of the fires of 1967. By the 1990s, community organizers and the city had generated new multifamily housing, a new shopping center, and a community recreation center. Eighteen months after Young left office yet another single-family subdivision, which immediately experienced brisk sales, opened with much publicity (see fig. 7.7).[64]

The New Center redevelopment project is also notable. In 1978, GM launched a project aimed at improving a six-block area north of its headquarters. The project included a new commercial center, a refurbished hotel, and new multifamily residential units. The company and the city built new entry gates, pedestrian walkways, courtyards and garages, and rehabilitated just over 100 historic homes and townhouses for sale on the private market. Professionals working at GM and the nearby university and hospital eagerly purchased the large and imposing houses.[65]

Fig. 7.7. Potential buyers lined up to inspect new model houses at Virginia Park Estates, July 23, 1995; the subdivision borders 12th Street, epicenter of the 1967 civil disturbances. The surprisingly strong market for this 45-lot subdivision and for another, Victoria Park, proved that the private market for new single-family houses in Detroit is not dead. J. Thomas, photographer.

Although these projects were impressive, the administration almost ignored distressed and borderline neighborhoods sprinkled throughout the city. Even some citizen district council areas could not conquer abandonment and decay. Resentment over the apparent tradeoff between downtown and the neighborhoods was palpable. As the leader of one neighborhood coalition commented: "While we have been trying to attract upper-income people to the riverfront, mostly white folks, the quality of life for neighborhood residents has been ignored. If you continue to ignore those issues, then riverfront residents will tire of their property tax bills going up, and of the feeling of insecurity they have if they go outside the gates of their property, and will leave." [66]

Several reasons could explain the city's lack of enthusiasm beyond a few showcase projects for neighborhood redevelopment. Neighborhood redevelopment projects seldom included a major private sponsor, except for stellar cases such as GM's New Center, and so no one matched government funds with extensive private financing. Federal policy made it easy to ignore neighborhood concerns, because CDBG usually required only weak citizen input. Neighborhood redevelopment meant extensive consultation with community leaders, or at least with residents, and in some sense sharing power. Detroit's political structure, with its strong mayor and at-large council members, was not designed to encourage such sharing.

TABLE 7.2   VOTER SURVEY ON YOUNG AS MAYOR

Accomplishments	
Developed downtown Detroit	20%
Integrated the Detroit police force	19
Managed the City through tough times	16
Stood up for Detroit with the suburbs	12
Revitalized the auto industry with two new plants in the city	8
Brought African Americans into control of city government	7
All of them	7
None of the above	5
Other	1

Failures	
Ignoring city neighborhoods	41%
Not working hard enough to create jobs and development	13
Not fighting hard enough against corruption in city government	11
Cutting city services too much	11
Alienating suburban and state governments	8
Not doing enough to stop white flight	2
All of the above	5
None of the above	4
Other/don't know/refused	5

Source: Market Strategies, Inc., as commissioned by Detroit Free Press/WXYZ, *Detroit Free Press,* June 24, 1993, p. 8A.

On the summer day in 1993 that Coleman Young announced he would not run for a sixth term, a telephone survey asked a random sample of registered city voters to list Young's biggest accomplishment and his biggest failure as mayor. Seventy-seven percent of the respondents were African American, a reasonably accurate reflection of city population. Respondents listed Young's major accomplishment as developing downtown Detroit, although integrating the police force was a close second. The mayor's biggest failure, by a wide margin, was "ignoring city neighborhoods" (see table 7.2).

Redevelopment and the State of the City

As we have seen, the results of Young's strong efforts to promote modern redevelopment were limited. By the 1990s, the city had made a visible difference in several major redevelopment areas. Nevertheless, systemic difficulties persisted. Although we have already pointed out some of these difficulties, this section will expand upon the overall economic and social challenges facing Detroit.

With its downtown and riverfront, Detroit experienced major development successes. Construction of Joe Louis Arena was an im-

Fig. 7.8. Millender Center: the lower horizontal tube is a pedestrian walkway connecting Millender with the City-County Building. The top rail is part of the People Mover system, which passes through the building; a train is here entering the Millender Center station. The complex includes retail shops, a hotel, a parking ramp (lower left hand corner), and apartments (towers in upper left). J. Thomas, photographer.

pressive feat. Also prominent were the pivotal Millender Center, which linked with the RenCen and other downtown buildings using futuristic skyways and light rail. The River Place, Harbortown, and Riverfront developments offered signs of renewal, as did the newly expanded Cobo Hall. All were good accomplishments given the odds against development in Detroit. But these projects hid major problems of decline.

Tourism offers an example. By 1990, the number of conventions booked for the central business district was up from previous years. Additions to Cobo Hall had expanded its exhibition space from 400,000 to 700,000 square feet, making it the nation's seventh-largest exhibit hall. But downtown hotels offered only 2,575 rooms, a fraction of Chicago's 25,000 and Manhattan's 100,000. The city solicited new hotel developers, but a soft market made investors wary. Metropolitan Detroit ranked last among the nation's 25 largest metropolitan areas in its ability to fill hotel rooms. The area's occupancy rate was 54.8 percent, compared with 70.9 percent for the New York area and 63.4 percent for the Chicago area.[67]

Those tourists that did come to the Motor City were often surprised to find Detroit more pleasant than its media image suggested. But they also found limited opportunities for shopping and other diversions. Away from the immediate riverfront and oases of downtown development in the RenCen, Millender Center, and Greektown, the ordinary retail district was weak. The city's festival mall,

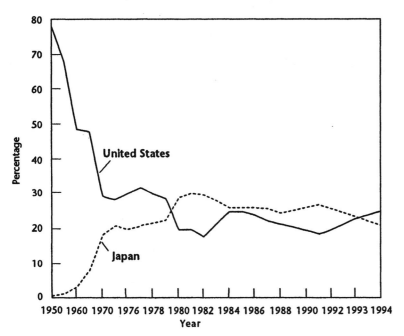

Fig. 7.9. *World production of motor vehicles (cars only) shows the clear dominance experienced by U.S. manufacturers as recently as the 1950s. Japanese production rose sharply, however, particularly after the early 1970s. Data from Motor Vehicle Manufacturing Association.*

Trapper's Alley in Greektown, could not keep tenants, and much of its retail space lay empty. A survey of attendees at one convention found that 78 percent would not return to Detroit for a personal vacation. Most respondents rated the city's hospitality, hotels, transportation, and restaurants at 7 or above on a 10-point scale but gave downtown shopping only a 4.13. Among 20 large U.S. cities, Detroit ranked dead last in 1989 in retail sales per capita; its sales were less than half of the median amount spent per citizen in each of the major cities.[68]

The industrial sector also faced difficulties. The permanent dark cloud hanging over industrial redevelopment was the massive change in the automobile industry, which affected the Detroit metropolitan area especially hard. Industrial changes, once cyclical, became permanent; never again would Detroit regain the dominance of automobile manufacturing it had experienced in the 1940s. The world automobile industry had changed too drastically.

The reasons for such changes are many. Detroit's competitors in Japan gradually gained important market share (see fig. 7.9). The Japanese excelled at producing reliable, durable, and affordable cars that were simultaneously fuel-efficient. Although for many years the United States produced most of the world's cars, this situation changed markedly in the early 1970s after the worldwide oil crisis, when Japanese firms became serious competitors for the world's car customers.

Some researchers have said that the most important reasons for this change were poor management and lack of technological innovation from the American automobile Big Three. David Halberstam, for example, tells a compelling saga of the tenacity and creativity displayed by Japanese automobile manufacturers in their relentless drive to enter the U.S. auto market. In contrast, for many years U.S. manufacturers did not invest sufficient funds in updating their operations and responding to the outside environment, preferring instead to create short-term profits. Firms such as Chrysler, GM, and Ford grew too big to respond to the need for innovation. Furthermore, quality control lagged and U.S. firms turned out inferior products riddled with defects.[69]

While Halberstam's account offers interesting insights into the personalities involved, many researchers have documented the problem in more systems-oriented ways that focused on economic systems rather than personalities. Richard C. Hill, for one, has written about some of the underlying causes for the continued dependency of Detroit's industrial sector upon the automobile industry. Hill has suggested that the global reorganization of that industry generated major changes in four areas: product design, concentration of capital in fewer firms, the labor process, and the international division of labor. Revisions in each of these spheres had major implications for automobile cities such as Detroit.[70]

As products changed, the familiar approach of using the same old manufacturing facilities to build superficially different car models could not continue. Product changes came too fast and were too driven by technology for that approach to survive. As technology reigned supreme, competition among the oligopoly's firms heightened, and weaker firms dropped out. The old pattern of interaction between large U.S. industries and large unions also died. Union membership declined as plants closed and capital moved into new regions able to offer cheaper wages and more labor flexibility. Those firms in former "Third World" countries had unique labor cost advantages over their "First World" counterparts; and so the global car arose, with components built in various sites around the globe. Domestic firms became international, and the true country of origin for any particular car became almost impossible to identify.

Even though they took major steps to adjust to this new environment, GM and Chrysler, the city's major industrial redevelopment partners, experienced continuing problems with productivity and plant efficiency throughout the 1980s and well into the 1990s. The domestic automobile industry became competitive again, because it managed to make important internal reforms, and because a weakened U.S. dollar made many Japanese cars too expensive. Part of the way U.S. auto makers became competitive, however, was to reduce employee counts drastically, to close older plants, and to become even more decentralized throughout the region, nation, and world.

During the same time, Japanese firms had begun to build automobile plants in the United States to reduce the costs of shipping cars and in anticipation of possible trade problems. But they seldom opened manufacturing plants in Michigan. One exception was Mazda's new assembly plant in Flat Rock, Michigan, a small suburb lo-

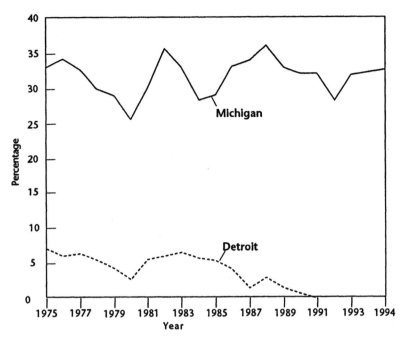

Fig. 7.10. This view of car assemblies in Michigan and Detroit shows that the State of Michigan has been able to retain its percentage of U.S. production. Assemblies in City of Detroit, however, has declined markedly. Data from Motor Vehicle Manufacturing Association.

cated in the southern section of Detroit's metropolitan area. To attract the plant, the state and Flat Rock offered broad incentives to Mazda. Like other Japanese firms, however, Mazda remained firmly tied to the corporate mandates of the mother firm in Japan.[71]

The attraction of staying in or moving to Michigan was weak for all firms, not just auto-related ones: Michigan's average industrial wage rate was the highest in the nation, and high-wage industries dominated the state. The mix of wage rates and industry type put the state at a competitive disadvantage. Little evidence suggested that Michigan's labor force was better educated and more highly skilled or more productive than workers in other areas, thus justifying higher wages. Anthony Downs called the Detroit area's wage structure "unrealistic in the world competitive market."[72]

For the city, the situation was even bleaker. As Hill indicated, Detroit's basic dilemma was that it was no longer able to compete in the world's market economy. Capital, he noted, was mobile, but Detroit was not. While the automobile industry could recover in part by decentralizing, modernizing, and seeking new markets, Detroit could not.

As figures 7.10 and 7.11 show, the entire state of Michigan was able to keep up a fairly steady, if fluctuating, proportion of U.S. motor vehicle assemblies of cars after 1975. However, Michigan's proportion of U.S. production of commercial vehicles plummeted. The City of Detroit's assemblies of both cars and commercial vehicles declined, even after construction of two new assembly plants (one of which, Poletown, was partially located in Hamtramck).

The relative position of the central city to its suburban neighbors

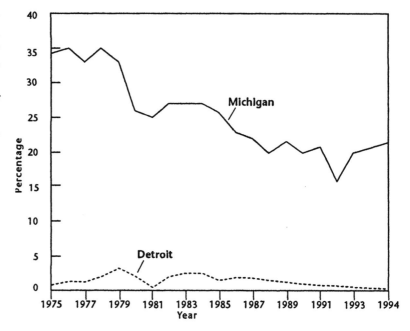

Fig. 7.11. Michigan has not fared as well in assembly of U.S. commercial vehicles as it has in car assemblies. Detroit has experienced minor dropoff in this area. Data from Motor Vehicle Manufacturing Association.

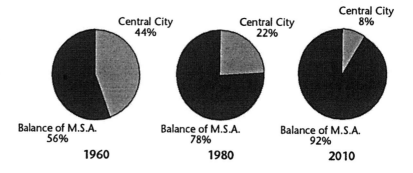

Fig. 7.12. This view of actual and projected job locations for the seven-county Detroit Metropolitan Statistical Area suggests that the City of Detroit will retain only a minor share by the year 2010. The Metropolitan Statistical Area (M.S.A.) expanded from three to seven counties during 1960–90. Courtesy Southeast Michigan Council of Governments.

remained poor, and worsened. The city held 44 percent of area jobs in 1960; this had dropped to 22 percent by 1980. The Southeast Michigan Council of Governments (SEMCOG) projected, based on 1989 data, that the central city would retain only 8 percent of regional jobs by 2010 (see fig. 7.12).

While the city's strongest efforts focused on the central business district, riverfront, and industrial redevelopment, neighborhoods experienced mixed success. Virginia Park, New Center, Riverplace, and Jefferson-Chalmers showed new life, and riverfront projects had no trouble attracting affluent young professionals.[73] Outside of targeted areas, however, residents felt the effects of decline. By 1990 only 1,027,000 people lived in the city, a loss of 800,000 people in 40 years. As Young noted, "If you keep the same city limits as we have, if half of the population is gone, then half of your buildings are going to be deserted."[74] Indeed they were. The city lost 143,172 housing units between 1960 and 1990. During the 1980s, housing demolition permits exceeded construction permits by 41,800.

Federal funds continued to drop. In 1980, federal funds of $392.9 million accounted for over 26 percent of the city's budget. During the 1980s, the federal government discontinued its general revenue sharing program and reduced funds for job training, CDBG, housing subsidies, mass transportation, health, and other areas. Detroit received $30.4 million a year from CDBG funds for 1974–77 and $60.7 million a year for the next four years. But appropriations levels dropped thereafter, falling to $40.1 million a year by 1990–91.[75] By 1990 federal revenues had fallen to 8 percent of the city's budget at $161 million. State funds had increased significantly during that decade, from $269 million to $444 million, but not enough to make up for the loss of federal funds.

In an attempt to maintain services, Detroit increased its tax rate. By 1990 the city's tax rate was 6.4 times the average paid by residents of other municipalities in the state. Because the number of tax returns fell so drastically during the 1980s, city revenue remained stagnant in constant dollars. High taxes drove more businesses and residents from the city. High per capita expenditures on city services did not guarantee good services, as city parks, streets, and library services continued to deteriorate.[76] The State of Michigan's 1993 action to replace most residential property taxes with a sales tax increase was an important corrective action, but the results would take years to appear.

Increasing poverty and unemployment wreaked a toll on the remaining population. In 1989 Detroit's unemployment rate of 15.7 percent was the highest of major American cities and more than double the median of those cities. Many people were no longer counted as part of the work force. The labor force participation rate, 49.6 percent, was the lowest of major U.S. cities. The city's median household income, $19,394, was the lowest of major U.S. cities.[77]

The social fabric of the city began to come apart. Faced with seeming hopelessness, many city youth turned to drugs as a quick way to get money. After crack—a cheap, viciously addictive drug—became popular, neighborhoods lost more houses to the drug culture. Dealers rented or appropriated vacant houses as places of business. These houses almost invariably deteriorated, as their addicted residents used them almost like disposable shelters. The result was lethal for stable residential areas. A new, violent subculture arose, much more extensive and damaging than the "skid rows" characteristic of previous decades. Guns and shootings proliferated, and the high murder rate for children and youth became a national scandal.[78]

With the drug culture came drug addicts, gangs, police, gun warfare. African-American males seemed particularly vulnerable to this drug culture, because for many the historic options for blue collar employment were gone and the only sure route to prosperity appeared to be drugs. High school graduation guaranteed little, and school dropout rates soared. Declining male employment is strongly associated with other social problems, particularly out-ofwedlock births among young women. Thus unemployment helped lead to the spiraling welfare dependency devastating many inner city neighborhoods.[79] By the 1990 census Detroit's most predominate family type was a female-headed household with children, 22 percent of city households. Of all Black families with children in the city, 61.5 percent were headed by single women. To some extent these figures reflected simple lifestyle changes, but some observers drew a clear connection between the falling marriage rate and the declining economic status of Black males ravaged by unemployment.[80]

An Uneven Match

Coleman Young's election was symbolic of the triumph of Black politics over racial oppression. Young's persona and operating style soon dominated Detroit. Like the other messiah mayors, he knew how to overcome short-term fiscal crises. A skilled politician, he devised ways to consolidate his political base, which rested upon city staff and African-American institutions. Young understood the symbolic importance of construction projects, and he seized upon redevelopment as the route to city salvation. A capable and focused captain of the urban regime, he created new solutions to old problems of economic decline and industrial redevelopment.

Yet no one mayor could change the national context, which was one of continued support for suburban growth and industrial mobility and vacillating assistance for central cities. The federal government retreated from high-profile attempts to remedy the problems of older, distressed central cities. CDBG dispersed "urban" monies far beyond older central cities, funding housing and development efforts in suburbs as well as cities. The United States accepted the supposed inevitability of the decentralized settlement patterns that government policies helped establish in the first place. Detroit turned to development projects using public-private partnerships, courting the private corporate sector for money with which to match limited federal funds.

This strategy did not solve the city's problems. Even with shining new downtown and riverfront buildings, Detroit's retail and service sectors suffered. Industrial projects yielded impressive new plants and valuable jobs but did not stop industrial decline. With limited resources and myriad problems, with little chance of competing with the riverfront strategy for investment support, and without Young's strong support, neighborhood redevelopment suffered. The city sponsored several successful projects, but many nontargeted neighborhoods declined even as new multifamily housing arose elsewhere. Continued social problems, such as drugs, crime, and unemployment, signaled that something was drastically wrong.

In Detroit and other cities, new mayors gained office when the historically mighty central cities were only shadows of their former selves, beset by the problems of old age and infirmity. The only mayors of whatever race who could survive this era were the ones who could make symbol stand for substance. The Young administration was very good at symbol. Much more difficult was the task of bringing about the substance of social and economic development.

Planning a
Better City   8

The last chapter hardly mentioned urban planning at all, and for good reason. The city had turned away from long-range public planning. Changes in federal financing made redevelopment an entrepreneurial game, based almost completely upon putting together "deals," or development partnerships, between private developers and local government. In that context, localities offered grants, loans, and tax incentives like so many bargaining chips. They made impromptu arrangements without the elaborate "workable programs," master plans, or similar tools of previous eras.

Local realities in Detroit also reduced planners' influence. Planners worked as staff for each redevelopment project, but their voices were strangely muted. Detroit City Council retained a small planning staff under the new charter, but both council and its planners had relatively little power compared with the mayor. Mayor Young's background and political style made him supportive of development but unfriendly to the concept of public planning. This reduced the city's ability to communicate its vision for improvement or to develop a cohesive initiative for Detroit's well-being.

And, thus, the pendulum swung back. As Detroit faced the major challenges of the 1990s and beyond, the concept of planning became important once again. Collections of people ranging from groups of corporate leaders to neighborhood organizations began to envision a better future, identify goals and objectives, and develop programs to meet those objectives. Events proved that if local government would not plan for a better future, then its citizens would.

Planning Modern Detroit

The 1970s and beyond were in stark contrast to the period just after World War II. During that earlier time, various housing acts, state enabling legislation, and the national planning literature all made central city planning important and necessary. Publicity given to planners such as Edmund Bacon in Philadelphia offered high visibility to planning initiatives and to the profession. The planning literature had an air of confidence, as it instructed students and professionals how to guide urban growth and carry out the great crusade against urban deterioration.

The 1960s caused a major crisis. Urban renewal programs alienated both scholars and inner city residents. Several important books critical of urban renewal and planning emerged, such as Jane Jacobs's *Death and Life of Great American Cities* and Herbert Gans's *The Urban Villagers*. These books rightly pointed out many injustices that had been done, and they tempered planners' tendency to ignore social context and to follow unjust policies blindly. Yet they often left the practicing planner with suggestions about what not to do rather than guidelines about what to do.[1]

Professional planning magazines and textbooks offered little practical help. Many planners worked for booming suburbs and small municipalities rather than faltering central cities. Others worked for regional planning agencies; these experienced their own ups and downs but nevertheless remained viable for tasks such as transportation and environmental planning. Planning for large central cities drifted in the backwater of professional attention. Some writings gave insights into issues of equity and distribution facing planners in central cities.[2] Others promoted special techniques such as linkage policies, which required downtown developers to provide social services such as subsidized housing or child care, but these policies assumed a strong market with willing developers.

Only gradually did practical articles and books appear on how to survive in a political cauldron such as city hall or successfully promote economic growth in the midst of decline or carry out enlightened neighborhood planning and development. For the professionals working for a planning agency within a distressed central city, the drought was lengthy. It was particularly difficult to understand how to attack population loss and economic decline. One Detroit planner worked for the City of Detroit for close to 30 years, beginning in the late 1950s. His comments are instructive:

The tools of planning are based on an era and a viewpoint that all we have to do is control and direct population and employment. We'd already seen major reductions in both employment and population in [the 1960s]. But it hadn't really worked into our psyche that this was going to be a continuing trend. Planners were not prepared and did not have tools to deal with a shrinking population, an employment situation where businesses were leaving. There was no literature on it, still isn't, I'm willing to bet. The planning profession is only very recently, kicking and screaming, going into an era when we're thinking what do you do to promote change and to deal with the realities of shrinking economies.[3]

Lack of knowledge was not the only problem. The changing local policy environment made operation very difficult. In the 1950s, urban renewal was a clear policy activity with straightforward requirements for long-range planning. Local policy was centralized, particularly for technical decisions, a category which at that time included planning and urban renewal. But as time progressed, re-development became less clear. City problems became more complex and solutions fuzzier. In that environment, city planners could hardly offer direction to others when they had so little themselves.[4]

Changes in federal legislation made planning less imperative as well. CDBG allowed funding of local planning but neither required it nor emphasized it. CDBG required formal application and performance reports, but these stressed complying with federal regulations rather than creating broader goals and strategies for community benefit. UDAG brought back the old style of grant competition for federal approval of individual projects, making packages of incentives more important than long-range planning.

As the Detroit experience showed, central city planning operations were also vulnerable because of changing political mandates. In Detroit, a new charter, developed when urban planning was most vulnerable politically, institutionalized important changes in its bureaucratic position. Not only did the city's 1973 charter split planning into three offices (the planning commission attached to city council and the CEDD and planning departments, attached to the mayor's executive branch), it also set up a strong mayor system and removed department directors from civil service protection (see figs. 7.5, 7.6). All department heads became political appointees, serving at the pleasure of the mayor, who therefore did not have to hire professional planning directors.

Depending upon one's perspective, this new organizational system was either a good way to balance power or a good way to weaken the influence of urban planners. The charter revision commission gave the balance of power as its formal rationale. The mayor could appoint and therefore easily direct his executive branch planning director as well as his CEDD director.

When considered from the perspective of the city council, having its own planning commission staff was very useful. That staff not only advised the commission and the council about planning-related ordinances, development proposals, and budgetary items, it also helped the council articulate and promote its own planning and development concerns. Furthermore, under this system the council hired its own planning director and commission staff to balance (or counteract) the mayor's planning director and department staff.

The council found its planning director in the form of a person who had worked for the commission almost from its inception. When Marsha Bruhn joined the commission in 1974, she had already worked as a planning assistant in the City of Covina, California, and as president of the Staten Island Citizens Planning Committee in New York City. A recent recipient of a master's degree in planning, she followed in the footsteps of other planners in the profession who "came up through the ranks," becoming a senior planner in 1975, and a principal planner in 1978. She served under three planning commission directors who did not find favor with the council; none lasted more than two years. The council appointed Bruhn as its city planning commission director in 1983, and she kept the position well over a decade.

Bruhn speculates that she survived because she had worked in the office for eight years before becoming director, and because she understood better than previous directors "what it meant to work for a policy-making body." To do so required skills in fitting planning concepts into a political process. It meant attending council meetings regularly and becoming fully acquainted with the council's priorities. It meant understanding that, although staff planners served a citizen-based planning commission, their employer was in fact Detroit City Council.[5]

In Bruhn that council found a director with whom it could work on a long-term basis and who could help it promote its neighborhood agenda. In 1976, the council had set up the Neighborhood Opportunity Fund (NOF), a program that offered small, competitive CDBG grants to community-based organizations. Throughout the years the council used NOF to counter the administration's big-ticket redevelopment agenda. Because the council controlled the budget, it made sure that the program received increased funding even as overall CDBG funds dropped. Between 1976 and 1993, NOF awarded over 1800 grants, totaling $111.8 million, to community-based organizations.[6]

The council directed planning commission staff to review NOF applications and to insure proper monitoring and follow-up. The staff helped organizations apply for funds and offered workshops in community development and fundraising. In the late 1980s, commission planners helped the council design a Nuisance Abatement Program, which was implemented only after the council fought Mayor Young in court. The ordinance stated that if a resident could prove that a property was abandoned, he/she could apply directly to the council for permission to repair the property. If the property was improved within a three-year period, ownership switched to the petitioner.

Bruhn was instrumental in helping to set up and monitor the NOF and Nuisance Abatement Programs. These efforts put her and her staff constantly in touch with community residents. The council planners became ombudsmen, guides through the labyrinth of the city's planning and development bureaucracy. Bruhn began to hire staff based in large part upon their sensitivity to neighborhood planning.

The only problem with this setup was that the power still lay with the executive branch, under the direction of the mayor. The charter gave the mayor control over implementing city services, because he supervised the city's departments. Although the city council was free to create and fund programs, the mayor's staff implemented them. For example, Bruhn's staff monitored NOF and helped com-

munity groups apply for the funds, but the mayor's CEDD administered the program. This strongly affected the program because, on
the executive side, support for neighborhood redevelopment was
not as strong. Furthermore, the staffs of the two branches were
grossly unequal in size: Bruhn never had more than 14 staff; CEDD
alone ranged close to 300, with dozens more in the planning department.[7]

From the perspective of the executive branch, the influence of
planning was very small indeed. One planner speculated on the reason: the charter gave the mayor "too much control. It was a step
backward when we went into this strong mayor system, because he
appoints the number one and number two person of all the departments and he is able to show favoritism to the people who contrib-
ute. Planning concepts are put on the back burner and the political
concepts get put on the front burner."[8] Young chose to focus on
project development without the benefit of strong planning support, which was associated by some with the hazy future. He had
pledged during his 1973 election campaign to take action, and he
wanted to work with powerful actors. In Detroit, this meant Detroit
Renaissance, Inc., and its corporate leaders. It meant fighting piece
by piece for an arena, a hotel, an apartment building, an auto plant.
It meant making ad hoc deals for project development rather than
planning for overall context and strategy.

And so it is no surprise that Young adopted as his favored agency
CEDD, rather than the planning department. He could appoint the
director of both, but over CEDD Young placed strong personalities,
practical bureaucrats. His most effective CEDD director was Emmett
Moten, the aggressive African American who put together the Poletown deal and who knew how to work with the private sector. Those
planners based in CEDD focused on specific projects or supervised
city ordinances.

Over his planning department the mayor placed a series of planning directors who would not—or, because of personality or training, could not—challenge Moten or CEDD in strength and influence. Although few of these planning directors were prominent, at
least one was very visible to the public. Planning Director Corinne
Gilb had impressive academic credentials: Recipient of a doctorate
from Radcliffe-Harvard, Dr. Gilb taught at Wayne State University when Young hired her in 1979.[9] Gilb's academic areas were
American Studies and history, however, and she had neither formal
nor informal training in the field of urban planning.[10] Although
bright and dedicated to her job, she was not the kind of leader familiar with the nuts and bolts of her operation. As a White graduate
of an Ivy League school, she could provide little political rapport
with Young's constituency. In contrast to Bruhn—well trained and
experienced in the field—Gilb came into the planning profession at
the top, as Young's planning director.

Of the six or seven planning directors that served under Young, only one came from professional planning roots. This caused morale to plummet among professional staff. A Black city planner exclaimed: "Imagine that! Imagine putting a non-lawyer over a law department! A non-engineer over engineering! This is part of what makes planning in Detroit so frustrating."[11]

In the days before charter revision, the mayor's planning director had impeccable planning credentials but had sometimes promoted controversial ideas. People linked the visionary Blessing with the "grandiose" planning popular in a bygone era. City planning meant successful projects such as Lafayette Park and Elmwood Park, but also less successful projects such as the Cultural Center plan, based on sketches of huge reflecting pools and sculpture gardens replacing Black historic sites. City planning meant Blessing's proposals for the physical redesign of the inner city, complete with parks and plazas, promoted at a time when people were fighting for jobs and their homes. It meant design-based opposition to revision of the Civic Center and construction of the Renaissance Center. It meant the destruction of inner city Black neighborhoods.

The old style of planning had generated a lot of racial mistrust, which existed independent of perceived professional competence. History came back to haunt the profession, as a representative of the victim class gained power and authority within city hall. The Black political constituency did not support planning, and their mayor distrusted it as well. The planners "were people who cleared areas where Black folks lived," according to one Black planner.[12] Another Black planner, a well-respected former planning commissioner, complained that it was difficult to remain credible with "a predominantly Black electorate which harbors some justifiable negative attitudes toward planners based on past indiscretions."[13]

One former planner called the mayor "contemptuous of the whole [planning] process. He thinks that the things that need to be done in the city are wheeling and dealing: Let's see what we can wrangle for our city."[14] A prominent regional planner commented: "Under the present mayor, planning is zero, and this is a very difficult thing. The mayor wants to carry the plan too much in his head; he doesn't want anybody out there getting in his way."[15] A Black planning professional bluntly bemoaned the results: "We are affected by the . . . doctrine that there can only be one 'planner' whose plan(s) we must all accept and defend."[16]

In spurning the planning process, however, Young also spurned whatever new ideas competent planners could have brought to the city. Planners in other cities—such as Robert Mier in Harold Washington's Chicago administration, and Norman Krumholz in Cleveland—had developed ways of increasing meaningful public participation and equitably distributing city resources. Like Young, Harold Washington was a Black mayor who came to power backed by the African-American community, in a city experiencing economic problems. But Washington actively forged a coalition with neighborhood groups and developed an inclusionary way of making development decisions. This yielded creative solutions to Chicago's economic problems even as it let the city pursue social equity goals.[17] In Cleveland, a series of mayors let Krumholz and his staff planners improve the central business district, transportation system, and other municipal services, and simultaneously promote social justice. Few such innovations were possible in a city where most decisions emanated from one person.

During her six-year tenure, Gilb helped the city create an overdue master plan. The 1974 charter required the mayor's planning department to write such a plan and present it to the city council by 1975. The last complete document was the 1951 master plan; after that, revisions were made piece by piece. Periodically, the planners put all the revisions into a policy document, which they did in 1973. But the city possessed no coherent statement of what its goals were, what kind of development it wanted to take place, or what strategies it would use.

A master plan is not absolutely necessary, and other large cities have worked without one. As with Detroit's 1951 master plan, global assumptions within master plans can sometimes prove wrong, and it is often difficult to identify the tools necessary to carry out the visions projected. Such plans are especially limited when a city is fully developed and has little vacant land left. As cities such as Detroit changed, however, designating future land use began to make sense. Abandonment and demolition left much land vacant, and city government owned some of it. By 1987 Detroit owned 40 percent of the properties in an area north of the downtown and flanking Woodward Avenue, 25 percent of the properties north of old Tiger Stadium, and 25 percent of the land surrounding the small city airport. Other vacant sites included old urban renewal and central business district parcels. These were potential sites for a new stadium, an expanded airport, or private development.[18] It became possible to envision changes which a master plan could guide.

Just as crucial was the need to build a democratic process for determining the city's future. While developing a master plan, a city government usually receives feedback from neighborhood residents and other concerned citizens about what the future of the municipality should be. Frank So, deputy director of the American Planning Association (an association that resulted from the merger of the American Society of Planning Officials and the American Institute of Planners), has noted: "If you don't know where you're going, it doesn't matter what road you take. At least this way there is a public process to talk about the future of the city."[19]

Developers also favor such plans. As one Chicago developer commented, "It is good for a city to express a new set of goals, putting their house in order. It also shows that the political and private powers in the town have been able to compromise on a definite direction for their community." "A master plan says where a city is going,

Fig. 8.1. Brush Park, an area north of the central business district, west of the Brewster-Douglass public housing project, and east of Woodward Avenue. For many years the city owned much of the land here and has tried to implement an approved city redevelopment plan. J. Thomas, photographer.

tells investors they are welcome, sets rules for them and is a thermometer of civic health. Developers and investors like this. To them it means stability."[20]

The lack of a plan hurt Detroit's central business district. By the 1980s, developers had built several buildings which would have fit together better if an overall plan had been in place. In the early 1970s Detroit Edison built more than 3 million square feet of office space in the northwest area of the central business district. Ford's Renaissance Center, built on the district's southeastern edge, put anticipated expansion of Detroit Edison Plaza on hold and assured its isolation. The Riverfront Apartments sat next to the Joe Louis Arena but appeared cut off from the rest of the downtown by major thoroughfares and poor pedestrian access.

Scattered throughout the district were a new campus for Wayne County Community College, Trolley Plaza Apartments, the Renaissance Center, and several new office buildings. The number of successful projects was impressive, but they were so disconnected they appeared to have little impact. In contrast, the east riverfront, benefiting from a land use plan developed by the city's parks and recreation department and a private firm, displayed at least the promise of cohesion among Harbortown, River Place, the Renaissance Center, and three linked parks.[21] Furthermore, Elmwood III, the last phase of the Lafayette Park/Elmwood Park urban renewal complex, continued to evolve and grow; private developers built a variety of

EDISON PLAZA

Fig. 8.2. Detroit Edison's tower, one of the major buildings in this utility company's complex, is isolated from the rest of the central business district by parking ramps, lots, and distance. New developers tended to gravitate toward the riverfront rather than to this area. J. Thomas, photographer.

projects upon successively developed parcels, all within the context of an attractive overall project plan.

Delay after delay prevented completion of a new master plan for the city. In 1982 Councilman Ravitz complained about the "millions" spent on the master plan since 1974, only to yield "nothing on paper to show what direction we should go."[22] One councilwoman protested that without a master plan, the council could not judge development proposals. "The council is trapped. . . . Some [project] is brought before us, and usually they say it means jobs, but we don't have the whole picture. Then we are told it's an emergency and we have to approve it or lose it, but we don't get the chance to see how it fits."[23]

Young did not mince words about his disdain for the complaints: "I have some plans, but a plan ain't worth a damn unless you have someone to carry it out."[24] "I feel that to be too concrete in a plan is to build up hopes, to promote a cynical attitude and a lack of belief in government and in the city." It was also Young's position that a published plan encouraged land speculation and reduced the city's flexibility. What the mayor truly believed in was soliciting individual projects. "Projects! That's when a plan . . . takes on reality. I don't publish paper. We have gone out aggressively and seized (developers) by the hair."[25]

Young's planning director, Gilb, continued to press for a master plan, but her staff lost interest because of the lengthy delays and the

Fig. 8.3. Detroit People Mover, rounding the last turn to the Grand Circus Park station. Abandoned stores and movie theater are located just below tracks, but to the far left is the construction site of a new home for a local opera company. J. Thomas, photographer.

mayor's obvious lack of support. Before she left office in 1985, Gilb supervised completion of twenty background studies and a draft three-volume master plan. The first of the three volumes included social, economic, and land use policies. The second volume presented development goals for the central business district, and the third examined neighborhoods. But the documents lacked polish and firm grounding in reality. The recommendations were so vague that it was difficult to envision implementation. The central business district volume spoke optimistically about laying fiber-optic cables under Woodward Avenue but did not explain how this would revitalize downtown. It called for improved housing and a shopping mall but specified no site.

The *Detroit News* complained that the neighborhood volume offered "little but the threat of disruption and hortatory advice to the city to do what it ought to be doing anyway," and that the central business district volume was hardly better. Finding that no staff person in city hall would discuss the draft plan, including Director Gilb, the *News* dubbed it "Coleman's Orphan."[26] Council members were noticeably unenthusiastic. Ravitz spoke glumly of sending the project "back to the drawing board."[27] A regional planner called the background studies and the draft plan useless, all because the mayor lacked strong professional planning leadership. "Those are lost years," he commented, "and no one can figure that out."[28]

Fig. 8.4. Elmwood Village, one of several townhouse projects in Elmwood III, is located very close to recreational facilities in the complex's Coleman Young Community Center and senior citizen housing in Elmwood Towers. J. Thomas, photographer.

Moving toward Planning Detroit

The next few years witnessed a growing recognition that the city needed some cohesive way to resolve a variety of physical, social, and economic problems, including crime, business development, and housing. First came efforts within city government to write a realistic master plan. Simultaneously came a strategic planning exercise, launched by the corporate sector, that tried to outline and implement basic physical and social improvements. In addition, neighborhoods arose to plan for themselves, with or without the city's support.

The city finally developed a master plan after a tug of war between the council and mayor. When the city council's planning commission received the planning department's overblown three-volume draft plan, Director Marsha Bruhn's commission staff responded by editing the tome to identify all items they considered to be substantive. This process yielded a concise 80-page document. Thus challenged, Director Corinne Gilb's planning department countered with its own summary, which was 500 pages long but better organized than its first version. This started a process of drafts moving back and forth between the council's legislative branch and the mayor's executive branch.[29]

In 1990, the city finally pulled together a master plan that the mayor and the council almost agreed upon. Based in part on the work initiated by Director Gilb, this 300-page policy document gave general guidelines for development and planning in the central business district and ten planning sectors. It also gave statements of city policies governing social, economic, and physical development. This was formally adopted in 1992, one year before Young left office.

During the entire process of master plan negotiation between the mayor and his planning department staff and the city council and its planning commission staff, the mayor fought hard to prevent the document from containing any unnecessary details or specific plans for development.[30] Nevertheless the plan did give some insight into plans for the future. For the central business district, the plan proposed a new museum, extensions to the people mover, more skywalks, and a tram to span the river between Detroit and Windsor. Most of its other policies for downtown and other prime development areas were no surprise, as these were elaborations of existing or previously announced projects. For some sectors, however, the plan offered residents valuable insight into official intentions for their areas.[31]

In the meantime, out of simple frustration, the corporate elite launched its own strategic planning process. Corporate leaders had been among those most concerned about the lack of a master plan. In 1983 department store magnate Joseph Hudson, Jr., director of Detroit Renaissance, had commented: "I don't think that enough people and groups have expressed clearly enough the logic and the urgency of a comprehensive master plan. It does not now exist. It should exist."[32] Hudson's Detroit Renaissance organized a coalition of business leaders and seized the planning initiative. They turned to strategic planning, popular in organizations ranging from major corporations to small groups, as an alternative way to deal with the city's problems.

It is no surprise that corporate leaders promoted strategic planning, already standard in corporations, which used it to formulate targeted but effective responses to the outside environment. Gradually, municipalities began using the method as well, in cities as widespread as San Francisco, Philadelphia, and Memphis.[33]

Strategic planning is a more action-oriented, short-range alternative to master or comprehensive planning. Professional planning theory had been moving in this direction for some time, but the label "strategic planning" opened the door to corporate and federal sponsorship and provided access to more extensive guidance in the literature.[34] Strategic planning involves setting goals for an organization, examining the opportunities and threats facing it, assessing its internal weaknesses and strengths, and choosing a realistic course of action. It can "correct weaknesses, take advantage of opportunities, deal with threats, and build on strengths." For cities, strategic planning makes good sense because cities must carefully choose their actions in today's urban environment, characterized by spiraling problems and scarce resources.[35]

But the process only works under certain circumstances. The group that carries out the process should include key decision-makers and other important stakeholders, but getting this part right can be difficult for cities. Corporations, the pioneers in strategic planning, function within a clear hierarchy; cities do not, and the landscape of their important stakeholders is varied and complicated. Therefore, some cities have had problems implementing decisions reached through strategic planning.[36]

Detroit's corporate leadership pushed for a strategic plan because they decided to plan for Detroit if its political leadership would not. As the business-oriented *Detroit News* commented in a 1986 editorial: "there is an implicit warning to the city in the formation of this group. The presence on the panel of so many business chieftains, such as General Motors' Roger Smith, indicates that their patience is wearing thin. They want action, and they want it now. Detroit's high crime, high taxes, and poor delivery of basic services is no longer supportable even for the wealthiest corporations."

The most important decision-maker for strategic planning would have been Mayor Young, but his commitment to the process was lukewarm. Young argued that only his administration should determine the city's future. If this group must plan, he commented, it should limit its concerns to job development, the most pressing concern and the one area most dependent upon corporate involvement. As the local press noted in rebuttal: "the city is in a poor position to dictate what should and shouldn't be on the coalition's agenda. The city can ill-afford to wait for unemployment to vanish before attacking other problems, such as crime. Crime drives out jobs just as surely as joblessness creates the despair that can lead to crime."[37]

Because of its domination by corporate leaders, the strategic planning group raised widespread suspicion among other citizens as well. Ravitz noted the presence of the same business leaders who had helped cause Detroit's decline. The roster was originally short of African Americans and neighborhood leaders. The mayor successfully pushed for a more representative group, but local community activists were still thinly represented.[38]

Rather than tackle global problems, the strategic plan focused on several important key issues that could be addressed with small, focused programs. Appropriately, race relations headed the list as a major concern. Other problem areas were education, jobs and economic development, crime, and the city's media image. The group divided itself into teams corresponding to these areas. Each team conducted its own research, sought public consultation, and developed appropriate strategies. Altogether the five task forces put together 34 action plans designed to take Detroit into the next century. They attacked some of the city's most difficult problems and came up with strategies that reflected imagination and promise.[39]

The race relations team adopted as its goal making certain that all races and ethnic groups were treated equally. They declared boldly that "good race relations are the only way Detroit and the suburbs can prosper," and laid out a modest agenda for progress. Three years after the strategic plan had been released, a progress report assessed the results. It found modest advances in some areas and little in others. By 1990, a new race relations council shared office space with New Detroit, Inc. The group had offered a grant to Wayne State University to set up a race relations institute, and the university was searching for a permanent director. The strategic plan team dropped plans to investigate discrimination in housing because other groups initiated several similar studies. It also dropped plans to create an independent newspaper.

Education initiatives generated mixed successes. In 1989 the group helped create Detroit Compact, a program with strong corporate and state government backing which provided jobs and college scholarships to city students meeting academic, attendance, and behavior standards. A federal grant facilitated an expanded educational program for 3- and 4-year-old children. An effort to promote "school empowerment" only slowly succeeded in getting schools to sign up.

Progress seemed especially slow in the area that Young had labeled the most important, jobs and economic development. The goals for that team had been to expand Detroit's economic base, make racial minorities full participants in the economic life of the city, and make the city more attractive for tourists, workers, and residents. One action plan was to develop a new "Town within a City," a redevelopment project which would combine housing, commerce, and community services. This plan foundered, as did a fund designed to assist minority business. The group dropped plans to develop two business incubators and create a small business ombudsman. No progress was reported in a drive to get every member company of Detroit Renaissance to lure at least one new firm to Detroit, and a youth employment initiative was slow to start. The most successful effort was a neighborhood development effort, led by a new local chapter of the Local Initiative Support Corporation (LISC), which brought $2 million for housing and neighborhood development to the city.[40]

In 1990–91 the strategic plan staff were involved in sixteen projects in the five task force areas. By 1993, the number of projects had fallen to six: Detroit Compact, the race relations council, communication, physical appearance, the LISC program, and Family Approach to Crime and Treatment.

The strategic planning initiative faltered in part because it was a "top down" solution, initiated by the corporate elite. Sparsely represented were the grassroots leaders and residents who had demonstrated, more consistently than the corporations, their commitment to stay in Detroit. Funding was a problem; anticipated donations needed to supplement Detroit Renaissance's $7.5 million commitment did not appear. Young's incomplete allegiance was fatal, as he was the center of political power.[41]

Although the strategic planning effort flagged, the experience allowed various groups to come together to discuss race relations, crime, education, and business development. It provided a test model for the kind of coalition-building and problem-solving that would be necessary in the future. The strategic planning experience made it obvious that the city needed to improve in a number of areas, but that such improvement needed mayoral and community support.

Neighborhoods Plan for Themselves

Another promising movement came from the grass roots. As the city continued its development project agenda, as the top planning staff batted a master plan backward and forward, and as corporate leaders ruminated about strategic plans, a few hardy neighborhoods and community-based organizations took it upon themselves to leverage what government and private resources they could muster and plan for their own community improvement.

Detroit had never been known as an especially strong neighborhood town, since neighborhood organizations lagged behind those in their sister cities in sophistication and experience. Yet many of the city's most critical dilemmas were neighborhood-based. In some areas, middle and working class residents persevered, but they fought physical deterioration, crime, and a faltering public school system. Other neighborhoods had already succumbed to blight, abandonment, and social decline.

Top down plans may work for coordinating overall city action or for giving an overall vision for a city's future. Even these, however, benefit from participation of the populace. For addressing problems based within neighborhoods, initiative and participation by the people most affected are vital. Otherwise solutions provide only a veneer, a temporary stopgap, with no staying power. The city's planners had discovered this in their attempts to spur neighborhood conservation in the 1950s. If residents did not attach themselves to the improvement process, they were likely to leave. So it was important that Detroit's neighborhoods develop positive agendas for improving their communities.

Such efforts required some financial support. The Community Reinvestment Act, a regulatory law passed in 1977, helped U.S. community groups pressure lending institutions to increase their community-based investments. By 1988, the Detroit Committee for Responsible Banking, a community-based coalition, successfully persuaded bankers to invest more in inner-city housing and business development.[42] The Michigan Housing Coalition worked with the Chicago-based National Training and Information Center to convince five major financial institutions to provide a new $10 million home mortgage program, to support home ownership and counter the historic effects of redlining.[43]

Another source of neighborhood support was state government. The Michigan State Housing Development Authority (MSHDA) funded community-based housing initiatives even in those years when federal support for low-income housing practically disappeared. MSHDA staff helped create an important state neighborhood program, the Neighborhood Builder's Alliance. Although it only survived from 1989 to 1992, the neighborhood grants and technical assistance components of the Alliance provided financial and technical assistance to several of the state's community-based organizations, including several dozen in the City of Detroit. MSHDA's Neighborhood Preservation Program, still extant in 1997, encouraged groups to develop plans for improving their neighborhoods and funded multihousing development.

Several community-based organizations used these and other resources to rise to the challenge of restructuring their neighborhoods. Some were CDBG citizen district councils created by the city. But other groups arose as independent forces for social change. Supported by the Reverend Eddie Edwards of the Joy of Jesus mission, the Ravendale neighborhood group built on the concept of block clubs to rally residents to clean up the neighborhood, fix up houses, and reject the drug culture. These efforts gained nationwide attention when Ravendale experienced dramatic improvements, all without government funds.[44]

While some community groups launched directly into improvement activities, others worked within the context of their own neighborhood plans. One of the first was the Michigan Avenue Community Organizations (MACO), which for much of its history relied upon the organizational philosophy of activist Saul Alinsky. MACO was an umbrella organization that included southwest neighborhoods lying on either side of one of the city's major streets, Michigan Avenue. MACO promoted housing and commercial rehabilitation, but it commissioned its own formal neighborhood plan to guide development initiatives.

Core City Neighborhoods, Inc., also retained a planning consultant to help it set out a vision and an action plan. Long-term strategies included housing rehabilitation, economic development, and crime reduction. One goal was to build 1,110 units of new housing and a shopping center. Short-term strategies were to subcontract with the city to mow weeded vacant lots and to work with the Michigan Housing Coalition to gain open access to home mortgages for low-income residents.[45]

Another successful group was the east side Church of the Mes-

siah Housing Corporation, which rehabilitated four large apartment buildings. Like several other nonprofit community development corporations that sprang up in Detroit and other cities, the Messiah group stepped in to develop low-income housing where private developers would not. In 13 years, it renovated 140 housing units.[46] An umbrella organization to which Church of the Messiah and ten other community-based organizations belonged, Islandview Village Development Corporation, built 17 new rental units; it also commissioned, and began to implement, an ambitious neighborhood plan which included a commercial development and additional housing construction.

Smaller community organizations began to contact universities to help them create neighborhood plans as a backdrop for community development. University of Michigan planning, landscape architecture, and architecture students worked in neighborhoods such as Corktown and Hubbard-Richard. Michigan State University urban planning and landscape architecture classes assisted with grant applications and neighborhood planning for several faith-based and other neighborhood groups, such as Fellowship, Inc., and New Hope Housing Development Corporation, as did planning students and faculty at Wayne State University.

Some organizations did not go through a formal planning process but built on extended agendas that revealed vision and organizational sophistication. Both Warren/Conner Development Coalition

Fig. 8.6. Row of rental units developed by Island-view Village Development Corporation, an umbrella organization that includes several churches and neighborhood organizations near East Grand Boulevard. This street lies a few blocks south of the old Mack-Concord conservation project. J. Thomas, photographer.

and Focus:HOPE, Inc., ably meshed social services and economic development. Warren/Conner's Youth on the Edge of Greatness program trained youth in crime prevention, economic development, and neighborhood cleanup. The development coalition opened a new store in a devastated east side commercial district, and it managed housing rehabilitation, leadership training programs, and a path-breaking program providing supportive services to the chronically jobless.[47]

Focus:HOPE, Inc., in a class by itself, began as a civil rights organization after the 1967 riots. Headed by the charismatic Father William Cunningham, the group started with food distribution; by 1989 it served 70,000 people per month. Cunningham soon realized the poverty was such that food distribution could never end.

In the 1970s Cunningham bought an old factory building abandoned in the neighborhood, hoping to create jobs, but found no one qualified to run it. That led to tutorial programs, to training programs, and to what has become a professional route upward for inner city youth given little chance by the public school system. In 1981, his group opened a Machinist Training Institute, which graduated 581 skilled machinists by 1989. Preparing trainees for the institute was Focus:HOPE's Fast Track program, which helped high school graduates rapidly improve their math and reading skills. These projects soon transformed the neighborhood. Industry Mall, covering 25 acres, contained two Focus:HOPE industrial firms, Fast

Fig. 8.7. Entrance sign for one of several buildings owned by Focus:HOPE, its Center for Advanced Technologies, with building in background. This training center has received visitors, including President Clinton, from all over the world. Note center logo for Focus:HOPE, composed of Black and White hands touching, symbolizing the organization's focus on racial unity. J. Thomas, photographer.

Track, a new Montessori School, and the Center for Advanced Technologies. Organizers of the showcase center, which opened in 1994, plan to turn high school graduates into world-class engineers and technicians.[48]

These groups could not, by themselves, turn around the city. The forces of decline were too strong for that. For decades residents and firms had been leaving, and more still would leave if given the chance. Nevertheless, these experiences suggested that community-based initiatives had a place in the fight for the city's survival. They indicated that neighborhoods might be saved even if the city had given up on them. They showed that local residents, if properly organized and motivated, could rebuild houses and drive out drug dealers; that community groups could launch successful housing, commercial, and even industrial development projects; that neighborhoods could plan for their future even if the city would not.

Joining Forces for Empowerment

All of these trends came together after a new mayor took office in Detroit in January, 1994. Dennis Archer, former state supreme court justice, was a man of diplomacy and capability. Although not a consummate racial politician in the sense that Young had been, he too had lived part of his childhood in Detroit's African-American community, and he had developed good human relations skills as a lawyer and judge. Archer brought intelligence and civility to his job and campaigned on the need to cooperate with suburbia and the business community.

After his election, Archer consulted widely with several transition teams, one of which focused on planning and development. They suggested that he form a master plan task force, later renamed the "Land Use Task Force." Creating this task force as one of his first acts of office, Archer charged it with creating a vision of land use for the city by the end of July, 1994. He appointed one of his assistants as the key staff person in charge of overseeing its research and deliberations. The resulting document laid out a preliminary but sensible outline of future land use for the city.

Another notable action was his appointment of Gloria Robinson as director of both the Department of Planning and CEDD. These merged, after July 1, 1994, into the Department of Planning and Development, immediately eliminating many of the overlap problems and turf battles that beset the previous administration. This gave the city two (instead of three) planning/development offices, the mayor's and the council's. Planning Director Robinson was well qualified for her job. Not only had she earned undergraduate and graduate degrees in urban planning, she had also worked many years as a professional planner, heading Wayne County's planning division at the time of her appointment. Her professional standing among her peers was unquestioned.[49]

Archer's appointment of the task force and of Robinson symbolized not only a recommitment to professional planning, but also, perhaps, the redemption of the profession. As a bonus, Robinson was African American, a clear sign that it was possible to find a competent, professional planning director among the city's dominant racial group. Her first job assignment was crucial. Archer appointed her as the lead organizer for the city's application for designation as a federal empowerment zone.

The city used the application to plan strategically for some of its poorest neighborhoods. Funded by Congress in August 1993, Empowerment Zones/Enterprise Communities (EZEC) formed a major component of Clinton's urban policy. The program was only vaguely similar to the concept of enterprise zones as first proposed by Peter Hall of Great Britain and championed, by some, as a conservative response to urban decline. Originally, enterprise zones provided tax incentives and wage concessions for business investors in specially designated depressed areas. Although successive Republican administrations failed to pass U.S. enterprise zone legislation, several states did.

Under Clinton, the concept of enterprise zones evolved into something akin to Model Cities. Advised by Congress and by experts in state enterprise zones, his administration decided to fund only nine empowerment zones, with six of these in urban areas. Each of the fortunate winners would receive a bonanza: up to $100 million in Title XX social service grants over a two-year period, various tax incentives, waivers on certain regulations, and priority standing for other federal grants. A greater number of urban and rural "enterprise communities" would receive less funding but get tax benefits as well.[50]

HUD and the U.S. Department of Agriculture held informational conferences in February 1994 explaining the application process, with applications due on June 30, 1994. The administrative rules gave great freedom to localities to specify how they would use funds, for a range of economic development, social service, and community improvement activities, but specified that applicants submit a strategic plan for intended expenditures. They also required that the planning process be inclusionary and community-based. This marked the first time in many years that a federal program aimed at community development had mandated strongly participatory planning.

The brand new Archer administration brought together an empowerment zone coordinating council to create a strategic plan for the application. On that council, the administration reserved nine seats for citizens associated with neighborhood or community development groups, and it held elections to select these representatives and nine alternates. Other members of the coordinating council represented major nonprofit institutions and other levels of government. Three co-chairpersons, including two community-based representatives and Planning Director Robinson, guided deliberation. The coordinating council in turn created six task forces, each of which tapped the ideas of hundreds of participants.

It was as if the Archer administration was, upon the orders of Contest Judge Bill Clinton, making a stew. Into the pressure cooker went newly appointed Robinson and other city staff; community-based organizations, some of which had been battling the city for years, seeking attention and financing; the state, county, and school district, each with a spotted history of cooperation with the city; local institutions, banks, and corporations; and a few temporary or borrowed professionals, brought in to assist the process. Added to all of these were ordinary residents of the zone, trying to play a role in one of the biggest events in urban policy history. Less involved at first but critical in later stages was the city council. The hope was that from these motley ingredients would spring another chance for the City of Detroit, or at least for its zone, reaching as it did around the heart of the city.[51]

That all these people had to agree on a plan very quickly only seemed to add impetus. Rallying around the new mayor, the private sector committed an astonishing $1.9 billion in funds to support the city's ten-year plan for its zone. Robinson, citizens, and staff successfully fought through time constraints and group conflicts — the intense steam of the pressure cooker — and put together an exceptionally good strategic plan. HUD's Secretary Cisneros labeled the

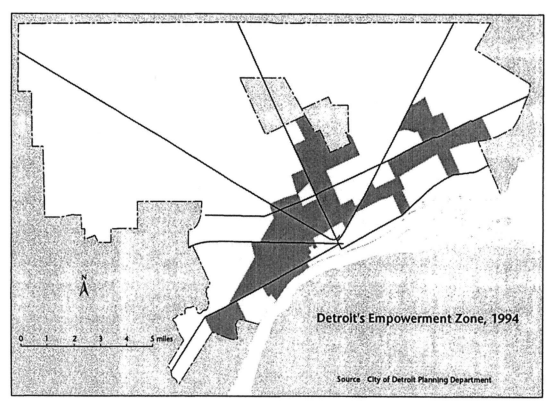

Fig. 8.8. The shape of De-troit's Empowerment Zone, 1994, shows the effects of attempts to meet federal requirements and simultaneously include major employers—such as General Motors and the Detroit Medical Center—and prominent community-based organizations. Courtesy Detroit Department of Planning and Development.

result the top application in the nation, and Detroit became one of the six urban winners.[52]

Detroit then began the difficult task of preparing to implement the plan. Among the hardest challenges: holding together the fragile coalition of city and community-based organizations, jaded by years of conflict and noncooperation.In addition, winning brought out all the unresolved conflicts between the city's legislative and executive branches, and among the community-based organizations and faith-based groups working in the zone. Working toward implementation proved very difficult in the first two years, after the euphoria of winning wore off. Yet in many ways Detroit was already victorious. A city that worked for years without a viable planning apparatus, a city that had labored and failed to develop a unified strategic plan or a sustained development initiative, a city that had forced its community organizations to fend for themselves, had come together to plan for a better future.

The Fall and Rise of Planning

Detroit approached the end of the century with a fresh determination to improve the city. A renewed effort arose for city improvement, and planning appeared to have a role to play in this effort. Unlike previous decades, when planning was strictly associated with land development, regulation, and design, the new agenda was more flexible, more strategic, aimed more toward cooperation and self-initiative.

This came about only after a period when the planning and development processes within the city had become uncoupled. Changes in federal policy lessened the importance of professional urban planning. Professionals survived a long period of disorientation and lack of guidance. Painfully aware of the potential injustices wrought by centralized planning, they still had little concept about how to solve the contemporary city's problems. Detroit's planners were handicapped even further by divisions within city government, by their own history, and by the legacy of racial antagonism.

The city's corporate leaders were prime beneficiaries of the city's pro-development mentality, since this gave them almost unqualified support for whatever projects they wanted to build. Even they finally realized that the pendulum had swung too far. The central business district showed the effects of lack of cohesion, with construction disjointed and the city's overall intentions unclear. The growing specter of economic and social problems made a conscious plan of action imperative.

A movement began to plan for improvement. The city council and Young's office finally reached sufficient unity of thought to develop a mutually acceptable master plan. Corporate and community leaders gathered together and consulted about the city's race relations, education, economic development, crime, and educational system. While the long-range results of the Detroit Strategic Plan were few, its promise was great.

Neighborhoods, long neglected, launched their own planning and development campaign. Often building upon CDBG financing, some formed community-based housing corporations, while others focused on more general neighborhood improvement. Several groups commissioned formal neighborhood plans to guide their growing activities. Sophisticated organizations such as the Warren/Conner Development Coalition and Focus:HOPE broke new ground in combining social and economic development with physical renewal.

When Dennis Archer was elected mayor, he launched a well-publicized effort to re-envision land use within the city. He also appointed a professional planner as director of a merged department of planning and economic development, in a major step to revive professionalism and reduce overlap. In a stunning testimony to professional competence and a cooperative spirit, key actors came together and produced a winning application for federal empowerment zone designation.

It began to appear that the capacity existed to plot a renewed future for the city, even in the face of decline. At the same time, however, major systemic problems still faced the city and the region. One of the most intractable was racial disunity.

Racial Disunity

9

Many things could stand in the way of the future well-being of cities such as Detroit, which is merely an archetypical example of the problems that confront other U.S. cities. Among the potential barriers to improvement, perhaps the most difficult to resolve will be the lingering effects of racial disunity. One of the most important lessons in this account of postwar Detroit's redevelopment efforts has been that race conflict and change have formed major barriers to city improvement.

The last chapter summarized the way in which planning evolved at the municipal and neighborhood level during the period after the early 1970s. That chapter ended on an optimistic note, suggesting that the City of Detroit, its prominent citizens, and its community-based organizations were rethinking their plan for a better future. This built on a previous account of several limited but visible project successes during Coleman Young's twenty-year administration. These two chapters only briefly referred to the mighty forces of social disorder.

This chapter confronts once again a force of social disorder. Unless society begins to resolve racial disunity, this and other cities will experience more decades of fundamental decline.

As table 9.1 shows, the Detroit metropolitan area has one of the nation's highest rates of "racial isolation." Such rates come from measuring the numbers of people of a particular race who live in a census block composed of at least 90 percent of their own race. While the amount of racial isolation lessened between 1980 and 1990, it remained a significant problem. Other metropolitan areas continued to experience racial isolation as well, but in the Detroit area isolation increased to an unusually high level.

Another way of measuring racial segregation is by using an index of dissimilarity, which measures the minimum percentage of either group that would have to move between census tracts in order to achieve even spatial distribution. By this measure, residential segregation of African Americans was as high in the Detroit metropolitan area in 1990 as in 1980. In fact, Black segregation changed hardly at all between 1960 and 1990, standing at high readings of 87, 89, 87,

TABLE 9.1 ISOLATION OF BLACKS IN U.S. METROPOLITAN
AREAS IN DESCENDING ORDER OF ISOLATION

Metropolitan Area	Blacks in Isolation, 1990	Change in Isolation, 1980–1990
Chicago	71%	−9.1%
Cleveland	67	0.4
Detroit	61	4.0
Memphis	58	−0.6
St. Louis	54	−3.3
Baltimore	53	0.1
Philadelphia	53	0.1
Buffalo	48	2.6
New Orleans	47	−3.2
Kansas City	44	−6.0
Atlanta	43	−6.1
Milwaukee	42	−7.0
Average for 50 areas	37	−6.7

Note: "Isolation" defined as living in a census block group that has at least 90 percent of the same race. Authors analyzed data for nation's fifty largest metropolitan areas.
Sources: Dan Gillmor and Stephen K. Doig, "Segregation Forever?" *American Demographics,* January, 1992, p. 50.

and 87 on a 100-point scale for 1960, 1970, 1980, and 1990.[1] As figure 9.1 indicates, Detroit's segregation index is higher than that of other metropolitan areas, although many of them experience similar conditions.

These population statistics are all the more remarkable considering the fact that the number of middle-class Blacks leaving the city had increased. As housing "opened," Black families moved to key suburban municipalities. Racial segregation continued in spite of this because of the pattern of residential exodus: Blacks tended to move only to certain "safe" suburbs in the metropolitan area. Simultaneously, other suburbs gained no Blacks because of hostility or Black unwillingness to be the first to integrate. Hence, suburban exodus did not appreciably reduce racial isolation within the seven-county metropolitan area (see fig. 9.2).

Who is to blame for the state of racial disunity in the Detroit region is a matter of some debate. Attention has tended to focus on personalities, particularly since the general public had a visible figure upon which to lay blame: Mayor Coleman Young. Because Young was an outspoken advocate for Detroit with a brusque style and earthy language, it was easy to focus upon him as the cause of racial antagonism. For example, Young had no qualms about verbally bashing suburbanites in full view of television cameras. But suburban politicians contributed to the general ill will, attacking Detroit and its citizens in sometimes virulent tones as well. This cre-

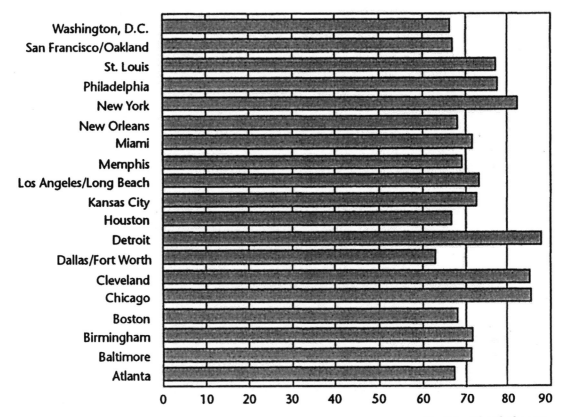

Washington, D.C.
San Francisco/Oakland
St. Louis
Philadelphia
New York
New Orleans
Miami
Memphis
Los Angeles/Long Beach
Kansas City
Houston
Detroit
Dallas/Fort Worth
Cleveland
Chicago
Boston
Birmingham
Baltimore
Atlanta

0 10 20 30 40 50 60 70 80 90

Fig. 9.1. The Black segregation index for selected metropolitan areas in 1990 shows how extensive is the problem of racial segregation. New York City, Detroit, Cleveland, and Chicago vie for the dishonor of highest levels of segregation. Data from Population Association of America.

ated a confrontational environment of well-publicized verbal volleys from public officials that inflamed quiet private prejudices.[2]

If Young were indeed the main cause of estrangement, Archer's election should have resolved all such problems. During the 1993 election, Mayor Young endorsed Archer's opponent Sharon MacPhail, a charismatic African-American woman who did not hesitate to spar with the White power structure. In contrast, Archer was a natural diplomat. White citizens and institutions would have been hard pressed to find a capable Black mayor more open to negotiation and cooperation, although Archer also had strength of character and will. Once elected, Archer soon found that his willingness to cooperate did not automatically eliminate suburban noncooperation. During his first year in office, battles with regional leaders —particularly over a proposed merger of city and regional transit systems—were bruising affairs.[3]

The current dilemma is far broader than personalities or political leadership, which only symbolize the chasm that separates the region and the races. The divisions are deep-seated, symptomatic of a virtual spiritual malaise. This racial disunity threatens the future of the city and the metropolitan area. This is evident in the problem of *discrimination,* a major cause of geographic and economic segregation. Racial disunity is also manifest in the lingering problem of *disparity* between the races. Finally, *regional fragmentation* is both a

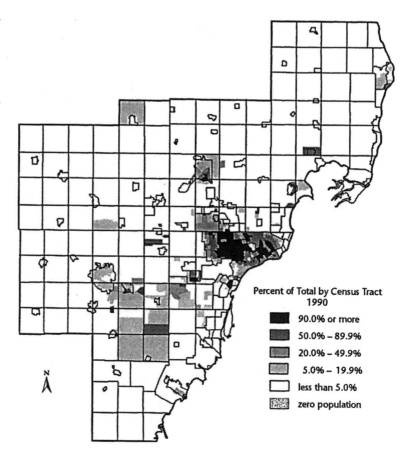

Fig. 9.2. This map of Black population in Detroit's metropolitan area, for 1990, shows how concentrated African Americans are in both the city of Detroit (core dark area) and selected suburban communities. Courtesy Southeast Michigan Council of Governments.

Percent of Total by Census Tract
1990

90.0% or more

50.0% – 89.9%

20.0% – 49.9%

5.0% – 19.9%

less than 5.0%

zero population

manifestation of, and a barrier to resolving, racial disunity. Each of these three phenomena must be overcome before any real revitalization can take place for Detroit.

Discrimination

The problem of discrimination is old and familiar. Residential discrimination is still a live and viable force within the metropolitan area. Researchers at the University of Michigan, administering one survey questionnaire in 1976 and again in 1992, found much higher intolerance among White respondents than among Blacks. The survey used picture representations of hypothetical neighborhoods and asked how various racial mixtures of residents would affect mobility. Black respondents were, on the whole, willing to move into racially mixed neighborhoods. When the mixture was half Black and half White, for example, 99 percent of Black respondents were willing to enter in 1976 and 97 percent in 1992. Blacks were also willing, by similar percentages, to move into areas where their race made up 20 percent of the population. They hesitated only to be the first Black person to move into a neighborhood; 38 percent would do so in 1976; even fewer, 28 percent, would do so in 1992.

TABLE 9.2   WHITE REACTION TO MIXED NEIGHBORHOODS,
DETROIT METROPOLITAN AREA

	1976	1992
If Blacks were 20% of neighborhood		
Would feel uncomfortable living there	42%	30%
Would try to move out	24	15
Would not move in	50	26
If Blacks were 50% of neighborhood		
Would feel uncomfortable living there	72%	66%
Would try to move out	64	52
Would not move in	73	56

Sources: University of Michigan Detroit Area Study, reported in *Detroit News/Free Press,*
October 10, 1992, p. 10A. Charlotte Steeh and Reynolds Farley, "Detroit: A Metropolis Di-
vided by Race? Report to Respondents" (Ann Arbor: University of Michigan Detroit Area
Study, March 1993), p. 6.

As table 9.2 shows, many Whites were not willing to accept residential integration even as late as 1992. Over the sixteen-year period, tolerance among Whites had grown. In 1992, 15 percent of the
White respondents would have tried to move out of a neighborhood that was 20 percent Black; in 1976, 24 percent of White respondents would have done so. By 1992, compared with 1976, tolerance had also increased for a hypothetical neighborhood with
a half-and-half racial mixture. Even though tolerance improved,
however, two-thirds of the 1992 White respondents would have felt
uncomfortable living in a neighborhood where half of the families
were Black. Over half would move out, and over half would not
move in.[4]

This situation left metropolitan neighborhoods still vulnerable to
racial turnover. Blacks were willing to move to neighborhoods with
few Blacks, and in real life they opened up several suburban communities. Whites were less willing to move into integrated neighborhoods, and they were quite likely to move out if integration
went too far. A common scenario was for a few Black families to
move into an area, prompting the most intolerant Whites to move
out. This increased the percentage of Black families. Eventually even
the most tolerant Whites moved out, or refused to move in, which
had much the same result. It took only a little White prejudice to
trigger the racial change cycle.

In spite of federal legislation prohibiting discrimination, social
gatekeepers prevented Blacks from moving freely or having free access to home financing. Surveys showed that discrimination against
potential renters thrived. HUD sponsored a series of tests designed
to detect such inequitable treatment. The Detroit Fair Housing Center found that when it sent White home-seekers and Black home-
seekers to the same apartment units separately, the Whites were favored in some manner in 50 percent of the test visits. Sometimes

TABLE 9.3   MEAN SOCIAL DISTANCE RATINGS AMONG VARIOUS PARENT GROUPS

Hamtramck Residents	Most Polish Americans	Most Arab Americans	Most Albanian Americans	Most Black Americans
Polish American	6.55	3.90	4.16	3.58
Arab American	2.67	6.48	2.69	2.33
Albanian American	4.85	2.80	6.77	1.78
Black Respondents	5.54	3.91	3.58	6.05

Pontiac Residents	Most Puerto Ricans	Most Mexican Americans	Most Black Americans	Most White Americans
Puerto Rican	6.90	6.80	6.68	6.80
Mexican American	5.80	6.45	5.20	5.78
Black	5.51	5.58	6.18	5.71
White working class	3.00	2.80	2.50	6.60
White middle class	5.80	5.98	5.68	6.45

Notes: The question was, How willing are you personally to accept these people as a close neighbor in your neighborhood or apartment building? Scale ranged from 1 to 7. Choosing 1 indicated almost definite nonacceptance; 4 signaled neutrality; 7 indicated very definite acceptance. The lower the number, the higher the intolerance.
Hamtramck is an inner-city suburb of Detroit and Pontiac, a Detroit-area suburb.
Source: Wallace E. Lambert and Donald M. Taylor, *Coping with Cultural and Racial Diversity in Urban America* (New York: Praeger Publishers, 1990), 80, 103, 128, 152.

the Blacks did not even know they had been discriminated against, so subtle was the snub. Only questionnaires asking the specifics of their experiences and comparing them by race revealed the truth. Apartment managers gave different information about whether or not apartments were actually available or offered different incentives for moving into them. Many victims successfully filed suit and publicized the results, but this did not deter other apartment managers from discriminating. New bias cases arose to replace the old.[5]

The categories "Black" and "White" hide great distinctions of class and ethnicity. We can use "Black" as synonymous with African-American in most, but not all, cases. And the "White" label covers a wide variety of people. When recent studies have identified respondents by way of more subtle categorization, what emerges is pervasive prejudice against other races, ethnic groups, and nationalities as potential neighbors, friends, or co-workers. Among some ethnic groups, tolerance of others is almost nonexistent.

Table 9.3 shows this dramatically. When researchers asked parents in two different suburban school systems how willing they were to accept members of other races as neighbors, the results varied widely. The chart reflects responses on a 7-point scale, where a score near 7 reflects a very definite willingness to accept the other group, a score near 1 reflects a very definite unwillingness to do so, and a 4 reflects neutrality. In Hamtramck, a suburb completely surrounded by the city of Detroit, the mixture of Polish-, Arab-, Albanian-, and African-American citizens lived together in a state of unease. Each group was most willing to live near its own kind.

This tendency was especially marked among Arab Americans, who barely tolerated living near Polish, Albanian, or African Americans. Conversely, Albanians were not particularly willing to accept Arab Americans as neighbors, and they were even less willing to accept African Americans.

In Pontiac, a multiethnic suburban city 20 miles from inner city Detroit, but still within the metropolitan area, the racial and ethnic mixture was different but discrete. This included Mexican Americans, Puerto Ricans, Vietnamese, Blacks, and Whites. Table 9.3 shows that Mexican Americans, Puerto Ricans, and African Americans showed a fairly high tolerance for neighbors of other races, as did middle-class White respondents. Working-class Whites did not.

The researchers also asked about their respondents' willingness to accept other racial groups as family members through marriage, as close personal friends, and as co-workers. Most respondents were unwilling to accept other racial groups into their families. Tolerance of other races as personal friends was a little higher. But respondents indicated surprisingly low tolerance even for "co-workers or partners at work." Tolerance scores were neutral for Polish-American citizens, who accepted other groups as co-workers. Even more tolerant were Puerto Ricans, Mexican Americans, Blacks in both cities, and middle-class Whites. Arab Americans scored near 2, indicating low tolerance, for Polish-, Albanian-, and African-American co-workers. Albanians scored slightly intolerant of Arab-Americans and African-American co-workers, at 3.20, and White working-class respondents were slightly intolerant of Puerto Rican, Mexican-, and African-American co-workers.[6]

This study is particularly important because it indicates tolerance levels displayed by Hispanics, one of the country's fastest growing minorities, and by Arab Americans, an important minority group within the Detroit metropolitan area. Metropolitan Detroit has one of the nation's primary concentrations of Arab Americans. Already conflicts have risen between this group and inner city African Americans, particularly since Arab Americans own many inner-city grocery and convenience stores.

Disparity

Another well-known problem of disunity relates to the disparities in life chances and well-being among the races, particularly Blacks and Whites. The fundamental imbalance that exists creates an inherently unstable environment. Just as lasting peace is not possible within the world so long as some nations have enormous resources and others do not, so prosperity is not possible within the metropolitan area as long as life opportunities and living conditions vary so greatly by race.

Disturbing disparities of poverty and wealth exist in the metropolitan area. Poverty affects a wide variety of social indicators, such

Fig. 9.3. Hart Plaza, in Detroit's Civic Center, with Renaissance Center in background. Sign advertises August 1995 African World ethnic festival. A series of ethnic and other music festivals draw large crowds in the summer. J. Thomas, photographer.

as lifespan, health, unemployment, income, educational attainment, and crime victimization. For each of these indicators, central city populations suffer more than their share. Even within central cities, quality of life varies markedly by race. Those Whites who remained in the city, however, reached poverty rates in 1989 that approached those of Blacks in 1969 (see fig. 9.4).

Health and mortality rates illustrate the reduced opportunities facing inner-city Blacks. A reliable indicator of health status is the infant mortality rate. While the Black infant death rate improved in the State of Michigan from 1970 to 1990, the differences between Blacks and Whites rose from 1970 to 1990. In 1970, the number of Black infant deaths per 1,000 live births was 30.6, compared with a White rate of 18.5. Thus Blacks experienced 1.7 times the rate of infant deaths of Whites. By 1990, the Black-to-White ratio climbed to 2.7, as Blacks experienced 21.6 infant deaths per 1,000 live births in the state compared with 7.9 for Whites. The Black-to-White ratio exceeded 2.4 every year between 1980 and 1990. Data for the City of Detroit for 1990 were also discouraging. In that year the Black infant death rate stood at 23.0, or 2.6 times the White rate.[7]

Even more dramatic have been the falling life opportunities for urban youth. Drug addiction increased sharply in Detroit and Wayne County from 1981 to 1991. Treatment admissions for cocaine—popularized by its derivative, the viciously addictive drug called crack—rose dramatically from 1980 to 1991. In Detroit, 1233

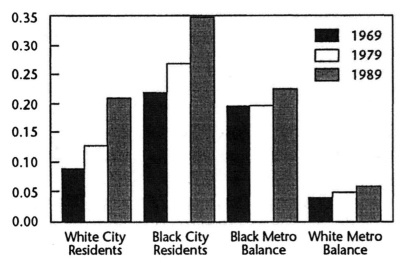

Fig. 9.4. *This chart of time trends in metropolitan poverty, by location and race, shows the extent to which Black inner city poverty has grown. Rates for both Black and White city residents have increased, however. Poverty rates are much lower in the balance of the tri-county area, but have recently inched up for African-American suburbanites.*

Black women were admitted for crack addiction in 1990–91, compared with 107 White women. Black men were more severely affected; 2371 Black men within the city were admitted for crack addiction in 1990–91, compared with 185 White men. Even in the larger Wayne County, White admissions were low. The drug plague that hit inner-city Blacks contributed to an increased homicide rate, as did an unchecked proliferation of firearms. In what four researchers called "an American childhood tragedy," homicide rates among 15- to 18-year-old Black males in the city and suburbs of Detroit climbed far beyond homicide rates for White males. Those rates escalated sharply in the 1980s.[8]

Many White suburban residents appear to have inoculated themselves against compassion for the conditions facing inner-city Blacks. This is most evident in interviews, when suburban residents display the extent of their disengagement. One prominent Oakland County elected official expressed this most succinctly: "In no sense are we dependent on Detroit. The truth is, Detroit has had its day. I don't give a damn about Detroit. It has no direct bearing on the quality of my life." The interviewer asked, "What about the quality of life for Detroiters?" The official responded, "It's like the Indians on the reservation. Those who can will leave Detroit. Those who can't will get blankets and food from the government men in the city."[9]

It became easier to hold such attitudes as the social structure collapsed within the city, causing escalating crime rates and falling city services. In part because of this, some observers rejected the argument that racial prejudice continued to fuel exodus to the suburbs. Even the term "White flight," such protesters claim, overlooked the influence of the American love affair with suburban life styles and disenchantment with deteriorating inner-city life.[10]

The truth is less simple. Flight to the suburbs has differed markedly by race largely because of racial discrimination. Furthermore, racial disparity weaves a circular web. Racial isolation aggravates poor social and economic conditions, which lead to desperation and its manifestations (drugs, crime), which lead to more isolation. As explained most cogently by William Julius Wilson, when society isolates racial minorities and low-income people within inner cities, a "concentration effect" takes hold. When only low-income workers or welfare recipients live in a neighborhood, children have no positive role models. Their isolation in ineffective school systems can make it appear education offers no way out. The lure of drugs and crime becomes irresistible as legitimate means of employment fade. Marriage fragments—or never takes place—as males lose earning power. And all of these problems can cause more isolation.[11]

Yet flight to the suburbs does not divorce suburbia from the city. Those U.S. metropolitan areas with strong and healthy central cities are healthier than other metropolitan areas because distressed central cities pull their suburbs down. When researchers at the University of Louisville looked at the prosperity of suburbs in 1979, as measured by per capita income, the Detroit suburbs ranked sixth. By 1987, however, suburban prosperity had declined in Detroit and other metropolitan areas with high levels of inner-city distress.[12]

Furthermore, as Detroit area leaders gradually have come to realize, Detroit's bad reputation affects business prospects. As business leaders travel abroad, they find that few foreigners make distinctions between the City of Detroit and Oakland or Macomb counties. The city's poor crime image affects all areas of the metropolitan area.[13]

One thing is certain: The chasm separating the well-to-do from the destitute is determined in large part by race. If citizens allow racial intolerance or disinterest to temper their support of improvement efforts, the future of the central city is bleak. And if the social and economic conditions of the central city do not improve, the entire metropolitan area will suffer. Improving the social and economic status of inner-city African Americans, therefore, must become part of the race unity agenda.

Fragmentation

The third part of the agenda is to recognize the relationship between political fragmentation and racial disunity within the region and to take deliberate steps to overcome that fragmentation.

The regional level is important because the metropolitan area really has become the essential unit of analysis. Many of the problems Detroit faced came from the failure to view the metropolitan area as unified community, where everyone was responsible for the good of the whole. This was the reason that regionalists, planners, and labor activists wanted to restructure the region in the 1940s. Yet it was easier for suburban communities to incorporate than for central cities to expand. Local reliance upon the property tax encouraged middle- and upper-income taxpayers to cluster in safe municipalities protected from the masses by restrictive zoning ordinances. The American attachment to local control or "home rule" could not be shaken.

Mild forms of regionalism exist. As in many metropolitan areas, special regional districts provide several important municipal services. In 1940 the people of five metropolitan counties established the Huron-Clinton Metropolitan Authority, which built and maintained several area parks and recreational facilities. Other special districts provided hospital facilities, trash incineration, and transportation services. Municipalities established cooperative agreements among themselves to provide services. Many area municipalities relied upon the City of Detroit to provide water services, sold on a contractual basis.[14]

Attempts to provide stronger forms of regional governance and planning persisted. The Ford Foundation provided the first $1 million to finance the Metropolitan Fund, a nonprofit research group that sponsored a number of important studies over the years beginning in the 1960s. Some of these studies led to major organizations, such as the now defunct Southeastern Michigan Transportation Authority (SEMTA), and the Southeast Michigan Council of Governments (SEMCOG).

SEMCOG became the regional planning agency, but it had the same weaknesses as other councils of government and regional planning agencies. Membership for metropolitan municipalities was strictly voluntary, for example. When regional promoters tried to develop a stronger form of metropolitan cooperation, they failed. In 1975 the Metropolitan Fund advocated replacing SEMCOG with a stronger regional governing body. Every area unit of government would have been forced to belong to this new regional body, the Southeast Michigan Planning and Development Agency, which would have coordinated economic, housing, and transportation development. State Representative William Ryan introduced enabling legislation, the "Area Unity Bill," House Bill 5527, in 1975. The bill generated widespread political opposition, however, and did not pass.[15]

For suburbanites, the proposal brought out fears that suburban residents would have to pay to support Detroit. At the time, opposition to cross-district school busing was heated, and groups of White housewives staged acrimonious protests against a school desegregation court order. Suburban fears of inner-city Blacks ran at an all-time high, making it a bad time to suggest regional governance. The distrust was mutual. Many city residents suspected that the largely White metropolitan advocates were trying to dilute hard-earned Black political power within Detroit. Young verbalized the mistrust borne of decades of grievances: "These people who fled to the suburbs to escape Detroit's problems in the first place aren't going to help support Detroit now. . . . I'm not willing to deal with

Fig. 9.5. Bronze street sculpture which created quite a stir after its 1986 unveiling. Many chose to see it as an angry "Black" fist, symbolizing inner city antagonism, but Los Angeles sculptor Robert Graham designed it as a monument to Detroit boxer Joe Louis, and the magazine Sports Illustrated donated it to the city. Building in the background is the Civic Center's City-County Building. J. Thomas, photographer.

people who have refused to deal fairly with me. I'm going to turn over my autonomy to people like that? I have to look askance at this whole proposal."[16]

The fight for regional planning and increased cooperation continued through the years. Periodically proposals arose for improving fiscal cooperation or mass transit in the Detroit area. Regional transportation remained an active effort, as did other forms of regional cooperation under SEMCOG. In general, however, the region remained fragmented. SEMCOG never gained the clout necessary to enforce cooperation. The tension between urban and rural interests remained a persistent problem.[17] Pro and con positions over state legislation affecting Detroit almost always took on racial overtones. It became almost impossible to understand the acrimony of debates over proposals to create a regional water authority independent of Detroit, institute mass transit, change the tax structure, or sever the city from county government without understanding the racial tension that underlay all arguments.

For example, when suburbanites opposed a Detroit subway proposal, one Oakland County commissioner noted that a deep-seated antipathy to Detroit fueled the opposition. As she pointed out, Oakland County residents expressed their anger toward Detroit "by attacking Coleman Young." Indeed they did. The Oakland Press published a special anti-subway supplement that included a collection of racist letters, boldly signed by their authors. One suggested that the subway "would be an open invitation for murders and muggings. Who wants any part of Black Detroit?" Two letters suggested a "lynching party" for Young, and another that Young dig his subway vertically, straight to hell.[18]

In spite of such feelings, signs appeared that Detroit area leaders were willing to rethink regional cooperation. An important incentive for doing so was the anti-growth movement, which arose because of the increasing economic and environmental costs of suburban sprawl. SEMCOG used federal transportation funds to sponsor a series of public meetings in 1991, under the umbrella of the Regional Development Initiative (RDI). The purpose of RDI was to develop proposals to halt sprawl and improve the unevenness of economic development. Forum topics revolved around social impacts, the economy, transportation, the environment, public finance, and management and governance.

The day-long RDI sessions on social impacts frankly acknowledged that social conditions, including crime, education, and racial fragmentation, posed a significant barrier to regionalism. SEMCOG offered participants a series of choices for action strategies and asked for a "vote" on each one. One draft strategy attacked discrimination, urging a renewed commitment to fair and open housing practices. Others suggested actions focused on inner-city conditions. Participants identified managing the rampant gun problem and improving drug enforcement as important alternatives. Fairly popular as well was a "regional attack on poverty," via a regional sales tax dedicated to job training and creating economic opportunities. To remedy poor race relations, the initiative proposed a strong effort to teach and celebrate multicultural education in the schools. This was not a strong strategy but was meant to join with existing efforts, such as the ongoing programs of New Detroit, Inc.[19]

Prominent regional actors were still not ready to accept regional governance. Governance proposals for consolidation or regional government drew little support at the 1991 RDI sessions.[20] But at least those sessions revived the possibilities for more extensive regional coordination. They also identified the negative effects of the lack of such coordination and highlighted the important role of race in bringing about such reforms. Clearly, according to RDI, greater racial unity was a part of the agenda for regional unity. The reverse is also true: regional cooperation is a necessary component of a race unity agenda, as long as the metropolitan area remains fragmented by race and class.

When David Rusk, author of the popular book *Cities without Suburbs*, addressed 765 registrants at the Greater Detroit Chamber of Commerce's 1993 annual conference on Mackinaw Island, he told the attendees that southeast Michigan would never solve its problems without increasing cooperation between city and suburbs. This would have to include, he noted, revenue sharing between the mostly affluent and White suburbs and the mostly poor and

Black central city; affordable housing programs across the suburbs; and regional cooperation on transportation, zoning, and planning. Someday, he suggested, the two poles of city and suburbs should even consider sharing political power. Mostly people listened seriously and debated his concepts enthusiastically. But Oakland County's White county executive called Rusk—respected author and former mayor of Albuquerque, New Mexico—"Marxist" for making such suggestions. The African-American head of New Detroit, Inc., judged Rusk's remarks "racist" for implying that cities with majority Black populations could not function independent of their suburbs. Perhaps Rusk's suggestions had come too close to the truth.[21]

Conclusion: Moving toward a Finer City

10

Evident over the span of fifty years covered by this book were the severe limitations of federal and local policies and tools, as well as the devastating effects of racial conflict and change on the task of saving America's central cities. Also evident were successive, often successful, and sometimes heroic attempts in Detroit to overcome these handicaps and to improve the city and its neighborhoods. These accounts become even more compelling when we reflect upon their highlights.

In my introduction, I noted how important it is for intellectuals to consider "models of possible worlds" if their work is to be fruitful. The last two chapters suggested some of the underpinnings of such models, although these lessons were often implicit rather than explicit. In this final chapter I hope to clarify some important principles for effective planning *and* for racial unity. In most cases these principles grew out of the Detroit experience, but they also stem from the wisdom of other scholars and the experiences of other cities. They offer some guidelines about how to plan for better cities and how to resolve lingering problems of racial disunity.

Policy and Planning

The unsurprising part of this story, the aspect most like the findings of researchers in other cities and in the nation as a whole, is that federal policy was tragically ill suited to the needs of the central city. Detroit's experience only confirms this basic truth. Yet reflection upon the events chronicled here suggests that it is possible to undertake steps that can help create a better future.

A Review

Consistently, throughout the period after World War II, the nation did very little to change the realities confronting distressed central cities. After a brief flirtation with regional reconstruction plans during the New Deal, the U.S. government settled into erratic support of regional planning agencies and cooperative bodies. Federal highway, home mortgage, and tax policies promoted an endless exodus outward. Simultaneously, the U.S. government tolerated racial discrimination in suburban housing programs.

Cities had to cope with weak, underfunded, and harmful public housing policies that sometimes left them with public ghettos worse than the original private ones. The urban renewal program encouraged cities to evict their own citizens, providing paltry relocation assistance, but did not give them the power to reconstruct anything. For all the effort to woo them, private developers were notoriously unwilling partners. Even central business district owners, primary initiators of the postwar redevelopment agenda, proved to be unreliable collaborators. The fact that Detroit managed to redevelop Lafayette Park, Elmwood Park, the Detroit Medical Center, and other similar projects is testimony to the city's tenacity.

One program component of urban renewal in the 1950s foreshadowed community development efforts of the 1970s and 1980s. The conservation program had the potential to help Detroit save existing neighborhoods and stem the flow of middle-class residents. In the context of federal and private incentives for movement outward and of racial flight, the weak conservation initiative was almost doomed to fail.

Also limited was urban renewal's assistance for commercial and industrial development. After 1954, federal legislation allowed some support for downtown redevelopment, but not enough to resolve Detroit's problems. The legislation was woefully insufficient to help the city respond to the collapse of the industrial sector while federal policies aided the flight of commerce and industry. These issues tempered the positive effects of economic redevelopment projects even after Mayor Young provided the strong local leadership needed.

The 1960s proved bitterly disappointing. The Johnson administration raised high hopes that the federal government would eliminate poverty and rebuild the ghetto. But the War on Poverty, the Community Renewal Program, and the Model Cities effort all suffered from weak and inconsistent federal commitment. Some important vestiges remained in later years, such as the War on Poverty's Head Start and community action agencies, but other promising initiatives, such as the joint physical and social improvement efforts under Model Cities, did not last.

With the era of Community Development Block Grants, the weak support of the federal government for distressed inner cities gained semipermanent status. Although CDBG was a reliable source of funds, given out via a formula that somewhat favored those cities suffering from distress, in real terms allocations dropped year by year. Other auxiliary financing programs, such as UDAG and housing subsidies, came and went sporadically, depending on congressional whims and presidential politics. Empowerment zones arose as an important new initiative in 1993, but their effectiveness was untried as of the writing of this book.

Given these federal policies and programs, it may seem futile to focus upon local policy. Indeed, federal policies wielded an almost overpowering influence over U.S. cities' fate. Detroit's tendency to build a few large inner-city public housing projects repeated trends evident in Chicago and Philadelphia. Detroit's approach to urban renewal bore striking resemblance to that of other cities, which operated under the same federal laws, allowances, and monitoring procedures. After the mid-1960s, the city continued to flow with the tide of federal policy. Community renewal programs, Model Cities, CDBG, UDAG, and various housing and redevelopment grant programs all arose on the national scene. Detroit, accordingly, applied for them and implemented them in a manner that was, on balance, hardly better or worse than in other similar cities.

Although federal policy dominated action, all cities had a certain amount of flexibility within their boundaries. The Detroit experience showed that local conditions were at least as important as national trends, since the city made unique responses to its particular circumstances. The 1947 Detroit Plan and antiblight enabling legislation eerily foreshadowed the specifics of federal redevelopment legislation. The local politics that propelled Mayor Albert Cobo into office profoundly affected the city's public housing policies. And urban planning activities, although funded in part by federal dollars, illustrated the potential for local autonomy and creativity.

For example, in the 1940s, satellite cities proposals would have allowed Detroit to expand its boundaries and keep middle-class residents and commerce. Detroit's mayor did not have the political power necessary to change state annexation and home rule laws, and thus conditions locked the city into boundaries dating back to the 1920s. Nevertheless, the concept had merit.

A more successful local initiative was urban planning, beginning with the 1944 postwar improvement plan but best exemplified by the 1951 master plan. That plan had shortcomings, but it was a powerful tool for redeveloping postwar Detroit. As the city's 1964 award for comprehensive planning confirmed, the plan laid the groundwork for postwar reconstruction of schools, parks, roadways, and other municipal facilities. The plan gave an overall vision and consistency to the capital improvements launched by city government and offered cohesion to subsequent redevelopment projects.

Other unique local planning initiatives included Ravitz's dramatic and creative but short-lived conservation campaign to galvanize community self-improvement, Blessing's urban design program, and Phillips's attempt to marry Black activism and historic preservation. Each of these initiatives was full of innovative ideas that, in another context or another time, would have yielded far greater benefits. Conservation's community organization campaign

Fig. 10.1. Chene Park Commons, in Elmwood III, another example of a series of fine apartment or townhouse projects in this former urban renewal project area. This builds on the traditions established by Detroit's planners in Lafayette Park and Elmwood I. J. Thomas, photographer.

proved to be a political liability, and the mayor quickly killed it. A similar fate awaited the urban design agenda, when it appeared ill-suited to the city's growing social problems. Phillips could not save his historic Black neighborhood from decline. Nevertheless, the positive effects of these efforts lingered. Community organization and historic preservation remained important movements within the city. And a visual tour of Detroit's redevelopment projects — Lafayette Park, Elmwood Park I–III, the Detroit Medical Center, University City—reveals the noble legacy of Blessing's urban designers. During the 1970s and 1980s, planners seemed to fade from the picture. Efforts continued in two branches of government, but division weakened them. The city moved away from long-range planning and toward project development. But soon it became necessary to turn once again to planning tools in order to take deliberate steps toward a better future. Corporate leaders put together a 1987 strategic plan that identified a number of key areas for action. The two branches that housed planning came together to adopt, at long last, an updated master plan. Community groups organized to develop their own plans and rehabilitate their own neighborhoods.

When Dennis Archer became mayor in January 1994, he confirmed the necessity of planning for the future. He convened a land-use task force, appointed a professional planner as head of the newly consolidated Department of Planning and Development, and gave her the lead in developing the strategic plan necessary for the city's empowerment zone designation. Once again, it seemed, the city was ready to plan for the future.

The overall impression that one gains from this account is of tenacity. In spite of counterproductive federal policies and unfriendly state laws, in spite of false steps and inadequate tools, in spite of political turmoil and social upheaval, local efforts continued. At no time during this half century did such efforts stop, although sometimes they slowed and became practically invisible. Someone was always trying to plan and develop a better city, and someone always will, for the foreseeable future.

Effective Planning

What can we learn from this history about how distressed central cities should recreate themselves? Should they pursue project development, federal funds, form over substance? Cities will always pursue project development and federal funds; given their political and economic contexts, they have little choice. The quality and effectiveness of that pursuit is what is at issue, as well as the beneficiaries. This study has made a strong case for the importance of planning for a better future. But that planning must be different from what was envisioned, for example, just after World War II. The basic components are the same: developing a vision, building support, setting goals, designing implementation strategies, seeing tasks through to completion. But the process must be very different. The following areas—concerning vision, social justice, participatory planning, and professionalism—begin to explain how.

Vision. A first principle is basic to human nature and human progress. Faced by dilemmas, whether of growth or decline, it will always be important to develop a vision of a better future and then to work toward making that vision real. Groups as well as individuals must have some idea of where they want to go if they expect to get there. For cities, this is the first and most fundamental planning maxim: Decide upon the desired characteristics of a better future. For that vision, recognize existing weaknesses, but also build on strengths, aim toward realistic and attainable goals, and work for the best possible qualities of good community life.

Implicit in the process of developing a vision is assessment of both the strengths and the weaknesses of the current state. This book has explained many of the weaknesses of the contemporary central city, which we need not repeat here, and has spent less time enumerating the strengths or assets. Yet recent studies such as one by Northwestern University have highlighted the importance of focusing upon a community's assets, rather than its problems, as a basis for improvement. Apparently distressed cities such as Detroit may have many such assets. Detroit's include strong public and nonprofit institutions, an accessible location, and a record of successful redevelopment projects. Some of its community leaders actively encourage citizens to think in terms of positives: the high number of people who are employed, as opposed to unemployed; the high number who do not commit crimes, who do take care of their homes, and who do not practice racism. Assets also include a network of nonprofit corporations and many opportunities for redevelopment on vacant sites.[1]

Not only must the vision for the central city expand upon existing strengths, it must also be realistic, building upon what currently exists, rather than scrapping everything and hoping to start anew. This means that the vision may be more modest than, for example, Blessing's vision of a "new city." But modesty has the virtue of attainability. To obtain a vision capable of improving current conditions, it will be important to build an action agenda that is both realistic and attainable.

The basic requirements of good community life are the same throughout the nation and in some ways throughout the world. Many urban visions are, therefore, not very different from each other. When city and community leaders sat down to develop a "vision" for the Detroit empowerment zone, as required by application procedures, the image they developed for one of the most distressed sectors of their city was quite similar to the image any other city or municipality might develop. Good community life means, essentially, life that supports families with adequate housing and community facilities, with sufficient economic opportunity for households to live comfortably and prosper, in an environment safe from crime, pollution, and other dangers. The hard task is to identify ways of bringing such visions to life successfully.

Historically, the tendency has been to attack one or two components of good community life at a time, separately, without synergy or conjunction: housing, or municipal and community services, or crime, education or economic development. Different experts focused on their segment of improvement, to the virtual exclusion of others. The lesson that should have been learned by now is that good community life depends upon all of these qualities. Yet it is impossible to be "comprehensive" in the sense of doing everything at once. Instead, visions of a better future must be holistic, requiring cooperative and simultaneous action on several fronts.

Social Justice and Equity. A second principle: Planning must depend upon social justice, defined here as fair and deliberate treatment of all parties but with a particular concern for improving the lives of the disadvantaged. This is very similar to the definition of social justice developed by philosopher John Rawls. Rawls argued that each person should have an equal right to basic liberties, compatible with similar liberties for others. He acknowledged that social and economic inequalities would exist, but proposed two conditions: that these inequalities be to everyone's advantage but particularly to the advantage of the least well off and that all positions and offices be open to all.[2]

Fig. 10.2. Street life and a street mural, "The Spirit of Detroit Never Dies," replacing empty storefront space along Woodward Avenue. Part of the visioning process for the future of Detroit has to take account of the irrepressible optimism that characterizes many of its citizens. J. Thomas, photographer.

Focusing largely on the second Rawlsian principle, concerning assisting the least well off, and upon the traditions of progressive reform and advocacy planning, Norman Krumholz has developed, tested, and promoted the concept of equity planning. A planner's version of social justice, equity planning is a conscious attempt to focus professional activities upon helping those at the bottom of the socioeconomic ladder. Nationwide, equity planners have begun to make small but important changes in the systems of social oppression over which they had some control. Such planners have improved choices for their city's least advantaged citizens in such areas as redevelopment, economic development, and community and municipal services. Such laudable activities have taken place in Cleveland, Dayton, Chicago, Jersey City, Boston, and San Diego.[3]

The story of redevelopment in Detroit confirms that it is indeed important for planners and other municipal decision-makers to promote social justice. Not to do so means to risk becoming tools of oppression, cogs in the machines of segregation, isolation, and favoritism for the well-to-do and for the majority. Such behavior also may create a backlash, as the oppressed turn against the instruments of oppression and seek self-determination or revenge. If one needs examples to frighten oneself into accepting social justice, such examples abound. But much more positive sources of motivation exist than these!

Several activities carried out by Detroit's planners helped promote social justice, although this was not always the prime motive. Today several redevelopment project areas provide neighborhoods with housing available for low-income families in complexes mixed by income and race. Historic and contemporary attempts by numerous neighborhood planners to organize, support, and help represent working-class communities deserve mention as do countless ongoing efforts to overcome financial disinvestment, promote neighborhood housing and business development, and rebuild distressed areas. Much of the planning activity carried out for Model Cities and the empowerment zone must be labeled, by default, equity planning.

The tasks for urban professionals are to embrace the concept, to see its potential as opposed to its drawbacks, to understand how to do it well. As the Detroit experience showed, making good, livable, and stable neighborhoods for working-class and poor city residents is a worthwhile activity but a difficult and challenging task. Society's failure to provide and support such neighborhoods is part of the continuing urban crisis. However, since continued decay and deterioration pull down whole metropolitan regions—their suburbs included—equity planning is actually in the best interests of society as a whole. Focusing on the disadvantaged has become one of the most important agenda items for urban professionals, not merely a sideline task for urban rejuvenation.

Because of this, an allied issue is the need to develop in students a passion for social justice. For some years I have participated in the direct support initiatives discussed earlier in which universities assist neighborhoods to develop their own plans. Urban planning students work for Detroit neighborhood organizations for one or two semesters, carrying out surveys, collecting ideas for improvement, finding funding sources. While this assists the residents, it also develops a sense of social responsibility within the students and helps "humanize" their view of low- and moderate-income central city areas. Similar efforts are taking place throughout the country, most notably in East St. Louis, Illinois, through efforts of the University of Illinois, Champaign-Urbana. These activities create attitude shifts needed in urban professionals of all kinds.[4]

Hopefully, in the future, urban planners will automatically act as "equity planners," almost unconsciously organizing their work under the assumption that they must protect the disadvantaged and promote their interests. And they will possess the skills necessary to convince others, including their political bosses, of the inherent value of helping to uplift those made low in the land.

Participation and Consultation. Working for social justice and equity planning is a fine and noble activity but only in the context of self-determination. The world of policy-making does not, and should not, depend upon the liberality and enlightenment of politicians and professionals. The more the affected populace participates in identifying the issues and developing solutions, the better, for it is their community at stake. Therefore, planning for a better city should be an inclusionary process, based on meaningful participation, and it is even more commendable if it springs from successful grassroots action. This principle makes "trickle down" revitalization untenable, even if done in the name of equity.

The practice of focusing professional skills on visible, high profile projects, while residential areas sink in the quicksand of social disorder, will not be effective. Instead, an inclusionary vision of a finer city must marry physical, social, and economic development in a way that positively affects the lives of everyday citizens as well as business, corporate, and institutional leaders. The best way to assure that ordinary citizens receive positive results is to involve them in the process of building solutions.

Although this can sometimes be difficult, particularly given the level of apathy and noninvolvement characteristic of today's civic life, we know something about how to overcome the difficulties. Much apathy comes from the public's impression that participation is not real, that political leaders and bureaucrats only pretend to encourage true involvement. Participation attracts more people when it does become meaningful and genuine.

Another difficulty is uncertainty about how to stimulate and utilize meaningful participation. Government agencies stumble over what they see as bothersome and meaningless requirements for public hearings and advisory committees. Those which attempt inclusionary planning are likely to experience conflict, distrust, and time-consuming negotiation. This, however, does not mean the principle is not valid, only that we need better means of carrying it out. One way is to explore new means of consulting about issues of mutual concern. Although some scholars have pioneered concepts of mediation and negotiation,[5] the need is to extend even further to discover effective means to consult and to carry out collaborative action.

Such collaboration is important because it may actually be necessary in order to carry out effective city improvement. Chapter 9 described a series of organizations that proceeded to plan for Detroit's future when city government would not. Of the groups described—ranging from corporate leaders, to city agencies, to community-based organizations—some of the most persevering have been the community-based organizations. That chapter told only a tiny fraction of their story, and only for Detroit. There are other examples in places such as New York's South Bronx and East Brooklyn, where community-based groups are busy remaking their environment.[6] Many of these groups are faith-based or connected in some way with religious organizations. Because the best of these groups have the pulse of the soul of the neighborhood, their solutions are naturally holistic, including social and economic development, housing assistance, physical rejuvenation, and spiritual uplift.[7]

It could be that the most important task for cities hoping to rejuvenate themselves is to tap into this grassroots movement, to complement, support, and stimulate the holistic efforts that such groups are already undertaking. In this way it could be possible to create synergy of action, such as happened in Detroit when community-based groups and the city joined together to apply for empowerment zone designation.

Professionalism. A fourth planning principle apparent from this account is that cities will have to put, and keep, their professional houses in order. The need for this is even more compelling in distressed central cities, which cannot afford incompetent leadership or ineffective bureaucrats. In fact, such cities need the most competent staff, because the challenges are so daunting.[8]

In some early years Detroit's planners were able to accomplish great things in their areas of expertise, particularly design, but also economic development and community planning. In spite of the fact that their skills were not always sufficient to solve the problems at hand, Detroit gained much from their accomplishments. In the years after that period, however, planning in Detroit suffered when it lost mayoral support and professional leadership. Plummeting staff morale was almost inevitable during those lean years, leading to even less staff effectiveness.

One lesson from that experience is that it is necessary to hire and support competent people. These people must develop the most up-to-date skills in their areas of service, upgrading themselves continually through staff training and enrichment, and cultivating good human relations and negotiation skills. The human relations skills are important because participatory professional activity, whether in planning or other areas, is extremely difficult, as is work in a city government under constant pressure to perform well in trying circumstances.

Furthermore, city planners must have the training, the skills, and the sensibilities needed to address today's concerns. Contemporary city halls still need staff to promote central business districts and riverfront development, to beautify city streets and design redevelopment projects, and to enforce the zoning ordinances. But staff should also know how to finance housing rehabilitation, encourage job training and entrepreneurship, promote community organization and development, and support a sense of community pride.

Professional staff must also exemplify the best of professional ethics, including honesty, trustworthiness, competence, and concern for the good of the polity. This question of ethics is a fundamental one and extends far beyond avoidance of dishonest or unprofessional behavior. It suggests, instead, that planning professionals will have to be the best people they can be, exemplifying the finest qualities and values that human beings can manifest. This is true in part because they must do a difficult and sometimes thankless job, one that requires true dedication, imagination, and skill.[9]

The danger in making such prescriptions is that the reader may find them too vague, too full of platitudes and dull suggestions. In fact, they have great immediacy, in part because they could be addressed fairly quickly, through hiring, promotion, training, and staff-enrichment policies. It was my brief experience as a consultant working as a staff member within Detroit's planning department, during the 1994 empowerment zone application period, that most vividly brought to life the importance of such prescriptions. For that position I had an opportunity to work with a wide range of staff within city government and various governmental and nonprofit organizations. Detroit has many excellent staff members in such offices as the (newly merged) planning and development department, planning commission and transportation, public works, and housing departments, many of them stalwart workers who manage to excel under trying circumstances. As in any office, however, those city workers with the finest professional and human interaction skills make the most difference in the successful prosecution of the mission of their departments, and those without such skills can severely hinder progress. A city loses when it does not set aside money to assure up-to-date training and to attract, and keep, the best possible staff.

Given the state of chronic fiscal emergency and budget-cutting in Detroit and similar cities, city staff will need special resiliency, and city administrations must provide special support, social and psychological if not financial. One way to provide such support is to restructure city government so that allied staff can work together, unfettered by counterproductive fragmentation within the bureaucracy (which hindered Detroit for so many years). Another way is to appoint competent department heads, leaders in their field, who know how to build team spirit and tap into the talents of their staff. But, whenever possible, cities must also give those leaders access to the resources necessary to ensure attraction and retention of capable people, as is beginning to happen at long last in Detroit's planning operation.

Race Relations

Even the best plans, the best strategies, the best staff and leaders can only go so far. Overshadowing the efforts of this half-century have been continuing social and economic dilemmas. Of all these, one of the most difficult has surely been racial disunity. The history of Detroit's redevelopment journey would have been entirely different if racial disunity had not been such an important and destructive subplot. As with our discussion of policy and planning in the first half of this concluding chapter, a review of the historical background of today's situation will allow us to suggest ideas for positive change, offered with what is, I hope, an acceptable mixture of creative vision and tempered assessment of reality.

A Review

Racial conflict afflicted Detroit even before World War II. Federal and local policies took an existing problem of racial prejudice and gave it the force of demolition and destruction. In the opening years of the public housing program, Detroit's Whites would not tolerate public or war housing neighbors who were Black. Stung by the Sojourner Truth war housing controversy and influenced by the bitter 1943 riots, the city's housing commission resolved not to mix the races. Detroit stopped dispersing public housing throughout the city, and instead expanded existing inner-city projects, cementing the structure of the inner-city ghetto. Suburban refusal to provide public housing confirmed this tendency. Racial prejudice kept public housing from being more widespread, less concentrated, and less identified with inner-city poverty than it should have been.

The urban renewal program brought another variation on the theme of redevelopment and race. As did public housing, urban renewal caused major hardships for the African-American community, destroying many existing neighborhoods and oppressing families and businesses alike. Combined with the equally destructive highway construction programs, urban renewal permanently distorted lives. Clearance failed to improve the lives of Black citizens and perpetuated their isolation.

Poor race relations affected redevelopment as surely as redevelopment affected race. White reluctance to live in integrated neighborhoods stymied the intentions of mayors, planners, and neighborhood activists. Conservation, an effort to save borderline neighborhoods, buckled before the forces of White flight. Neighborhoods changed racially, replacing the White middle class with the Black, and then changed again to low-income status. The inherent imbalance implicit in a metropolitan culture that freely accepted White families in suburban communities but set up legal and extralegal means of keeping out Black families was hard to overcome. These social forces counteracted whatever benefits redevelopment policies accomplished.

Even with the apparently biracial citizen protest movements against urban renewal, the shadow of racial conflict hovered. Outrage among African Americans and civil rights groups helped spur a citizen protest movement that strongly moderated the city's reconstruction program. Civil rights activists charged that the redevelopment agenda did not consider the needs and concerns of the Black community. The protest movements were, in some ways, an extension of the growing influence of civil rights groups and politicians.

By the mid-1960s, chronic unemployment, poor commercial facilities, and inadequate schools and public facilities stalked inner-city communities. Social and economic inequality did not die with the antipoverty and urban programs of the 1960s, which first increased expectations and then dashed them. The racial mentality exhibited by the city's police force only made matters worse. The central city became a virtual prison, constructed by the force of housing discrimination, spatially defined by invisible racial barriers, forcibly maintained by the police, and peopled with souls suffering from increasing poverty and deteriorating social conditions.

One response to this situation was the violence of the 1960s. Rooted in decades of social and economic discontent and racial discrimination, the 1967 civil disturbances worsened the conditions the city was trying to improve. Society's failure to deal with an agitated Black populace caused the physical destruction of the cities that planners were trying to build up. Almost overnight, the problems changed from overcrowding and passive misery to physical destruction of homes and businesses, newly enkindled racial fears, and additional impetus for White residents and commercial establishments to flee. Left in their wake were desperate neighborhoods that smoldered decades after the fires were out.

Coleman Young's election quieted the protests of the African-American community, which saw him as one of their own. Racial politics help explain why Young came to power and why he remained in office so long. They may partially explain why he distrusted urban planning, which he associated with the racial oppression of urban renewal. Furthermore, race helps explain why Young was able to pursue a redevelopment strategy so favorable to private developers and corporations, since his policies probably would have drawn stringent opposition from a conservative White mayor. Young carried out the "messiah mayor" agenda of relying on visible symbols of city progress to hide the reality of inherent social and economic problems, but he also nurtured his political base and satisfied his constituency.

Archer came into the mayor's office able to build on the considerable number of successful redevelopment projects built by Young, committed to bringing a new level of professionalism, but less connected to the formula of "racial" politician. He began to build ties to the city and region's White citizens and to the area's business sector, even as he organized to attack problems of chronic disinvestment. But he nevertheless inherited a city severely isolated from its region by discrimination, prejudice, disparity, and political division.

While it may have seemed that racial conflict diminished in the 1970s and 1980s, in some ways it had actually become worse. A more appropriate term than conflict is "disunity," which better describes the quiet and simmering distrust, disassociation, and distancing from mutual concerns. This new generation of racial disunity, which existed both in spite of and because of the presence of an assertive Black mayor, continues to this day. It must be exposed for the devastating effect it continues to wreak.

A Race Unity Agenda

Urban society in America is so severely fragmented by race that this situation deserves special, independent consideration. Even giving increasing attention to such laudable techniques as equity planning and consultation does not resolve the deep-seated dilemmas of racial disunity. How can we resolve this issue?

Obviously, it is not possible, in the space of a portion of a chapter, to lay out all the requirements for resolving this profound social problem. But the components for a solution emerged in a previous chapter. These components lay in three allied areas: discrimination, disparity, and regional fragmentation. Although each area of concern will be difficult to conquer, together they offer a plausible outline for a reform agenda.

Discrimination. Overcoming discrimination will be necessary to allow mobility for all the region's citizens, regardless of race. Discrimination has supposedly been outlawed, but studies show continued problems for Black home-seekers, as well as strongly prejudiced behavior by Whites and members of other ethnic minority groups. Although attitude surveys suggest that progress has been visible within the last few years, racial prejudice still affects accessibility to both housing and employment. If prejudiced action is not attacked, all people within the metropolitan area cannot progress, and perhaps the metropolitan area itself cannot progress.

Open housing and other civil rights legislation has not resolved all problems, but it has at least tempered conscious incidents of discrimination. All efforts to end racial discrimination and prejudice must take place in the context of enforced civil rights laws prohibiting discrimination in housing, employment, and public services, and flagrant cases of civil rights violations must be exposed and, if necessary, prosecuted. Enforcement, however, is essential but not sufficient.

Important battles have been won, and discrimination is largely outlawed. Yet society (as represented by the U.S. Supreme Court and U.S. Congress) appears to be moving away from aggressive, affirmative approaches to resolving historic discrimination. Part of the response to this environment should be to supplement the usual route of civil rights legislation and enforcement. Changes are needed in both behavior and attitude. People break no law when they move out of a neighborhood because another group enters, or when they refuse to accept members of another racial group as friends or as co-workers. That their actions are legal makes them no less effective in dividing the metropolitan area. Problems will persist as long as people have the freedom to express or act upon their prejudice, to seek homogeneity rather than heterogeneity, and to deny access to housing, employment, or community facilities for those who look different. Attacking both discrimination and prejudice, therefore, must become part of the race unity agenda.

Fig. 10.3. Part of the Motown Museum, site of the original studio of this company from 1959 until 1972, when Motown moved its headquarters to Los Angeles. The "Motown sound" was a major contribution by Detroit's African-American culture to the world at large. Part of the inscription reads: "Motown provided an opportunity for Detroit's inner-city youth to reach their full potential and become super stars." J. Thomas, photographer.

Several steps will be necessary to overcome such prejudice, all of which involve educating the general populace. Some people will never accept such "education," because discrimination and disparity are in their self-interest, and they see no reason to change. Social privilege has been institutionalized, creating a legion of beneficiaries, who fight for their privileges when they see them threatened. But many do receive periodic doses of diversity in race relations education, during their school or university years, in their civic or religious organizations, or in job-related training programs. Part of the agenda for such education should be to help people better understand the negative effects of historical discrimination upon urban areas, as with several examples presented in this narrative. Another tack would be to demonstrate and celebrate the positive effects of racial diversity, such as the rich cultural contributions made by African Americans and other racial and ethnic groups to the city, the region, and the nation.

Perhaps even more important is to understand how society has progressed once people have overcome discrimination and prejudice. Stories illustrating such progress can become beacons of light, proof that a better future is possible. Just as this account gave negative examples of racial discrimination, so too did it give positive examples of cooperation. One example is Mack-Concord, which in spite of unfortunate failure to maintain racial balance also experienced the power of cooperation, when urban planner Mel Ravitz first organized White and Black residents and watched barriers melt. An even better example is the experience in Lafayette Park and Elmwood I–III, which census figures show are some of the most racially integrated residential areas in the city. At first the city was afraid that the White market would not respond, but today's complex proves that racial integration can work.

These are older examples, drawn from this history, but there are more contemporary examples in many residential complexes, neighborhoods, and municipalities. These instances of diversity, harmony, and unity deserve examination and publicity. Someone in the region needs to devote attention to educating the region's population about the benefits of overcoming racial discrimination and prejudice. A previous chapter referred to the work of the region's fair housing center and of various fair housing organizations throughout the Detroit metropolitan area. As Dennis Keating has shown in his study of Cleveland, such organizations can play a significant role in improving race relations and are an important part of the whole picture.[10]

In Detroit, however, organizations such as a metropolitan race relations council have died for lack of funding and support. A few groups have taken up the slack, some of them faith-based. Examples of these in metropolitan Detroit are members of the Bahá'í Faith, consistent supporters of race relations institutes and conferences in the region over the past few decades. Their public conferences and smaller race unity meetings and training sessions have drawn multidenominational support and have upheld the standard of racial unity before the general public.

Much larger-scale efforts could only help, particularly if they target metropolitan school systems, which are educating the next generation. Part of these efforts must expose different races to each other, so that the hysteria, fear, and distancing that now come from both sides can be overcome. But this exposure must take place in a context of tolerance, with lack of judgment or superiority, from the majority culture, and a willingness to consider moving beyond past grievances, from the minority culture. For each "side" is estranged from the other, requiring delicate work to build human relationships.[11]

Disparity. Reducing the disparity between the social and economic status of the races is another crucial component of the race unity agenda. Different rates of poverty, infant mortality, and drug use are just the sordid tip of an enormous iceberg of disparity in educational attainment, income, employment, and life chances. Without a program of social improvement that addresses such disparity, the image, marketability, and prosperity of the entire metropolitan area will suffer.

As with discrimination, reducing disparity requires at some least minimal understanding of its origin and evolution. A more general understanding of these issues is important because society—made up of citizens who could support change—consistently fails to provide assistance on a scale large enough to make a difference. Disparity is connected to discrimination, since the isolation that was based on race was also based, in part, on income. Systematic, policy-supported isolation generated many of the problems we see today, according to Wilson and Rusk.[12]

But understanding is not enough; the general populace must also develop a heightened sense of social responsibility. This is a basic principle of good society that dates back to the beginnings of several religious traditions and many secular ones as well, and appears in many variations of "the Golden Rule": The fortunate should feel a responsibility to help the less fortunate and should act on this feeling. This is far different from the common practice of blaming the poor for their state of affairs or of sanitizing one's assistance by "giving at the office."

To see this most clearly, consider the opposite of today's state of affairs: Suppose major institutions, including corporations, churches, religious organizations, and clubs, were to adopt several substantial assistance projects for distressed communities, in rural or, particularly, central city areas. Suppose that each member of these organizations were to pledge to monitor and support one family per year. Suppose, furthermore, that all of these people pressured their political representatives to help end poverty and disparity among the races. A greater sense of social responsibility among the general populace would go a long way toward resolving today's problems. It is this mentality, in part, that governs Krumholz's "equity planning" concept, which aims to develop an active sense of social responsibility among urban planners.

While such efforts can only help, they do not answer the question: Help to do what? What exactly should such service activities accomplish? What should the government do? This throws us back to the fundamental dilemma of urban social reform: What will resolve the problem of urban disparity?

If a first principle for reducing disparity is to broaden a sense of understanding and social responsibility among the population at large as well as urban professionals, certainly a second is to improve key social and economic systems. Major social support is needed to improve the quality of life for inner-city residents. But how to do this is problematic. For some time people have debated whether to help inner-city people move outward, giving them access to suburban jobs, housing, and educational systems, or to improve their lot where they stand. The first is called the dispersal theory; the second focuses on development.

In the past, most policy initiatives have tried to bring development to Blacks in the inner city, letting the metropolitan area off the hook, absolving metropolitan residents of any responsibility for sharing their neighborhoods and places of work.

Mark Alan Hughes has suggested that neither the dispersal strategy, which advocates moving inner-city Blacks outward, nor the development strategy, which advocates assisting them where they are, has worked. Instead, we need a "mobility" strategy, in both the labor and housing markets. An effective labor strategy should disperse inner-city Blacks to suburban jobs, but also insure that equally qualified Blacks receive the same wages as Whites. This step alone would greatly improve Black income. A housing strategy would disperse inner-city Blacks into suburban housing, and also assure middle-class Blacks entry into middle-class White neighborhoods.[13] Translated to the Detroit metropolitan area, this would mean getting inner-city residents out to suburban jobs, continuing open housing efforts, and fighting for equal pay.

Others have suggested that basic conditions will not improve without broader actions which remedy deeply seated problems. The issues facing Detroit are systemic and global in origin. As Goldsmith and Blakely noted in *Separate Societies*, firms have adjusted to the global economy by moving abroad, reducing their unskilled work force, and relying more on financial than productive activity. These changes caused job dislocation and structural unemployment among the working class. Blacks were particularly hard hit because of their history of suffering racial discrimination and geographic isolation. Therefore Goldsmith and Blakely suggest that reforms must be undertaken in industrial policy, educational policy, and family support systems. Such policy initiatives would get at the roots of the problems facing cities, as well as greatly improve the lives of impoverished city residents.[14] Goldsmith and Blakely focus on national policies. But the local version of such a strategy would be to improve economic development, make more effective educational systems, and support strong and healthy families.

An aggressive industrial policy, according to Goldsmith and Blakely, should encourage a highly qualified labor force, support technological innovation and investment, and increase productivity. Improving the physical infrastructure would be an important component of such a policy. At the local level, improving economic development requires finding new ways to create a strong, export-based economy and enabling improved access to entrepreneurship for workers. One requirement is diversification, which means constantly searching for allied but new sources of industrial and service sector growth. Consistently, businesses have targeted tax and land policies as key barriers to prosperity and growth; these too can be reformed. The concept promoted in EZEC legislation—to promote "one-stop capital shops"—also has promise because urban businesses have long suffered from labyrinthine federal, state, and city policies.

The other two areas Goldsmith and Blakely emphasize are education and family services. They suggest reinforcing investments in education and in community-building, complementary systems that can markedly affect quality of life. Supporting good community schools would join with effective programs in two major areas: early childhood education, such as Headstart, and linking schools and work places, to make education meaningful and firmly linked to the world of work. In terms of family support, they suggest major improvements in social welfare policies but also improving family access to health care through an enlightened health care policy. In addition, they call for comprehensive family support for dependent adults.

If national policies in these areas had been better, the effects upon Detroit would have been positive. Consider how helpful it would have been for municipalities to experience more national support for meaningful and equitable education; this could have evened the chances of upward mobility and prevented creation of vast pools of obsolete workers. In the future, worker education is a key area of social reform that must be improved. The old style of general education, which assumed that a high school diploma was enough to gain a factory job, no longer works. It will become necessary to connect education with actual work experience in actual work environments, which is routinely done in secondary schools in Germany and elsewhere. Particularly important in the U.S. will be to reform inner-city school systems so that they serve as stepping stones rather than warehouses.

Cities such as Detroit have also suffered from the incompletely waged War on Poverty, abandoned long before it was won. Finding better ways to support poor families would have made a major difference in low-income neighborhoods and in the city as a whole. These are important, basic systems that observers are already realizing are firmly interwoven and interdependent. And yet, we have already mentioned a number of other areas of potential improvement, such as housing, community services, and public safety. The need is for holistic solutions, but each of these issue areas is complex and requires special skills and resources to resolve. How is it possible to attack all successfully?

Here again, we return to the considerable advantages of strategic planning, which is focused, and community-based efforts, which are inherently holistic. About strategic planning we have commented at some length in a previous chapter. Its basic lesson is to identify a few key systems, identify a limited number of important actions, and concentrate on these. Such an approach is the only way to function in the midst of such complexity.

Community-based efforts deserve a bit more comment. In the chapter on planning, we referred to several efforts in Detroit. Prominent among these was Focus:HOPE, the organization that began as a food distribution program and expanded into early childhood education, machinist training, manufacturing, math and English

Fig. 10.4. Rooftop detail of newly constructed Montessori Center for Children, sponsored by Detroit's Focus:HOPE, offers a visual reminder of the promise of racial unity. J. Thomas, photographer.

tutoring, and advanced engineering. Focus:HOPE is an important example for several reasons. One is that it illustrates the power of heightened social responsibility, in this case from its co-founders, Father William Cunningham and Eleanor Josaitus, and from their colleagues. In addition, the organization illustrates a holistic, organic approach to urban poverty, one that addresses the important need to expand economic opportunity; educate inner-city youth effectively, as a strategy for upward mobility; and simultaneously support families at various stages of development.

Conquering the economic disparity that plagues inner cities will involve considerable effort specifically directed at social uplift. Cornel West, perhaps the foremost African-American intellectual of this era, has become an important philosopher for today's Black community. It is his opinion that the fundamental "nihilism" which afflicts many low-income Black communities will have to be overcome.[15] This means that the concentration effects documented by Wilson must not be allowed to destroy the social fabric of the community.

At one time, African-American community leaders refused to acknowledge that any major internal problems existed. Their refusal was an attempt to undercut the larger society's all-too-anxious tendency to blame the victim, to imply that poverty and social disorder stem from inferiority or moral weakness, and to overlook racism as a factor in the oppression of minorities. But rising rates of teenage pregnancy and single-parent households, continuing problems of inner-city violence and social disruption, crime, drugs, and youth disaffection cannot go unchallenged.

We need effective ways to develop, particularly within many Black youth, a stronger sense of positive direction. Needed is more focused training in positive values, in conflict resolution, and in feeling a sense of nobility and self-worth—the kind of work that, in past days and in different cultures, was carried out by home, school, and religious institution.[16] It is futile to focus upon physical rejuvenation of the city while girls and boys die in the streets for want of viable solutions to the problems of drugs or gun control or for lack of training in human relations skills and violence prevention.

It would be dishonest to deny that these issues exist and deserve resolution, just because some in society misuse them as evidence that government should not intervene or that the problem centers around the moral failings of the poor. According to West, promoters of social justice must not concede dialogue about values and moral action to those sometimes identified as conservatives, many of whom profess spiritual sensibilities and yet, in contradiction, do nothing substantial to improve the plight of the poor.

This is another reason that community development will be an important part of the solution, particularly faith-based efforts. In city after city, including Detroit, community groups and faith-based organizations are providing innovative solutions for the problems at hand. Some of these groups are able to promote housing improvement and economic development projects but also to train children and youth and reinforce those positive values which still flourish in today's inner cities. While these efforts are not without their own shortcomings—some of which deserve special attention and resolution—they can play unique roles in the effort to reduce the poverty, disparity, and despair which continue to haunt inner cities.[17]

Broader geographic approaches are needed as well. In the last chapter we discussed the need to supplement a strategy of development within existing low-income areas, described in some detail in this account, with a strategy of mobility to communities of opportunity. The Model Cities approach to urban revitalization has continually focused on remaking the ghetto into something better. And yet it may be more effective to move low-income inner-city residents to areas of greater opportunity in the metropolitan area, either for work or for residence.

The Clinton administration has rekindled interest in residential mobility as a strategic initiative, building on the positive experiences of the Gautreaux Assisted Housing Program in the Chicago region. For that effort, thousands of low-income minority families who moved from public housing to more prosperous communities in the region experienced improvements in school performance, employment, and income.[18] These experiences suggest that eliminating isolation is an important potential solution to disparity and lack of opportunity.

Regional Fragmentation. And yet the fragmented metropolitan area nurtures and supports isolation. The major barrier is governance, but the issue is much larger: The governmental structure of metropolitan areas has allowed neighbor to become isolated from neighbor, race from race. Unless and until people come to see each other as equals, the problems of discrimination and disparity will not be solved.

The issue of governance will be among the most difficult to address. As noted in this account of Detroit's planning history, unsuccessful attempts to change the basic political structure of the northern U.S. metropolitan area date back to the 1930s and earlier. Recent attempts to open the dialogue of metropolitan governance have not yielded positive results. The Detroit region's leaders cannot merge bus systems, much less governments. The reaction to David Rusk's 1993 address to Michigan political leaders, referred to at the end of the last chapter, was symptomatic of the problem: Suburban advocates expressed no desire to give up their autonomy, and central city advocates were unwilling to give up theirs, too.

Prominent urban scholars offer few answers to this dilemma. One author who has offered specific policy suggestions is Rusk, who reopened the debate about U.S. metropolitan governance structures, in part by documenting how greatly regional disparity devastates regional economic health. Rusk lists specific steps that policy-makers could implement to mesh older, land-locked central cities more firmly with their metropolitan communities. State governments, for example, could empower urban counties or create newly consolidated regional governments. They could also improve cities' abilities to annex and limit the creation of new municipalities. Practical steps for the federal government would be to create incentives for metropolitan reorganization and to strengthen metropolitan requirements for federal grants.[19]

But the Detroit experience offers a cautionary tale about the likelihood such initiatives will succeed in older northern metropolitan areas. While the suggestions are good, little in the history of federal policy, or in the current federal environment, suggests that intervention would come from that governmental level soon. Neither does it seem likely that state governments—torn as they are by contentious legislatures, which dramatize very real divisions among metropolitan municipalities and non-metropolitan places—will step in to facilitate metropolitan governance. Practically every such initiative in Michigan has failed.

As we have noted, central cities with high minority populations are understandably loathe to give up political power. Robert Catlin addressed such a situation in his study of Gary, Indiana. From the perspective of Black political power, Catlin strongly attacked a particular proposal for metropolitan governance in Gary's metropolitan area, and he elegantly articulated the concerns of minority citizens. But Catlin and his clients were not completely opposed to the concept; they expressed a willingness to accept metropolitan governance, if proponents insured at least minimal autonomy for the Black electorate. Catlin suggested, therefore, that issues of minority political power could be negotiated.[20] The loss of suburban municipalities' autonomy, however, would be much more difficult to overcome.

As both Catlin and Rusk note, and as we have found in Detroit, less drastic (and less effective) means exist to reduce isolation. Many regional municipalities cooperate in several ways, through regional planning agencies or councils of government, regional water or sewer systems, or other services such as regional parks. These efforts must continue and expand. Other means include ties of friendship and cooperation between suburban and central city organizations and neighborhoods and joint efforts to reduce discrimination and disparity. The strategies listed for developing a greater sense of regional social responsibility can only build stronger regional unity. Occasionally, enlightened metropolitan leaders, such as Detroit's Mayor Archer, also help bridge gaps between city and suburbs.

In the final analysis, these are only palliative solutions. Signs suggest that the American populace is not eager to change metropolitan disunity, particularly in the North. Instead, individualism, home rule, and self-interest reign supreme. And so we return to the need to educate both the individual and social institutions in tolerance, in the practical implications of a greater sense of responsibility for fellow human beings, in the importance of social equity and human dignity. This will be a lengthy effort but will be worth the trouble. Together, individuals, families, communities, organizations, and governments must come together to plan finer, more unified, more equitable metropolitan areas.

It is a somewhat common practice to begin books with inspiring quotations. For this work, however, it seems more appropriate to end with one, at a point when vision is perhaps more sorely needed. This particular quote, by a Persian man who lived most of his life in the nineteenth century (1844–1921), comes from a book that laid out the essential prerequisites for civilization, many of which are not that different from suggestions we have made in this chapter. Although one of the primary purposes of the passage was to counsel against war, it is relevant for us because it reminds us that good cities are an essential part of good civilization. According to author 'Abdu'l-Bahá:

[Humankind]'s glory and greatness do not consist in his being avid for blood and sharp of claw, in tearing down cities and spreading havoc. . . . What would mean a bright future for him would be his reputation for justice, his kindness to the entire population whether high or low, his building up countries and cities, villages and districts, his making life easy, peaceful and happy for his fellow beings, his laying down fundamental principles for progress, his raising the standards and increasing the wealth of the entire community.[21]

Postscript

A lot has changed since this book was published in 1997, but a lot has remained the same. It is impossible to review all the changes that have taken place in the City in its planning and development efforts or in its region, even in cursory form. However, it is possible to comment briefly on major trends and challenges. In order to do so, I will pick up some of the same themes that the last three chapters of the original manuscript addressed. Three major areas in particular are important: changes in city context, urban planning actions, and future needs.

Changes in City Context

Both the 2000 and the 2010 censuses revealed major changes in the city and its region. The 1990s and 2000s had not been kind to the city of Detroit. The extent of population decline and industrial decentralization was such that the city became almost a fantasy land of ruins and vacancy, subject to the indignity of foreign and other "outsider" journalists and videographers descending to chronicle just how empty some of it looked. The U.S. Census Bureau found that population declined 25 percent between 2000 and 2010, one of the steepest drops in U.S. central cities, and much steeper than Detroit's 7.5 percent drop between 1990 and 2000. The number of households, defined as occupied housing units, fell by 19.9 percent in the decade leading up to 2010, again a steeper decline than the 10 percent loss in the 1990s. The news that one of the greatest industrial-era cities in the U.S. had dropped from 1.8 million people in the 1950 census to 714,000 in the 2010 census was a devastating blow to many city leaders and residents. It was a blow as well to the institutions that needed people in order to survive, such as the public school system, funded based on the number of children whose parents were willing to send them to Detroit Public Schools, and city government itself, which depended on property and income tax revenues that were plummeting. Yet anyone observing Detroit already knew long before the U.S. Census that the city looked much emptier than before.

Of particular importance during the 2000–2010 decade was the different racial nature of population decline. In previous decades whites continued to leave the city, but blacks were much less likely to do so. In the early 2000s, however, a lot of blacks left. This followed a national trend of increasing black suburbanization, a partial legacy perhaps of years of fair housing initiatives. Even so, racial segregation within metropolitan areas remained high. Detroit remained a majority black city, but the number of blacks had fallen 23.9 percent from 2000, a drop of 117,000 people. In the 1990s, the drop in black population had only been 0.3 percent, hardly any drop at all. The black suburbanization trend meant that more racial integration was taking place in certain suburbs. Other suburbs remained largely white, and the city largely black—hence persistently high metropolitan segregation rates—but also the majority race, blacks, had begun to leave the city as did others before them. The number of Asians in the city had increased by 2,300 from 2000 to 2010, and the number of Hispanics/Latinos had increased by 1,500. Welcome trends, but hardly enough to offset the losses. Whites, already much smaller in numbers than blacks, had declined yet again, this time by almost 41,000 people.

Much of the research needed to help explain the nature of these population changes has yet to be done, but some studies offer clues. A survey carried out in 2001 concerning quality of life had shown widely spread dissatisfaction among the Detroit area's central-city residents compared to suburban residents. The University of Michigan researchers considered how respondents rated quality of life at three levels: individual home, the neighborhood in which the home was located, and the locality in which the neighborhood was located. Because they had results from previous years' surveys, they could determine that city dwellers' ratings had declined since the mid-1970s. By 2001, on a seven-point scale, Detroiters rated their locality at a relatively low 4.2 compared to a higher rating of 5.24 from residents of the region for their localities. Detroiters were also not happy about their neighborhoods' conditions, rating them only slightly higher than they rated the city as a whole, and they expressed dissatisfaction in particular with the maintenance levels of other nearby homes, traffic, noise, and crowding. Many city respondents expressed a strong desire to move out of the city.[1]

Studies had also shown that racial prejudice remained a key factor in citizens' perceptions of the desirability of neighborhoods in both Chicago and Detroit. Carried out in 2004–5, this research, which used video footage that respondents rated for neighborhood desirability, showed that the race of residents photographed in a neighborhood influenced whites' perception of that neighborhood regardless of the income class of those portrayed. This built on previous surveys that had used responses to paper pictograms of neighborhoods with varying rates of racial integration to measure racial prejudice in housing over a number of decades. As late as

2005, whites were avoiding all-black neighborhoods and some were avoiding racially integrated neighborhoods; racial dynamics apparently still affected the housing market and caused turmoil in changing neighborhoods.[2] Hence, it is little surprise that published figures for metropolitan Detroit's dissimilarity index, a common measure of racial residential segregation, showed that in 2010 metropolitan Detroit had almost the highest level of white-black dissimilarity in U.S. metropolitan areas, a dubious distinction it had held in past decades. Metropolitan Detroit's white-black dissimilarity rating of 86.7 on a 100-point scale was surpassed only by the small metropolitan area of Gary, Indiana.[3]

The economic crisis beginning in 2007 contributed to population decline for the city and region as well. The mortgage crisis led to a wave of foreclosures everywhere, but particularly in vulnerable areas such as Detroit's neighborhoods, leading to more housing vacancies and eventually, if the City was able to raze the site, vacant land. Between 2005 and late 2011, mortgage lenders foreclosed mortgages for 63,150 homeowners in the city of Detroit, a city that only had just over 336,000 occupied housing units in 2000. These foreclosures had peaked in 2007 at just over 15,000 for that year, but continued to top several thousand units for each of several years after that. Tax foreclosures leapt as well. Some foundations and groups organized to prevent future foreclosures, but their task was enormous and their efforts by necessity limited.[4] Furthermore, the recession slashed the prices of homes throughout the region to a greater degree than anyone could remember. Suburban homes that were once unattainable for central-city families suddenly became easily affordable. When the price of a single-family home in a desirable suburb fell to the price that previously would only have been possible within the central city, moving out of Detroit became an attractive prospect for greater numbers of people and families. At the same time, the City was showing serious stress indications in its public services, including public education, but also other municipal services; for a higher tax rate than that of surrounding suburbs, citizens were often getting poorer service. They also paid much higher insurance costs because of crime and perception of crime.

Devastating on several levels, the economic downturn also pummeled the job market. The Detroit-Warren-Livonia metropolitan area, composed of six counties, had 2.2 million people in the civilian labor force in 2005 with a still-impressive 409,594 people working in the manufacturing industry. Five years later, estimates suggested that the number of people in the civilian labor force had only fallen by four percent for this region, but manufacturing employment had dropped by 27 percent, continuing a shrinking of this industry that had been taking place for a long time. The civilian labor force for city of Detroit residents during those five years fell by 14 percent, much steeper than the region's 4 percent loss, and not surprising given the city's population decline. Manufacturing employment for residents of the city of Detroit had fallen much harder than the region's to 25,174 people in 2010, 43 percent less than 2005 levels. Just after 2010, manufacturing recovered somewhat as the automobile industry picked up business. But this industry made only incremental gains in job numbers, which were unlikely to return to previous levels. Looking at class of workers rather than industry, those holding government jobs in the six-county metropolitan area had dropped only by 5 percent between 2005 and 2010, but in Detroit government workers dropped by 20 percent, to 31,229. This made government employment larger than manufacturing employment for city residents, an ominous sign given the non-export nature of government jobs. The government sector in coming years would have to lay off workers as well. The City of Detroit experienced a major fiscal crisis, and Wayne County and several area municipalities also experienced stresses that reduced their ability to provide jobs and salaries for area workers.

All of this had a devastating effect on the city's neighborhoods. Some collapsed altogether, leading to whole sectors of the city with residential blocks where only one or two houses stood instead of the previous 50 or 60. The Detroit Residential Parcel Survey, carried out in 2009 by a local consortium, documented over 91,000 vacant residential lots in those portions of the city that it assessed. Enlisted students and volunteers drove one city street at a time to tally field results.[5] They found that at least 26 percent of vacant residential lots were improved in some way, meaning that neighbors or others were using them for gardens, parking, recreation, lawns, or other uses, but the rest were not improved. They assessed housing as well, discovering many uninhabitable units. Their maps, soon published at their website, showed a city of vacancies.

Whole neighborhoods were disappearing. Prairie grass was growing where streets and houses and stores and community centers used to be. Neighborhoods that had weathered previous storms contained vacant or dilapidated houses where few or none had existed before, although some residential areas managed to survive nonetheless. Other once-stable neighborhoods sat on the fence, as it were, but once they tipped over toward abandonment it became increasingly difficult for home buyers to perceive them as viable places to live. Historic neighborhood institutions, such as community-based organizations and to some extent non-profit community development corporations (CDCs), were hard pressed to continue to exist, much less pursue a proactive agenda, in the midst of worsening environmental circumstances. Many CDCs that had depended upon developers' fees for newly constructed housing as their main source of income went out of business. Schools and community facilities closed in places where no one thought that they would ever close, as the public school system tried to cope with vanishing enrollments. Street lights stopped working in mostly uninhabited and in some inhabited stretches of the city.

As if these were not challenges enough, the city also suffered from a devastating political scandal that made local government appear paralyzed. Mayor Kwame Kilpatrick had succeeded Dennis Archer in 2002 and seemed at first to bring youthful energy to the city's top position. The business community supported him for two elections because of his commitment to continue to pursue a growth agenda for the central business district. But a series of scandals caused a new and unfamiliar crisis for the citizens of this beleaguered city. Starting with alleged wrongful firings of whistleblowers on City staff and followed by publicized text messages the mayor sent to his mistress who was also his chief of staff, the incidents soon extended into charges of official coverups concerning the firings and texts, and then later to charges of embezzlement for Kilpatrick and his closest associates. The entire incident cost the City millions of dollars in settlement and legal fees. When Kilpatrick refused to resign his position in a timely fashion, and at first no one seemed able to force him to do so, it became apparent that the City's existing charter did not make it clear how to hold top elected officials accountable. Kilpatrick's eventual resignation as a part of a plea bargain with the Wayne County prosecutor led to the Detroit City Council President finishing out Kilpatrick's term. Kenneth Cockrel Jr. served for eight months in 2008–9, and then voters elected Mayor David Bing. In the meantime, revenues continued to spiral downward, and deficits soon piled upon historic debts and deficits to create a major financial crisis requiring the State's intervention.

The resulting media circus exacerbated a still-palpable distrust between suburbs and the central city. The fissures included such matters as disagreements about regional support for public transportation, and unwillingness to invest in regional projects based in the city, with a few notable exceptions such as small regional millages approved by residents of three counties for the Detroit Zoo (2008) and the Detroit Institute of Arts (2012). The region had a high and increasing rate of concentrated poverty, a problem that confronted many other U.S. metropolitan areas as well, adding to the racial and political fragmentation.[6] At the same time, some groups made concerted attempts to bring city and suburban residents together, in a modest form of regional consciousness. For example, the Southeast Michigan Council of Governments (SEMCOG), the regional planning agency and council of governments, continued to function as a forum for research and consultation, although its voluntary membership format and suburban prominence continued to cause concerns. As another example, a grassroots organization that emerged in 1997, Metropolitan Organizing Strategy Enabling Strength (MOSES), was dedicated to organizing based on faith-based principles and congregations, and to bridging the gap between city and suburbs. MOSES also supported specific advocacy initiatives, such as Transportation Riders United, a group supporting public transportation, and the Michigan Suburbs Alliance, which encouraged intergovernmental cooperation among older suburbs.[7] Some people and organizations were therefore trying to gain better cooperation in the region in spite of great odds against success.

An elected Detroit Charter Revision Commission held admirably open and responsive public hearings and consultations about the specifics needed for a new city charter that built in safeguards against political ineptitude and, at the same time, made significant reforms in the way city government was structured. The new charter, which voters approved in the fall of 2011, set up a Detroit City Council elected partially by district to help ensure that seven of nine future City Council members would each be responsive to the neighborhoods that elected them. The new charter also made it easier to dismiss dishonest or incompetent elected officials.

Changes in Planning

In this context, planning and redevelopment were hardly the most dramatic stories in town. Planning as a municipal function usually operated in the background, helping to move forward projects that mayors approved and directed but did not actually, themselves, shepherd through the required paperwork, applications, grant applications, and financial packaging necessary to bring them into being. That took daily workers, in various departments, agencies, and firms, who were also concerned about location, surrounding streets, parking, zoning, and coordination among city agencies. But some planners and development specialists worked separately from specific development projects to help improve basic form and function.

The Mayor's Land Use Task Force that Mayor Dennis Archer had appointed in 1994, mentioned earlier in this book, was only able to create a broad sketch of necessary land use changes in the city. That small advisory group yielded to a much larger project carried forth in part because of financial assistance from the Kresge Foundation and other groups. Labeled the Community Reinvestment Strategy (CRS), this initiative involved voluntary work teams of residents and business owners from each of ten clusters in the city, with each cluster containing about 100,000 residents according to the 1990 census. CRS cluster boards, helped by local planning consultants, discussed future land-use needs for their particular cluster. The process yielded ten volumes of cluster strategies. The 1997 volumes are still available at local libraries and, as of this writing, posted on the website of the Detroit Department of Planning and Development (P&DD).[8] Although these had wonderful ideas about the future and about residents' needs, these ideas were not always tempered by market or political realities, and no mechanism existed for coordinating the clusters' efforts with each other[9]. To the great frustration of some participants, the CRS documents did not seem to lead to any tangible results. The City did not adopt them as policy, and they remained separate from the official master plan adopted in 1992, although the plan adopted in 2009 used some of the citizens' 1997 CRS ideas.

Evidence for the marginalization of the master planning process came when the planning division of P&DD created new master plan drafts in 2004 and 2005 that built on the citizen-driven CRS strategies but that the City Council, yet again, did not adopt. This was a stinging reminder of the detriments of the two-part planning system described earlier in this book. Essentially, the executive branch planners in P&DD were creating a planning document that the legislative branch planners and planning commission, Detroit City Planning Commission (DCPC), did not support or pass on to City Council to adopt. This led to a certain amount of frustration among planning division staff in P&DD, although the City Council adopted an essentially updated version of the revised master plan in 2009, when federal stabilization programs required such a plan. Looking at the City from the lens of master planning, then, the effort to create an organized and strategic vision for land use lagged. Other things were going on, however, including a much-needed revision of a woefully outdated zoning ordinance, a project begun in 1998 and taking several years after that.[10] Furthermore, a number of development projects were planned and built, and these were making visible changes in certain portions of the city. The 2011 charter kept the two-part planning system after revision commission discussions about the difficulties of changing it.

Although most city departments stopped publishing paper reports as the web made electronic reporting inexpensive, or because they were not required to, the DCPC did publish such reports for occasional years. These reports listed projects that the planning commissioners' planners worked on, and this undoubtedly meant that P&DD planners, particularly the Development division, were involved with them as well. The 1996–98 DCPC report described several projects, large and small. One of the larger ones was Comerica Park, a new baseball stadium for the Detroit Tigers. That report also mentioned work to support reconstruction of the public face of the Renaissance Center, renamed the General Motors Corporation Global Headquarters. Built as a fortress walled off from Jefferson Avenue and the riverfront, this building required significant revisions in order to make it open to the city and to the views that the river afforded. Modifications also required rearrangement of public roads near the site and, eventually, the project led to enhanced riverfront development that would extend from the GM riverfront plaza. Other projects mentioned included work to rezone properties necessary for temporary casinos and to help find permanent casino sites in the central business district.

Evident in that report as well was a theme that continued to emerge for several years. The DCPC was closely aligned with state-enabled local planning commissions and their functions. The commission itself, for example, held open meetings to which it invited the public. This required the commission to create a certain working relationship with residents and community-based organizations in neighborhoods. Hence it is not surprising that DCPC had a community organizing unit, which provided resources for helping to build community capacity in local neighborhoods, using in part federal resources such as the Community Development Block Grant program (CDBG). Reference to such community development efforts arose again in the 2001–2 report, and in the group's 2010–11 work program.[11]

The planning commission's 2001–2 report described its work on the Near East Riverfront project, Jeffries Housing Project West, and the Brush Park modified development plan, as well as continuing work with casinos. The Near East Riverfront was an effort to extend a river walk east from the old Civic Center, which included Hart Plaza, with the goal of eventually extending the walk east to the bridge that led to Belle Isle. Although eventually a Detroit Riverfront Conservancy (2003) formed as a nonprofit organization that could more easily move this forward, before 2003 the vision and the project were in the hands of planners and other departmental staff working for the City. The City had rezoned 57 acres in 1998 to allow casino development on the riverfront, but that plan fell through as the casinos built in other sections of the central business district. Rezoning for more appropriate uses for riverfront land took place in the early 2000s. The City also facilitated the HOPE VI-funded reconstruction and redevelopment of the Jeffries housing project, renamed Woodbridge Estates, located west of the Lodge Expressway. Other projects included an intermodal freight facility, modifications to the Brush Park redevelopment site (which led to construction of new townhouses and apartments), and enhanced code enforcement.

The Detroit Economic Growth Corporation is a quasi-public organization that has taken on several City development functions. It was its leadership, for example, that enabled the very complicated reconstruction of the historic but abandoned Book Cadillac Hotel into the Westin Book Cadillac. This venture included an array of grants, tax credits, pension funds, and private investment. The financial deal required a series of complex charts just to trace the complicated commitments.[12] The luxurious Westin Book Cadillac now stands as a magnificent testimony to the potential of the central business district's older, historic buildings to serve modern purposes. It is located one-half block from the Campus Martius Park, an award-winning small urban park nestled near a new Compuware corporate headquarters building.

All such efforts were in keeping with the vision dating back to the 1950s of making the central business district and its immediate surroundings a point of attraction for regional residents. Planners were serving as contemporary facilitators of the central business district strategy that had had mixed success throughout the twentieth century. Yet these projects and others, including the Ford Stadium (football) located and built next to Comerica Park, three casinos, the extension of the East Riverfront project, Campus Martius Park, and other similar initiatives, helped provide additional office, housing, and recreational opportunities in the center of a steadily decentralizing city. Such projects, from the City's perspective, were acts of self-preservation rather than lasting solutions to its problems, and in most cases they required significant investment of public funds. Scholars pointed out that stadium megaproject and casino strategies were palliative at best and could not help central cities remain viable, and surely they did not "save" central-city Detroit, but they provided at least some investment in a city that had experienced little investment from the private market.

This focus on those areas attractive to corporations and institutions, however, did not directly benefit the rest of the city, although some indirect benefits trickled down. As we have noted, during this period the city was undergoing a major contraction in housing stock and population. Public services were becoming expensive not just because the tax base was fleeing, but also because the fire, police, parks, and other departments had to serve large stretches of land in many of the neighborhoods where few people still lived, or had to travel or route services past those largely-abandoned areas to get to viable neighborhoods. Not enough city revenue existed to serve sparsely settled residents remaining on near-empty blocks in a city that contained only 40 percent of its 1950 population. When David Bing took office in 2009, he soon realized that the traditional way of handling the city's land and housing was not coping with large swaths of vacant land and abandoned housing. He began to work with foundations to put together a new planning initiative labeled Detroit Works.

It's too soon to judge the results of Detroit Works (financed mostly by private foundations). However, after a rocky start characterized by contentious community meetings, the initiative's basic message took hold: Detroit needed to make hard choices concerning which neighborhoods and job centers were viable, and which were not. Once the effort broke into a short-term and long-term phase, City planning staff concentrated on a short-term focus on public service improvement for certain key areas, and private planning consultants focused on long-term strategic vision and planning. The consultants drew up a series of technically proficient and well-conceived maps and documents that described current conditions and they suggested which neighborhoods were most viable for future investment. The consultants also made sensible suggestions, informed by community input, about appropriate strategies for different kinds of neighborhoods. They identified key job centers with potential for expansion and suggested strategies for economic growth in one of their strongest elements, and they addressed as well city systems, infrastructure, land use, and the environment. They created a long-range strategic framework plan that they vetted with area professionals as well as city residents in an enhanced participatory process.[13] Soon, news items appeared that suggested that City staff were making decisions about which community-based projects to support, or not, based in part on information gained from this research.

Future Needs

Understanding changes in context and in past and present planning activities sets the framework necessary to consider Detroit's future in other ways. What are the future needs of the city, and in what ways could planning and development help with those needs? Chapter 10 discussed such questions under two main headings, effective planning and race relations. Most of what the original book discussed then is still relevant, although changing circumstances have necessitated changing our understanding, somewhat, of what is necessary to improve the future.

Effective Planning

For this topic, the original four key areas discussed in chapter 10 continue to be important. Vision, social justice and equity, participation and consultation, and professionalism should indeed become watchwords, and the original text discussion of these values rings true for all four areas of concern. Yet the city and region's circumstances force a rethinking of what these values mean for Detroit.

For example, "vision," given the current context, is a major and necessary challenge. The task is not simply to develop vision, but rather to recognize the present realities and then develop a reasonable vision given the circumstances. One step for city leaders, in a process encouraged by the Detroit Works project, would be to abandon any thoughts or actions that presumed that Detroit could grow or be "revitalized" as a whole. In hundreds of "shrinking cities" around the world, city leaders and professionals are starting to let go of any preoccupation with "growth" and to realize that some places may never grow.[14] The task, rather, is to adjust to new realities, which requires a different approach compared to past efforts.

People are adjusting to depopulating Detroit neighborhoods in varying ways. In those neighborhoods that still have a critical mass, some people are using the opportunity of vacancy to create homesteads composed of several lots, where they can spread out and enjoy big yards for any number of purposes. In other areas, where no or very few surviving residents live, alternative uses for remaining land are necessary and promoters are planting and planning gardens and farms, but in other areas a return to nature is the most probable state. The vision for the city is not just of good neighborhoods, which are also important, or of a revived central business district or riverfront, which may indeed happen, but also of sensible use of the land, compact neighborhoods well cared for, and viable commercial nodes. The vision for the city, that is, should be of realistic adjustment to a much more spacious city than anyone anticipated, with a reduced tax base both protected and enhanced, and necessary public services provided well. The vision for the region still needs to be a metropolitan area characterized by greater cooperation than exists today, on several levels, but we will comment more on this topic below.

Social justice and participation are great goals—and always will be. Here again the Detroit Works process helped illuminate what is important about these topics. At early community meetings for Detroit Works, many residents focused their comments on the great injustice they felt over the environmental conditions with which they had to live, the public services not received, and the lack of attention the City gave their neighborhoods. They defined social justice as access to a good quality of life and some displayed little patience with the concept of future land use planning devoid of discussion of such needs. Yet City leaders had limited ability and resources to meet such basic needs. Department heads were present and they took names and addresses and promised to answer complaints, but the scale of the problems extended far beyond personal promises. The true social injustice in Detroit is the bifurcation that exists between city and suburb, since the city has indeed been abandoned to its fate in some ways, and between the wealthy and the poor, a variation of the same theme. This is different from residents experiencing some form of purposeful oppression and a city government oppressing them. City resources are limited, and City officials do not withhold them because departments don't know what the needs are or because leaders don't think it is important to meet these needs. New definitions of social justice need to take into account the prospects for regional equity, an idea that is beginning to take hold in many parts of the nation. When a city has hemorrhaged wealth and resources to its region, efforts to create social justice for meeting basic needs must tap the region.

Participation and consultation, likewise, are not the main issue, as they were in the past. Large-scale development projects that intrude on people's neighborhoods are rare if not non-existent for shrinking cities, and participatory strategies for those that do arise are pretty well established even if not perfect. Neighborhood planning must be participatory, but this has slowed as well as the housing crisis deepens. For other matters, participation breaks down when people do not see results forthcoming. The CRS process under Mayor Archer was highly participatory but appeared to lead nowhere. The issue is not just to make sure to involve people in consultation about the future of their own neighborhoods, but also to help set up situations where success is possible. Therefore, participation may be more tangible at the block or neighborhood level than for large planning initiatives. People want to see the results of their efforts, even if this is no more than a neighborhood watch group that reduces crime or a gardening club that grows and sells vegetables. So perhaps we need to adjust the scale at which we consider this particular value for planning cities such as Detroit.

Finally, professionalism remains essential. Our most vivid examples are of professionalism gone incredibly wrong. The Kilpatrick scandal, for example, and associated bribery and graft, were the extreme end of professional irresponsibility. These events were surely a good reason for all public servants to examine their professional ethics. More common than such extremes would be an agency that pretends to involve affected residents in a decision about their neighborhood, or the staff member who slows down work but makes sure he or she appears to be busy, or the person who does not even try to perform up to the standards the job demands. Working for the betterment of Detroit has become increasingly challenging, and much has gone wrong because of systems that don't work well, in part because of bureaucratic inertia and lax professional standards. For example, major problems have existed with Detroit's vacant land disposition system dating back many years, and these need to be fixed. Neighborhood stabilization money must be spent properly and promptly. Systems must work.

For those in the planning and development fields working in surrounding suburbs, regional agencies, or the state, the standards are just as high and in some ways higher. Urban planning professionals may have to help citizens see the importance of regional cooperation at more than a surface level. They may need to help educate suburban planning commissions and mayors about the value of well-integrated low-income housing, or of regional transit systems that serve both city and suburbs. They need to uphold the extensive ethical principles of their profession, even if to do so is not easy or convenient.

Race Relations

This subject—the need to enhance race relations in a metropolitan area such as Detroit—would require a separate book to explore the topic fully. In some ways the race relations situation seems to have stayed the same as before. Black-white racial segregation has remained high by some measures, for example, and the Detroit region remains fragmented partially by race. Surveys are showing continued tendencies toward racial exclusion in preferences for residential areas. Concentrated poverty has layered on top of racial exclusion to jeopardize high-minority communities even more. Organizations and movements for racial unity and collaboration seem palliative at best. Success in past efforts is hard to see.

The agenda for race unity remains much the same as it was fifteen or twenty years ago. It is important, however, to recognize changes in circumstances that may lead to changes in strategy. Black suburbanization has created more racially mixed neighborhoods in some suburbs than existed before. At the least, this movement should serve to modify some of the fragmentation based on race or political boundaries. A few Asians and Hispanics have moved to Detroit; in the case of Hispanics, their presence has made major contributions to the stabilization of sections of southwest Detroit. In some parts of the city, such as Midtown, Corktown, and the villages east of Indian Village, efforts to attract young white professionals have begun to succeed in small measure. These in-migrants may not show up in great numbers, but these neighborhoods are changing nonetheless. The trend of increasingly diverse metropolitan neighborhoods is taking place throughout a number of U.S. cities; one set of geographers has suggested the need to measure racial segregation differently. They discerned decreasing levels of low-diversity white neighborhoods in a number of metropolitan areas, including Detroit, between 1990 and 2000, even while metropolitan segregation experts were seeing little progress.[15]

Here perhaps is where, once again, we need vision. The old strategies for improving race relations have not overcome basic dilemmas such as political balkanization and deindustrialization, as well as collapse of key public services. Good race relations are no substitute for excellent public education for all, housing in viable neighborhoods, equitable access to transportation and public services, and jobs or the ability to become successful entrepreneurs. One of the most successful civil rights organizations in the region, Focus: HOPE, has got it right—it has led efforts that promote racial unity and it offers food distribution services. At the same time, and more importantly, it provides necessary education and training in subjects such as engineering to help young people living in Detroit escape poverty and learn an employable profession. Social justice, in this view, means economic justice as well as equal opportunity.

The lingering effects of racism and classism have done enormous damage to Detroit and its suburbs and to other cities like Detroit. We see the results of intransigence and disunity wherever we look. Any solution must overcome historical prejudices, non-cooperation, and unwillingness to implement necessary reforms. The path to a better future is increasingly clear. We need to take it.

June M. Thomas
August 2012

Notes

Manuscript Collections

Bentley DUL	Bentley Historical Library, Detroit Urban League Collection, Ann Arbor, Michigan
Bentley Kornegay	Bentley Historical Library, Francis Kornegay Collection, Ann Arbor, Michigan
Burton CRC	Burton Historical Collection, Detroit Public Library, Charter Revision Commission Papers
Burton DCPC	Burton Historical Collection, Detroit Public Library, Detroit City Plan Commission Manuscripts
Burton Mayors	Burton Historical Collection, Detroit Public Library, Mayors Papers
Reuther CCR	City of Detroit Commission on Community Relations Collection, Walter P. Reuther Library of Urban and Labor Affairs
Reuther David Cohen	David Cohen Collection, Walter P. Reuther Library of Urban and Labor Affairs
Reuther Detroit NAACP	Detroit NAACP collection, Walter P. Reuther Library of Urban and Labor Affairs
Reuther Reuther	Walter P. Reuther Collection, Walter P. Reuther Library of Urban and Labor Affairs

Introduction

1. My source for these principles comes most forcefully from the concept of equity planning, explained in Norman Krumholz's work (note 4 below) and from the social and economic teachings of the Bahá'í Faith. This faith teaches that social equity, racial equality, and the unity of humanity are fundamental principles of conscience.

2. David Harvey, *Social Justice and the City* (Baltimore: Johns Hopkins Univ. Press, 1973).

3. For an example of a normative theory of city performance see Kevin Lynch, *Good City Form* (Cambridge: MIT Press, 1984).

4. Norman Krumholz, "A Retrospective View of Equity Planning: Cleveland 1969–1979," *Journal of the American Planning Association* 48 (1982): 163–78.

5. Chester Hartman, "The Housing of Relocated Families," in *Urban Re-*

newal: People, Politics, and Planning, ed. Jewel Bellush and Murray Haus-kencht (Garden City, N.Y.: Doubleday, Anchor Books, 1967); Joe R. Feagin, *Free Enterprise City: Houston in Political and Economic Perspective* (New Brunswick: Rutgers Univ. Press, 1988); John H. Mollenkopf, *The Contested City* (Princeton: Princeton Univ. Press, 1983).

6. Robert W. Lake, ed., *Readings in Urban Analysis: Perspectives on Urban Form and Structure* (New Brunswick: Rutgers Univ. Press, 1983), pp. xiv–xv; David Harvey, "The Urban Process under Capitalism: A Framework for Analysis," in Lake, pp. 197–227; Feagin, *Free Enterprise City.*

7. Robert Dahl, *Who Governs? Democracy and Power in an American City* (New Haven: Yale Univ. Press, 1961); Floyd Hunter, *Community Power Structure: A Study of Decision Makers* (Chapel Hill: Univ. of North Carolina Press, 1953); Mollenkopf, *The Contested City.*

8. Stephen Elkin, *City and Regime in the American Republic* (Chicago: Univ. of Chicago Press, 1987), pp. 21–31.

9. Ibid., pp. 55–59.

10. Christopher Silver, *Twentieth Century Richmond: Planning. Politics and Race* (Knoxville: Univ. of Tennessee Press, 1984); Allen Jacobs, *Making City Planning Work* (Washington, D.C.: American Planning Association Press, 1980).

11. Douglas Yates, *The Ungovernable City: The Politics of Urban Problems and Policy Making* (Cambridge: MIT Press, 1977), pp. 34–35; Norman Fainstein and Susan Fainstein, "New Haven: The Limits of the Local State," in Susan Fainstein, et al., *Restructuring the City: The Political Economy of Urban Redevelopment* (New York: Longman, 1983), pp. 52–55.

12. Yates, *The Ungovernable City,* p. 88.

13. Arnold Hirsch, *Making the Second Ghetto: Race and Housing in Chicago, 1940–1960* (Cambridge: Cambridge Univ. Press, 1983); John Bauman, *Public Housing, Race, and Renewal: Urban Planning in Philadelphia, 1920–1974* (Philadelphia: Temple Univ. Press, 1987); Chester Hartman, *The Transformation of San Francisco* (Totowa, N.J.: Rowman & Allanheld, 1984); Robert Caro, *The Power Broker: Robert Moses and the Fall of New York* (New York: Vintage, 1975).

14. Catherine Bauer, "Can Cities Compete with Suburbia for Family Living?" *Architectural Forum* 105 (1956): 322, cited in Eugenie Birch, "An Urban View: Catherine Bauer's Five Questions," *Journal of Planning Literature* 4 (1989): 250.

15. Catherine Bauer, "Is Urban Redevelopment Possible under Existing Legislation?" *Planning 1946* (Chicago: ASPO, 1946), p. 70.

16. Victor Bringe, "Reporter's Summary," *Planning 1946* (Chicago: ASPO, 1946), p. 71.

17. Silver, *Twentieth Century Richmond;* Hirsch, *Making the Second Ghetto;* Carl Abbott, *Portland: Planning, Politics, and Growth in a Twentieth-Century City* (Lincoln: Univ. of Nebraska Press, 1983).

18. Hirsch, *Making the Second Ghetto;* Robert A. Catlin, *Racial Politics and Urban Planning* (Lexington: Univ. Press of Kentucky, 1993).

19. Friedrich Hayek, *Law, Legislation, and Liberty,* quoted in Elkin, *City and Regime,* p. vi.

Chapter One: Roots of Postwar Redevelopment

1. Quoted in DCPC, "The Planner," July, 1943, pp. 5–6, Burton Mayors, 1943, Box 2, "CPC" folder.

2. Mayor's Postwar Improvement Committee, "Post-War Improvements to Make Your Detroit a Finer City in Which to Live and Work" (Detroit: City of Detroit, 1944), pp. 30–31; International Union, United Automobile, Aircraft and Agricultural Implement Workers of America (UAW), "Memorandum on Post War Urban Housing" (Detroit: UAW, 1944), p. 11; "Problems of Large Cities," panel discussion, *Planning 1945: Part I,* "Proceedings of a Discussion Conference on Problems of Large Cities" (Chicago: ASPO, 1945), p. 15.

3. Carl Wells, "Proposals for Downtown Detroit" (Washington, D.C.: Urban Land Institute, 1942), p. 15.

4. Ibid., pp. 10, 20; John R. Fugard, "What Is Happening to Our Central Business Districts?" in *American Planning and Civic Annual* (Washington, D.C.: American Planning and Civic Association, 1940), p. 231.

5. Ladislas Segoe, *Local Planning Administration* (Chicago: International City Managers' Assoc., 1941), p. 224; see also Fugard, "What Is Happening?" p. 231.

6. Wells, "Proposals for Downtown," pp. 10, 20, 15 (quote).

7. Walter H. Blucher, "Urban Redevelopment," *American Planning and Civic Annual* (Washington, D.C.: American Planning and Civic Association, 1943), p. 159.

8. DCPC, "Planning Detroit 1944" (Detroit: DCPC, 1944), p. 6.

9. Blucher, "Urban Redevelopment," p. 159.

10. DCPC, "Planning Detroit 1944," p. 6.

11. James Sweinhart, "What Detroit's Slums Cost Its Taxpayers" (Detroit: Detroit News Reprints, 1946); Critique in John P. Dean, "The Myths of Housing Reform," in *Urban Renewal: People, Politics, and Planning,* ed. Jewel Bellush and Murray Hausknecht, pp. 25–35.

12. *Michigan Chronicle,* January 20, 1945, p. 1.

13. U.S. Home and Housing Finance Agency, mimeo report, January 21, 1948, p. 5, Burton Mayors, 1948, Box 4, "Housing Commission (1)" folder.

14. Walter White and Thurgood Marshall, "What Caused the Detroit Riot? An Analysis" (New York: National Association for the Advancement of Colored People, circa 1943), pp. 5–14.

15. Mayor's Postwar Improvement Committee, "Postwar Improvements," p. 13.

16. DCPC, "The Planner," March, 1942, p. 2, Burton Mayors, 1942, Box 2, "CPC (2)" folder; see also "Third Report of the Regional Defense Planning Committee of the Detroit Metropolitan Area," June 1, 1943, Burton Mayors, 1943, Box 2, "CPC" folder.

17. Eugenie Birch, "Woman-made America: The Case of Early Public Housing Policy," in *The American Planner: Biographies and Recollections,* ed. Donald A. Krueckeberg (New York: Methuen, 1983), pp. 149–75; Lawrence M. Friedman, *Government and Slum Housing: A Century of Frustration* (Chicago: Rand McNally, 1968), p. 100 (quotes).

18. Birch, "Woman-made America," pp. 165, 170.

19. Kenneth T. Jackson, *Crabgrass Frontier: The Suburbanization of the United States* (New York: Oxford Univ. Press, 1985), p. 221; Friedman, *Government and Slum Housing,* pp. 103–07.

20. Herbert Norman, Jr., "Crime in Detroit Public Housing," Ph.D. diss., Michigan State Univ., 1990, pp. 164–70.

21. Carl L. Bradt, letter to Lent Upson, August 2, 1938, Burton Mayors, 1938, Box 6, "Housing Commission (June)" folder; George Edwards, letter

to C. H. Veale, November 19, 1940, Burton Mayors, 1940, Box 4, "Housing Commission (1)" folder.

22. George Edwards, letter to James A. Urich, July 3, 1940, Burton Mayors, 1940, Box 4, "Housing Commission" folder.

23. George Emery, "An Analysis of Housing and Labor in Relation to the War Production Program in the Detroit Industrial Area as of December 1, 1942," Burton Mayors, 1942, Box 2, "CPC (1)" folder.

24. Lowell Carr and James Stermer, *Willow Run: A Study of Industrialization and Cultural Inadequacy* (New York: Harper & Bros., 1952), p. 68.

25. Carl Bradt, letter to Douglas Martin, March 5, 1940, Burton Mayors, 1940, Box 4, "Housing Commission (2)" folder; Bradt, letter to Nathan Straus, September 30, 1938, Burton Mayors, 1938, Box 6, "Housing Commission (June)" folder.

26. Donald R. Deskins, Jr., *Residential Mobility of Negroes in Detroit, 1837–1965*, Michigan Geographical Publication no. 5 (Ann Arbor: Univ. of Michigan, Department of Geography, 1972), pp. 103–05.

27. M. J. Morrison, letter to Mayor Richard Reading, November 2, 1938, Burton Mayors, 1938, Box 6, "Interracial" folder; Richard Thomas, *Life for Us Is What We Make It* (Bloomington: Indiana Univ. Press, 1992), p. 93.

28. Hirsch, *Making the Second Ghetto*, p. 41.

29. "Report from Guy Larcom re: Sojourner Truth," March 5, 1942, Burton Mayors, 1943, Box 5, "Housing Commission (1)" folder; Hon. Rudolph G. Tenerowicz, speech to U.S. House of Representatives, February 27, 1942, Burton Mayors, 1942, Box 5, "Detroit Housing Commission" folder.

30. Robert Conot, *American Odyssey* (Detroit: Wayne State Univ. Press, 1986), pp. 362–63 (quote).

31. Louise Nathan, January 11, 1937, letter to Richard Reading, Burton Mayors, 1938, Box 6, "Housing Commission" folder; Detroit Housing Commission minutes, January 3, 1938, ibid.

32. Detroit Urban League, "The Victory Pattern in Public Housing," April 29, 1943, Burton Mayors, 1943, Box 5, "Housing Commission (2)" folder.

33. Mayor's Interracial Committee, minutes, April 21, 1952, Burton Mayors, 1952, Box 3, "Interracial Committee" folder, p. 2; *Michigan Chronicle*, October 15, 1955, p. 10; David Greenstone, "A Report on the Politics of Detroit," (Cambridge, Mass.: Joint Center for Urban Studies, 1961), pp. v–40.

34. *Michigan Chronicle*, January 20, 1945, p. 1.

35. Hirsch, *Making the Second Ghetto*, pp. 122, 185, 224.

36. Bauman, *Public Housing*, pp. 125, 119 (quote), 119–35.

37. Bauman, *Public Housing*; Hirsch, *Making the Second Ghetto*; Jackson, *Crabgrass Frontier*.

38. Lewis Mumford, *The Urban Prospect* (New York: Harcourt Brace Jovanovich, 1968), pp. 153–66, 178; see also Roy Lubove, *The Urban Community: Housing and Planning in the Progressive Era* (Englewood Cliffs, N.J.: Prentice-Hall, 1967), pp. 17–22, and Mel Scott, *American City Planning since 1890* (Berkeley: Univ. of California Press, 1971), pp. 292–93.

39. Lewis Mumford, "The Garden City Idea and Modern Planning," introduction to Ebenezer Howard, *Garden Cities of Tomorrow* (Cambridge, Mass.: MIT Press, 1965), pp. 29–40.

40. Melvin R. Levin, *Planning in Government: Shaping Programs That Succeed* (Washington, D.C.: American Planning Association Press, 1987), p. 33; Lewis Hill, "Lewis Mumford's Ideas on the City," *Journal of the American Planning Association* 51 (1985): 407–21.

41. National Resources Committee, "Our Cities: Their Role in the National Economy," Report of the Urbanism Committee (Washington, D.C.: U.S. Government Printing Office, 1937), p. 80; see also Scott, *American City Planning,* pp. 310–16, 342–48.

42. William N. Cassella, Jr., "Regional Planning and Governance: History and Politics," in *Regional Planning: Evolution, Crisis and Prospects,* ed. Gill C. Lim (Totowa, N.J.: Allanheld, Osmun, 1983), pp. 17–28.

43. Regional Defense Planning Committee of the Detroit Metropolitan Area minutes, May 4, 1942, p. 4, Burton Mayors, 1942, Box 2, "CPC (1)" folder.

44. Carr and Stermer, *Willow Run,* pp. 65, 85.

45. Scott, *American City Planning,* p. 394.

46. DCPC, "The Planner," March, 1942, p. 4.

47. DCPC, "Twenty-Fourth Annual Report: 1942," p. 3.

48. DCPC, "The Planner," February, 1944, Burton Mayors, 1944, Box 2, "CPC (1)" folder.

49. DCPC, "Progress Report on City Expansion Study," June 26, 1947, Burton Mayors, 1947, Box 1, "CPC" folder (quotes from pp. 1, 2, 3, map on p. 4).

50. DCPC minutes, November 21, 1946, pp. 2, 4 (quotes), Burton Mayors, 1946, Box 2, "CPC" folder; DCPC, "Planning Detroit 1944," pp. 21–26.

51. See 1909 Public Act 279. Also see State Board of Registration for Professional Community Planners, *Michigan Laws Relating to Planning* (E. Lansing: Institute for Community Development and Services, Michigan State Univ, circa 1974), p. 23; John Bauckham, "A Capsule Summary of Municipal Annexation Proceedings," *Michigan Township News,* May 1983, pp. 20–22.

52. Conot, *American Odyssey,* p. 403.

53. Bruce Van Dusen, "Detroit Considers Plan for Suburb Satellite," *Detroit News,* October 1, 1967, in "Regional Planning" vertical file of Detroit Municipal Reference Library, Detroit Public Library.

54. R. D. Norton, *City Life-Cycles and American Urban Policy* (New York: Academic Press, 1979); "Clinic: Annexation," *Planning 1952* (Chicago: ASPO, 1952), pp. 108–13; Victor Jones, "Annexation," in *The Future of Cities and Urban Redevelopment,* ed. Coleman Woodbury (Chicago: Univ. of Chicago Press, 1953), pp. 550–72.

55. Citizens' Housing and Planning Council of Detroit, "Annual Report, 1947," p. 17; DCPC minutes, November 6, 1947, Burton Mayors, 1947, Box 1, "CPC" folder; Charles A. Blessing, letter to W. S. Poindexter, September 25, 1956, Burton Mayors 1956, Box 2, "CPC" folder.

56. UAW, "Memorandum," p. 9.

57. Ibid., p. 15.

58. Ibid., p. 100.

Chapter Two: Postwar Planning

1. Christine Boyer, *Dreaming the Rational City: The Myth of American City Planning* (Cambridge: MIT Press, 1986), pp. 222–25; Harland Bartholomew, "The Trend of Modern Planning," *American Civic Annual,* IV (1932), p. 179.

2. Flavel Shurtleff, "What the Plan Commissions Are Doing," *American Civic Annual,* IV (1932), p. 178.

3. "Statement of Walter Blucher, Executive Director, ASPO, January 20, 1944," U.S. House of Representatives, *Postwar Planning No. 2. Hearings before*

the Committee on Public Buildings and Grounds, 78th Congress, 1943–44, p. 204.

4. Alfred Bettman, Chairman, City Planning Commission, Cincinnati, Ohio, February 9, 1944," statement to U.S. House of Representatives, *Postwar Planning No. 2. Hearings before the Committee on Public Buildings and Grounds,* 78th Congress, 1943–44, p. 510.

5. DCPC, "Annual Report of the City Plan Commission, 1927" (Detroit: DCPC, 1927), p. 3.

6. DCPC, "A Building Zone Plan" (Detroit: DCPC, 1919), and "Carrying out the Master Plan: Report to the Honorable Common Council of the City of Detroit by Its Advisory Committee," in City Planning vertical file of Detroit Public Library, Municipal Reference Library, October 2, 1925, p. 15.

7. Segoe, *Local Planning Administration,* p. 345.

8. DCPC, "Annual Report 1940" (Detroit: DCPC, 1940), pp. 2, 7.

9. George Emery, letter to Guy Mahon, August 6, 1941, Burton Mayors, 1941, Box 2, "CPC" folder.

10. "Newsletter from the Citizens' Housing and Planning Council of Detroit," May, 1943, pp. 1–6, Burton Mayors, 1943, Box 5, "Housing Commission 2" folder; Caro, *The Power Broker.*

11. "Expert Calls City Laggard in Planning," *Detroit Free Press* clipping, no date, no page, in Burton DCPC, Box 16, "News Clippings 1943–44" folder; and DCPC, "The Planner," June, 1943, p. 8.

12. DCPC,minutes, April 25, 1940, p. 3, and March 20, 1941, p. 1, Burton Mayors, 1940, Box 2, "CPC" folder; see also Scott, *American City Planning,* p. 400.

13. George Emery, letter to Guy Mahon, August 6, 1941.

14. DCPC, "Twenty-third Annual Report, 1941," p. 11; George Emery, letter to Guy Mahon, August 6, 1941.

15. City of Detroit, "The Detroit Plan," February, 1947, p. 2.

16. *Detroit Free Press,* January 1, 1946, p. 9; Herschel Berman, "Who's Who and Why," *Detroit News,* October 17, 1944, no page, in Burton DCPC, Box 16, "News Clippings 1943–44" folder.

17. "New Planning Setup Asked," *Detroit News* clipping, no date, no page, in Burton DCPC, Box 16, "News Clippings 1943–44" folder.

18. Edward Walker, letter to Frederick Storrer, August 25, 1946, Burton Mayors, 1946, Box 2, "DCPC" folder.

19. Segoe, *Local Planning Administration,* pp. 43, 46.

20. *Regional Survey of New York and Its Environs,* Vol. VII (1929), p. 338, reproduced in Segoe, *Local Planning Administration,* p. 511.

21. Ibid., pp. 419, 510–14.

22. DCPC, *Detroit Master Plan,* 1951; Merle Hendrickson, interview, March 9, 1987.

23. Segoe, *Local Planning Administration,* p. 346; Merle Hendrickson, interview.

24. "New Planning Setup Asked," *Detroit News* clipping, no date, no page, in Burton DCPC, Box 16, "News Clippings 1943–44" folder.

25. City of Detroit, "Master Plan Report No. 5: Proposed Generalized Land Use Plan," May, 1947, p. 22.

26. Ibid., p. 18.

27. Ibid., pp. 7, 25–26.

28. "Statement of Alfred Bettman," p. 519.

29. Scott, *American City Planning,* p. 452.

30. DCPC, "Planning Detroit 1944," p. 21.

31. Mark Gelfand, *A Nation of Cities: The Federal Government and Urban American, 1933–1965* (New York: Oxford Univ. Press, 1975), p. 117.

32. Ibid., pp. 135–41.

33. John Petrick, letter to Edward Jeffries, July 31, 1946, Burton Mayors, 1946, Box 4, "Housing Commission" folder.

34. Detroit Housing Commission, "Monthly Report to the Commissioners," September, 1945, p. 7, Burton Mayors, 1945, Box 3, "Housing Commission" folder; George Emery, letter to Edward Jeffries, Jr., March 5, 1945, Burton Mayors, 1945, Box 2, "DCPC" folder.

35. UAW, "Memorandum," pp. 58–71, quote on p. 71.

36. DCPC minutes, February 1, 1945, and February 15, 1945; Conot, *American Odyssey,* p. 517.

37. DCPC minutes, April 26, 1945, December 19, 1946, February 15, 1945, February 22, 1945; Act 344 in Michigan Department of Economic Development, *Michigan Laws Related to Local Planning* (Lansing: Michigan Department of Economic Development, 1949), pp. 122–27.

38. Press release from Mayor Jeffries office, no date (circa 1944), Burton Mayors 1944, Box 2, "DCPC 1" folder; see also "Problems of Large Cities," p. 51.

39. Herschel Berman, "Who's Who and Why," *Detroit News,* October 17, 1977, no page, in Burton DCPC, Box 16, "News Clippings 1943–44" folder.

40. Bauman, *Public Housing, Race, and Renewal,* pp. 90–93.

41. "Problems of Large Cities," p. 52.

42. DCPC minutes, October 22, 1948, p. 3.

43. DCPC, "Master Plan Technical Report on Areas Proposed for Redevelopment," by Donald Monson, August, 1947, p. 10; Emery's comment, DCPC minutes, October 22, 1948, p. 3.

44. Hirsch, *Making the Second Ghetto,* p. 112.

45. City of Detroit, "The Detroit Plan," p. 2.

46. Charles Edgecomb, "Urban Redevelopment Is Under Way," *Planning 1947* (Chicago: ASPO, 1947), p. 153.

47. Ibid.

48. Bauer, "Is Urban Redevelopment Possible," pp. 64, 67.

49. Tracy B. Auger, "City Planning and Housing—May They Meet Again," *American Planning and Civic Annual,* 1940, p. 227.

Chapter Three: Eliminating Slums and Blight

1. Gelfand, *A Nation of Cities,* pp. 141–47; U.S. Congress, *Evolution of Role of the Federal Government in Housing and Community Development: A Chronology of Legislative and Selected Executive Actions. 1892–1974,* 94th Cong., 1st sess. (Washington, D.C.: U.S. Government Printing Office, 1975), pp. 25–26.

2. Ibid., pp. 141, 154.

3. *Michigan Chronicle,* August 18, 1945, p. 2, and May 31, 1947, p. 6; William L. Price, "Report of the Housing Situation as It Affects the Community in the Gratiot Redevelopment Area," March 20, 1951, p. 2, Burton Mayors, 1951, Box 4, "Housing Commission" folder.

4. George Duggar, "The Relation of Local Government Structure to Urban Renewal," in *Urban Renewal,* ed. Jewel Bellush and Murray Hausknecht, p. 185.

5. Ed Hustoles, interview, February 4, 1987; DCPC, "Detroit: Achievement Through Planning," July 1965, submitted originally in May 1964 for the AIP Honors Award in Comprehensive Planning, p. 5.

6. Roger Montgomery, "Improving the Design Process in Urban Renewal," *Journal of the American Institute of Planners* 31 (February, 1965): 12 (Montgomery), 11 (Smithson).

7. Bauman, *Public Housing,* pp. 95–96; *Detroit Free Press,* August 1, 1945, p. 2; *Detroit Tribune,* December 4, 1948, p. 4; *Michigan Chronicle,* October 13, 1945, p. 13, May 31, 1947, p. 6, and July 19, 1947, p. 6.

8. Louis Wirth, letter to Albert Cobo, April 7, 1950, Burton Mayors, 1950, Box 5, "Interracial Committee" folder.

9. Hirsch, *Making the Second Ghetto,* pp. 112–20, 129; DeHart Hubbard, letter to "Key People," June 23, 1945, Bentley DUL, pp. 5–12.

10. Merle Hendrickson, interview, March 9, 1987.

11. "Problems of Large Cities," p. 52.

12. Melvin Holli and Peter Jones, *Biographical Dictionary of American Mayors, 1820–1980* (Westport, Conn.: Greenwood , 1981), pp. 69–70; Conot, *American Odyssey,* pp. 403–5.

13. *Detroit News,* November 15, 1949, clipping in Bentley DUL 5-31; *Detroit Free Press,* January 3, 1950, p. A-8, and March 12, 1950, p. A-6; *Michigan Chronicle,* January 7, 1950, p. 3.

14. *Michigan Chronicle,* February 11, 1950, p. 4; "Statement by Orville Linck, Chairman, Detroit Chapter, Americans for Democratic Action," in a public hearing before the Common Council, July 11, 1950, Burton Mayors, 1950, Box 5, "Housing Commission" folder.

15. "Housing—Supplemental Report," May 11, 1950, Burton Mayors, 1950, Box 5, "Housing Commission" folder, p. 3; Conot, *American Odyssey,* p. 444.

16. Maceo Grutcher, Beatrice Johnson, and Walker Smith, letter to Allen Finley, May 6, 1950, Burton Mayors, 1955, Box 5, "Housing Commission" folder; see also City of Detroit, Housing Commission, "Planning Data: Gratiot Redevelopment (HHFA DM-1)," February 26, 1951, Bentley DUL A5-25.

17. Ibid.; Robert J. Mowitz and Deil S. Wright, *Profile of a Metropolis: A Case Book* (Detroit: Wayne State Univ., 1962), pp. 30–34, 43–44.

18. *Detroit Tribune,* September 2, 1950, p. 1.

19. Price, "Report of the Housing Situation," attachment entitled Survey Findings, pp. 5, 6.

20. J. Lawrence Duncan, letter to John Dancy, February 21, 1951, Bentley DUL 6-8; Mowitz and Wright, *Profile of a Metropolis,* pp. 38–39.

21. Detroit Urban League, "The Detroit Urban League's Brief on Urban Renewal Activity in the City of Detroit," November 29, 1956, pp. 9, 10 (quote), Bentley DUL, A8-28.

22. Shirley Terreberry, "Household Relocation: Residents' Views," in Eleanor Wolf and Charles N. Lebeaux, together with Shirley Terreberry and Harriet Saperstein, *Change and Renewal in an Urban Community: Five Case Studies of Detroit* (New York: Praeger, 1969), p. 428.

23. Harriet Saperstein, "Business Relocation: Owners' Views," in Wolf and Lebeaux, *Change and Renewal,* pp. 481–82, 455.

24. Ibid., p. 485 (quote), pp. 462, 464.

25. Basil Zimmer, "The Small Businessman and Relocation," in *Urban Renewal: The Record and the Controversy,* ed. James Q. Wilson (Cambridge: MIT Press, 1966), pp. 380–403.

26. M. M. Robinson, letter to Albert Cobo, January 17, 1953, Burton Mayors, 1953, Box 4, "Housing—Gratiot" folder.

27. Leo Adde, *Nine Cities: The Anatomy of Downtown Renewal, A Retrospective Review of Nine Cities* (Washington, D.C.: Urban Land Institute, 1969), p. 220 (quote), 219–25.

28. Walter Gessell, letter to Albert Cobo, September 29, 1955, Burton Mayors, 1955, Box 5, "Citizen Redevelopment Committee" folder.

29. City of Detroit, Community and Economic Development Department, "Elmwood III: A Prospectus for an Offering of Land" (Detroit: CEDD, circa 1975), p. 5.

30. "Urban Renewal Deplored as Pell-Mell 'Negro Removal,'" clipping in Reuther CCR, Box V: 3, "Clippings 1962" #1 folder.

31. James Inglis, letter to Detroit Common Council, December 12, 1949, Burton Mayors, 1949, Box 3, "Housing Commission (1)" folder.

32. Real Estate Research Corporation, "An Analysis of the Market for New Housing Proposed for Construction in the Gratiot Redevelopment Area," November, 1954, Burton Mayors, 1954, Box 4, "Housing Commission 1954" folder, pp. 16, 17, 25, 30.

33. City of Detroit, Housing Commission, "Urban Renewal and Tax Revenue: Detroit's Success Story," circa 1965, pp. 3–8.

34. Eleanor P. Wolf and Mel J. Ravitz, "Lafayette Park: New Residents in the Core City," *Journal of the American Institute of Planners* 50 (1964): 237.

35. Gilbert Silverman, letter to Louis Miriani, May 18, 1961, Burton DCPC, Box 6, "Correspondence 1957–63" folder.

36. Elkin, *City and Regime,* pp. 21–31.

37. DCPC, "Central Business District Study: Land Use, Trafficways and Transit: A Basis for the Development of a Long Range Guide for Growth in Downtown Detroit," Master Plan Technical Report, June, 1956.

38. Arthur Woodford, *Detroit: American Urban Renaissance* (Tulsa, Okla.: Continental Heritage, 1979), pp. 87–95, 111.

39. DCPC, "Changes in Central Business District Retail Sales Patterns, 1948–1954," January 7, 1958, p. 2, Burton DCPC, Box 6, "Changes in Central Business District" folder.

40. Detroit Metropolitan Area Regional Planning Commission, "Shopping Centers in the Detroit Region," (Detroit: DMARPC, September 1957), pp. 1–9.

41. Ibid.; DCPC, "Central Business District Study," Master Plan Technical Report (Detroit: DCPC, 1956); DCPC, "Commercial Renewal Study: A Measurement of Tendency Toward Commercial Blight," Master Plan Technical Report (Detroit: DCPC, 1958).

42. Juliet Sabit and Harold Black, "The Central Business District," January, 1962, p. 6, Burton DCPC, Box 6, "The Central Business District" folder.

43. Albert Christ-Janer, *Eliel Saarinen* (Chicago: Univ. of Chicago Press, 1948), p. 125; Rulpert Spade, *Eero Saarinen* (New York: Simon and Schuster, 1971), pp. 10, 11; DCPC, "Planning Detroit 1947."

44. Greenstone, "A Report on the Politics of Detroit," pp. v-12; Conot, *American Odyssey,* pp. 404, 445; Mowitz and Wright, *Profile of a Metropolis,* p. 162.

45. Sabit and Black, "The Central Business District," p. 6.

46. Ed Hustoles, interview, February 4, 1987.

47. Adde, *Nine Cities,* p. 221; William Sloan, letter to M. J. Wood, March 31, 1959, Burton Mayors 1959, Box 3, "Industrial Development" folder.

48. Richard D. Ahern, "Plans for the Future of the Central City," circa 1958–60, p. 8, Burton DCPC, Box 3, "Interoffice Memos" folder.

49. Sabit and Black, "The Central Business District," p. 5; Transit plans in DCPC, "Central Business District Study," Master Plan Technical Report, no page (Section IV).

50. David Hartman, "The Development of Detroit's Cass Corridor: 1850–1975 (Detroit: Center for Urban Studies, Wayne State Univ., 1975), p. 7.

51. DCPC, "Renewal and Revenue," pp. 41–43; Detroit Community Renewal Program, "Detroit: The New City. Summary Report" (Detroit: CRP, 1966), pp. 17–18.

52. Thomas Ticknor, "Motor City: The Impact of the Automobile Industry Upon Detroit, 1900–75," Ph.D. diss., Univ. of Michigan, 1978, pp. 140, 145.

53. Donald Moore, "The Automobile Industry," in *The Structure of American Industry,* ed. Walter Adams (New York: Macmillan, 1954), pp. 301–14; Paul Reid, "Expansion Trends in the Automobile Industry, with Special Reference to the Detroit Region" (Detroit: DMARPC, 1956), p. 28.

54. Rory Bolger, "Recession in Detroit: Strategies of a Plantside Community and the Corporate Elite," Ph.D. diss., Wayne State Univ., 1979, p. 49.

55. Reid, "Expansion Trends," pp. 15–18.

56. Coleman Woodbury, "Industrial Location and Urban Redevelopment," in *The Future of Cities and Urban Redevelopment,* pp. 156, 141, 220–25, 284–86.

57. George Emery, comments on a panel discussion, "Problems of Large Cities," *Planning 1945* (Chicago: ASPO, 1945), p. 4.

58. Detroit Metropolitan Area Regional Planning Commission, "Movement of Manufacturing Establishments, 1937–1949 and Factors Influencing Location of Plants," (Detroit: DMARPC, December, 1949), pp. 2–4; Paul M. Reid, "Industrial Decentralization: Detroit Region 1940–1950," (Detroit: DMARPC, June, 1951), pp. 5–7.

59. DCPC, "Industrial Renewal Program: Progress Report," 1958, pp. 2-4; See also DCPC, "Industrial Renewal," 1956, p. 13.

60. June M. Thomas, "Planning and Industrial Decline: Lessons from Postwar Detroit," *Journal of the American Planning Association* 56 (1990): 297–310; DCPC, "Planning," May 1945, p. 5.

61. DCPC, *Detroit Master Plan,* 1951, pp. 4–5, 10–11; Segoe's role in Merle Hendrickson, interview, March 9, 1987.

62. DCPC, "Planning Detroit 1944," p. 26; Mowitz and Wright, *Profile of a Metropolis,* pp. 84–86.

63. Ibid., pp. 89–94, 417, 536–37.

64. City of Detroit, Housing Commission, "Urban Renewal and Tax Revenue," circa 1964, pp. 9–11.

65. B. H. Zendel, letter to Mayor Albert Cobo, July 12, 1954, Burton Mayors, 1955, Box 2, "DCPC" folder; see also Thomas Leadbetter, letter to Albert Cobo, February 4, 1955; Mowitz and Wright, *Profile of a Metropolis,* pp. 104–6.

66. DCPC, "Industrial Renewal Program: Progress," pp. 2–4.

67. Draft of "Supplement to Redevelopment Report," July 28, 1954, Burton Mayors, 1954, Box 2, "DCPC" folder and unpaged table entitled "Estimated Net Cost of Eighteen Year Redevelopment."

68. DCPC, "Industrial Redevelopment: West Side Industrial District" (Detroit: DCPC, 1958), p. 4, and "Industrial Renewal Program," p. 13; Industrial

Development Subcommittee, Mayor's Committee for Industrial and Commercial Development, minutes, April 22, 1958, Burton Mayors, 1958, Box 4, "Industrial Redevelopment" folder; William Sloan, letter to Harry Durbin, April 3, 1959, Burton Mayors, 1959, Box 3, "Industrial Development" folder.

69. Mayor's Committee for Industrial and Commercial Development, minutes, October 28, 1964, Burton DCPC, Box 4, "Detroit Research Park" folder; Mayor's Committee for Community Renewal, "Proposal for Progress: Detroit's Application for a City Demonstration Planning Grant," March, 1967.

70. W. Morgan, "The Effects of State and Local Tax and Financial Inducements on Industrial Location," Ph.D. diss., Univ. of Colorado, 1964, cited in John P. Blair and Robert Premus, "Major Factors in Industrial Location: A Review," *Economic Development Quarterly* 1 (1987): 77.

71. Mollenkopf, *The Contested City*, p. 117; Gelfand, *A Nation of Cities*, p. 208.

72. Heywood T. Sanders, "Renewing the American City: The Eisenhower Administration and the Creation of National Urban Renewal Policy, 1953 to 1960," paper presented to the Annual Meeting of the Society for American City and Regional Planning History, September, 1987, pp. 2, 3, 10, 12.

73. Ken Morris, letter to Dwight D. Eisenhower, February 4, 1958, Burton Mayors, 1958, Box 4, "Industrial Redevelopment" folder; see also William B. Sloan, letter to Cecial Galey, May 16, 1958, Burton Mayors, 1958, Box 4, "Industrial Redevelopment" folder.

74. Robert Hoffman, interview, February 18, 1987; DCPC, "A Study of Economic Trends in Detroit" (Detroit: DCPC, 1962).

75. Greenstone, "A Report on the Politics," p. v-7; Otto Krohn, letter to Louis Miriani, January 22, 1958, Burton Mayors, 1958, Box 4, "Industrial Redevelopment" folder.

76. Wolf and Ravitz, "Lafayette Park," p. 235.

77. Barry Checkoway, "Large Builders, Federal Housing Programmes and Postwar Suburbanization," in *Readings in Urban Analysis: Perspectives on Urban Form and Structure*, ed. Robert W. Lake, pp. 183–86.

Chapter Four: Racial Flight and the Conservation Experiment

1. DCPC, "Master Plan Technical Report: Population Capacity" (Detroit: DCPC, 1954), p. 2; DCPC, "Planning Detroit 1953–1955," November, 1955, pp. 41–42.

2. "Population, Housing, and Economic Characteristics of The Detroit Standard Metropolitan Area," *Detroit News*, April, 1961, Burton DCPC, Box 8, "Population, Housing" folder.

3. Charles Wartman, "Ford Rehabilitates Village of Inkster for Negro Workers," *Michigan Chronicle*, August 22, 1953, pp. 1, 4.

4. Albert J. Mayer, "Public Housing, Urban Renewal and Racial Segregation in Detroit," June, 1962, pp. 32–34, Reuther Detroit NAACP, Part 2, Box 30, folder 9.

5. Detroit Urban League, "The Detroit Urban League's Brief," pp. 3, 4 (for data); see also City of Detroit, Commission on Community Relations, "A Report on Population Movement and Neighborhood Stabilization," July 16, 1962, Reuther Detroit NAACP, Part 1, Box 14, "CCR 1962" folder.

6. Paul Knox, *Urban Social Geography: An Introduction,* 2d ed. (Essex: Longman Scientific and Technical, 1987), pp. 165–245, 252–56.

7. Joe T. Darden, "Choosing Neighbors and Neighborhoods: The Role of Race in Housing Preference," in *Divided Neighborhoods: Changing Patterns of Racial Segregation,* ed. Gary A. Tobin (Newbury Park: Sage, 1987), pp. 25–26.

8. Jackson, *Crabgrass Frontier,* pp. 198–213, 208 (quote).

9. DCPC, minutes, September 19, 1946, Burton Mayors, 1946, Box 2, DCPC; Jackson, *Crabgrass Frontier,* p. 208.

10. Walter Reuther and James Thimmes, letter to Dwight D. Eisenhower, July 23, 1954, Reuther Reuther, #366–15; Maxwell Rabb, letter to Walter Reuther and James Thimmes, August 26, 1954, ibid; U. S. Congress, *Evolution of Role,* p. 84.

11. Michigan Association of Real Estate Brokers, "Failure of the Voluntary Mortgage Credit Program," circa 1956, p. 1, Bentley DUL 6-26; George Schermer, "An Approach to the Racial Factor in the Housing Market," address before the Greater Detroit Society of Residential Appraisers, October 23, 1951, p. 7, Burton Mayors, 1951, Box 4, "Interracial Committee" folder.

12. Joe Darden, Richard Hill, June Thomas, Richard Thomas, *Detroit: Race and Uneven Development* (Philadelphia: Temple Univ. Press), pp. 119–25.

13. *Detroit Free Press,* August 15, 1986, p. 9A; several issues of *Michigan Chronicle,* including January 25, 1947, p. 6, February 8, 1947, p. 4, March 29, 1947, p. 1, April 12, 1947, p. 6, November 29, 1947, p. 3, and February 3, 1951, p. 1.

14. *Michigan Chronicle,* August 25, 1945, p. 3, September 8, 1945, p. 6, March 15, 1947, p. 1, and June 20, 1953, p. 1.

15. Mayor's Interracial Committee, letter to John C. Dancy, August 27, 1948, Bentley DUL 5-28; *Michigan Chronicle,* September 17, 1955, p. 10; Richard E. Cross, letter to Louis Miriani, October 6, 1961, Reuther CCR, Series III, 2–5.

16. U.S. Congress, *Evolution of Role,* pp. 84, 88, 126.

17. Robert Sinclair, *The Face of Detroit: A Spatial Synthesis* (Detroit: Department of Geography, Wayne State Univ., 1972), pp. 48, 50; Robert Sinclair and Bryan Thompson, *Metropolitan Detroit: An Anatomy of Social Change* (Cambridge: Ballinger, 1977), pp. 29–31.

18. George Schermer, letter to Albert Cobo, September 14, 1950, Burton Mayors, 1951, Box 4, "Interracial Committee" folder; E. M. Staley, letter to Mayor Jeffries, March 3, 1942, Burton Mayors, 1942, Box 5, "Interracial" folder; see also George Schermer, "The Transitional Housing Area: A Statement Prepared for the 1952 Nation Association of Housing and Redevelopment Officials Conference," November 10, 1952, Burton Mayors, 1952, Box 3, "Interracial Committee," folder, p. 1.

19. Hirsch, *Making the Second Ghetto,* pp. 187–99, 203–7; Arthur Kornhauser, *Detroit as the People See It: A Survey of Attitudes in an Industrial City* (Detroit: Wayne State Univ. Press, 1952), pp. 87, 95, 100.

20. Wolf and Lebeaux, *Change and Renewal in an Urban Community,* p. 28.

21. Ibid., pp. 45 (quote), 25–33, 41.

22. Ibid., pp. 64–89.

23. Ibid., p. 408.

24. John Coogan, letter to Detroit Common Council, March 11, 1948, Burton Mayors, 1948, Box 5, "Interracial Committee" folder; anonymous citizen's letter to Detroit Common Council, March 10, 1950, Bentley DUL 6-2; last points from Greenstone, "A Report on the Politics," pp. VI-16, V-68.

25. *Michigan Chronicle,* January 16, 1960, p. 6.

26. Sidney Fine, *Violence in the Model City: The Cavanagh Administration. Race Relations. and the Detroit Riot of 1967* (Ann Arbor: Univ. of Michigan Press, 1989), pp. 68–69.

27. Richard Steiner and Dorothy Rubel, remarks on "Conservation of Middle-Aged Areas" panel, *Planning 1952* (Chicago: ASPO, 1952), pp. 189–96.

28. Martin Meyerson, "Urban Renewal" panel, *Planning 1955* (Chicago: ASPO, 1955), p. 169.

29. Maurice F. Parkins, "Conservation and Urban Renewal," *Planning 1959* (Chicago: ASPO, 1959), p. 157.

30. DCPC, "Residential Redevelopment Study: Selection of Areas and Assignment of Priorities" (Detroit: DCPC, 1954).

31. Quoted in Joseph Molner, letter to Detroit Common Council, September 23, 1955, p. 3., Burton Mayors, 1956, Box 5, "Neighborhood Conservation" folder.

32. Maurice F. Parkins, "Neighborhood Conservation: A Pilot Study," (Detroit: DCPC in cooperation with U.S. Housing and Home Finance Agency, 1958), p. 18.

33. DCPC, "Neighborhood Conservation: A Ten Year Investment and Program To Eliminate Deterioration and Prevent Blight and Slums in Detroit's 53 Middle-aged Neighborhoods" (Detroit: DCPC, 1955), pp. 3, 4, two unpaged charts following p. 7.

34. DCPC, "Planning Detroit 1953–55," p. 31.

35. Ibid., p. 53.

36. Parkins, "Neighborhood Conservation," p. 18, pp. 59–61.

37. Ravitz, interview, February 20, 1987.

38. Mel Ravitz, "The Sociologist as a Participant in an Urban Planning Program," *Journal of the American Institute of Planners* 20 (1954): 79; Parkins, "Neighborhood Conservation," p. 51.

39. Mel Ravitz, "Urban Renewal Faces Critical Roadblocks," *Journal of the American Institute of Planners* 21 (1955): 17–21, quotes on pp. 17, 21.

40. Mel Ravitz, "Report on Social Attitude Survey of Conservation, Pilot Neighborhood 6E," January 18, 1955, Reuther CCR, Series III, Box 2-8, pp. 2, 3.

41. Parkins, "Neighborhood Conservation," p. 54.

42. Ravitz, interview, February 20, 1987; Ed Hustoles, interview, February 4, 1987.

43. Mel Ravitz, "Block that Blight!" *Adult Leadership* (Adult Education Association of the U.S.A.), May, 1956, unpaged photocopy in author's possession.

44. Mel Ravitz, "Some Principles and Problems of Citizen Organization for Neighborhood Conservation," talk presented to Conservation Victory Banquet, October 15, 1957, p. 6 (quote), Reuther CCR III: 2–9; see also Mel Ravitz and Adelaide Dinwoodie, "Detroit Social Workers Mobilize Citizen Aid for Urban Renewal," *Journal of Housing* 13 (1956): 232–34; Racial Cooperation Success Story in *Detroit Free Press,* October 2, 1956, p. 3.

45. Joseph Molner, letter to Detroit Common Council, February 12, 1959, Burton Mayors, 1959, Box 3, "Neighborhood Conservation" folder; Greenstone, "A Report on the Politics," p. v-68; Ravitz, "Some Principles and Problems," pp. 2–5.

46. Albert Mayer, "Public Housing, Urban Renewal, and Racial Segregation in Detroit," June, 1962, p. 27, in Reuther Detroit NAACP, Box 30, folder

9; see also Mel Ravitz, "Community Development: Challenge of the Eighties," *Journal of the Community Development Society* 13 (1982): 2–9; Citizen Participation Committee, Detroit Committee for Neighborhood Conservation and Improved Housing, minutes, September 15, 1960, Bentley DUL A5-18, p. 1.

47. DCPC, "Renewal and Revenue," pp. 57–59. This report makes no distinction between survey results for Mack-Concord and two other nearby "control" communities; Stephen S. Olney, "Indications from a Professional Study of Urban Renewal in Other Cities," Burton DCPC, Box 8, "Master Plan: Memo" folder.

48. "Conservation: A Study of Conservation Programs in Detroit, Cincinnati, Philadelphia, Chicago and New Haven (Detroit: Department of Urban Studies, Univ. of Detroit, April, 1965), pp. 109–11, 136–37, 178–79, 222.

49. Ravitz, "Urban Renewal Faces," p. 20.

50. Written comment to author, February 19, 1991.

51. Mel Ravitz, "Urban Renewal, Ideas and Reality: A Speech Before the Michigan Chapter of the American Institute of Planners," June 9, 1962, Burton DCPC, Box 9, "Urban Renewal" folder.

52. "Conservation: A Study."

53. Ibid., pp. 185–95.

54. Ibid., pp. 149, 116.

55. Fine, *Violence in the Model City,* p. 69.

56. U.S. Congress, *Evolution of Role,* p. 84.

57. Charles Abrams, "The Housing Order and Its Limits," reprint from *Commentary,* 35 (January, 1963), pp. 2–4, in Reuther Reuther, Box 406–4; See also National Urban League, "The President's Housing Order . . . An Important First Step," *Commentary* 35 (1963): 10–14.

58. Detroit Commission on Community Relations, minutes, February 18, 1963, Reuther Detroit NAACP, Part 1, Box 21, "Detroit CCR, 1963" folder.

59. Mel Ravitz, vita, in author's possession.

60. Mel Ravitz, interview, March 11, 1987.

61. Process for passage in David Cowley, memo to Richard V. Marks, September 17, 1962, Reuther Detroit NAACP, Part 1, Box 4, "CCR 1962"; Ordinance described generally in City of Detroit, CCR, "1962 Annual Report," February 18, 1963, p. 4.

62. Fine, *Violence in the Model City,* p. 60.

63. Housing Committee, Detroit Commission on Community Relations, memo to CCR, April 21, 1966, p. 6, Reuther Detroit NAACP, Part 2, 10–18 folder.

64. Detroit CCR, "Draft 1967 Annual Report," p. 4, Reuther Detroit NAACP, Part 2, 10–18 folder.

65. Detroit CCR, "1962 Annual Report," p. 8, Reuther Detroit NAACP, Part 1, Box 21, "CCR 1963" folder.

66. *Michigan Chronicle,* February 22, 1964, p. 1.

67. Denise Lewis, memo to The Honorable Common Council, December 27, 1971, p. 9, Municipal Reference Library, Detroit Public Library, vertical file, "Detroit—Housing—Blacks" folder.

68. Darden et al., *Detroit: Race and Uneven Development.* pp. 139–49.

69. Greenstone, "A Report on the Politics," p. v-41.

70. Martin Millspaugh and Gurney Breckenfeld, "The Human Side of Urban Renewal: A Study of the Attitude Changes Produced by Neighborhood

Rehabilitation" (Baltimore: Fight-Blight, Inc., 1958), p. 228. Cited and discussed in DCPC, "Renewal and Revenue," p. 58.

71. Phyllis Myers and Gordon Binder, *Neighborhood Conservation: Lessons from Three Cities* (Washington, D.C.: Conservation Foundation, 1977).

72. Daniel Lauber, "Racially Diverse Communities: A National Necessity," in *Challenging Uneven Development: An Urban Agenda for the 1990s,* ed. Philip Nyden and Wim Wiewel (New Brunswick: Rutgers Univ. Press, 1991), pp. 49–84.

73. David Varady, *Neighborhood Upgrading: A Realistic Assessment* (Albany: State Univ. of New York Press, 1986), pp. 13–14, 32, 10–11.

Chapter Five: Revisioning Urban Renewal

1. DCPC, "Detroit Achievement Through Planning."

2. Fine, *Violence in the Model City,* p. 62.

3. June M. Thomas, "Neighborhood Response to Redevelopment in Detroit," *Community Development Journal* 20 (1985): 89–98.

4. Unidentified author, letter to Charles Blessing, undated (ca. 1955), Burton DCPC, Box 4, "Medical Center" folder, p. 3; Detroit Medical Center Committee, "A Proposal for a Detroit Medical Center," May 23, 1956, Burton Mayors, 1956, Box 2, "Detroit Medical Center" folder.

5. Detroit Medical Center Citizens Committee, "The Detroit Medical Center: A Proposal for the Re-use of Land Cleared under the Federal and City Urban Renewal Program," September, 1958.

6. Clarence White, "Community Organization, Participation and Interaction in Renewal Areas of Detroit," unpublished master's thesis, Wayne State Univ., 1964, p. 36.

7. Detroit Medical Center Committee, "A Proposal," 1956, pp. 7–8, 9.

8. Detroit Urban League, Community Organization Department, minutes, June 12, 1951, Bentley DUL A6-23; Medical and Hospital Study Committee, Detroit Commission on Community Relations, various 1954 reports in Bentley DUL A6-24.

9. "Urban League Recommendations Respecting the Proposed Detroit Medical Center Development," June 26, 1957, Bentley DUL A6-22; "Suggested Statement for Presentation at the Public Hearing Before the Common Council Regarding the Urban League's Position Toward the Proposed Medical Center Plan," circa 1956, Bentley DUL A6-22.

10. White, "Community Organization," pp. 56–60, 69–73, 109.

11. Rev. Louis Johnson, interview, June 29, 1984; see also White, "Community Organization," pp. 22–24.

12. Carl Almblad, interview, August 20, 1986.

13. *Detroit Free Press,* March 1, 1970, p. Bl; project initiation in DCPC minutes, August 24, 1960.

14. *Detroit Free Press,* August 17, 1965, p. 3A; "New Neighborhood Resolutions and Urban Renewal Resolutions," adopted at WCO Annual Convention, June 26, 1966, Bentley DUL Box 50, "Reference File organization: West Central Organizing Committee" folder.

15. *Detroit Free Press,* August 22, 1965, p. lB; *Michigan Chronicle,* November 6, 1965, p. 3A; "The Fifth Wheel," supplement to *The Daily Collegian,* April 11, 1967, p. 3; *Detroit Free Press,* August 17, 1965, p. 3A.

16. *Michigan Chronicle,* December 11, 1965, p. A5; Detroit Commission

on Community Relations, "Highlights of the Commission Meeting," September, 1966, p. 1; Cavanagh response in *Detroit Free Press*, August 17, 1965, p. 3A.

17. One-page sheet with resolution (February 15, 1966) and 1966 version of bill (Senate Bill No. 1054) in Reuther David Cohen, Box 2, folder 17.

18. *Detroit Free Press*, March 1, 1970, p. B1; DCPC, minutes, October 8, 1968; see also *Detroit Free Press*, December 16, 1971, p. 10B, and Detroit Housing Commission, Quarterly Report to the Commissioners, First Quarter 1971, p. 3; *Detroit News*, September 22, 1975.

19. Fine, *Violence in the Model City*, p. 57.

20. DCPC, minutes, May 8, 1952; Blessing information in *Detroit News*, June 6, 1956, p. 76; Charles Blessing, interview, July 18, 1986.

21. Blessing interview, July 18, 1986. This interview and another one on September 9, 1986, used for several subsequent facts; Charles Blessing, "Challenge and Response," *Journal of the American Institute of Planners* 25 (1959): ii.

22. James Rouse, letter to Blessing, March 1, 1961, Burton DCPC, Box 2, "Blessing Correspondence 1952–1961" folder; Blessing, letter to Norman Williams, August 14, 1962, "Blessing Correspondence August to October 1962" folder; Blessing, letter to Kevin Lynch, February 14, 1964, "Blessing Correspondence "Nov. 1963–Feb. 1964" folder; Robert Weaver, letter to Blessing, July 9, 1964, Burton DCPC, Box 6, "May–December, 1964" folder; Invitations in Burton DCPC, Box 2.

23. Blessing, "Challenge and Response," p. ii; minutes of the DCPC meeting March 27, 1963.

24. *Journal of the American Institute of Architects* 41: 39–44; Greek trip described in Blessing's letter to Morris Ketchum, September 27, 1963, Burton DCPC, "August 1963–October 1963" folder.

25. DCPC, "Detroit: Achievement Through Planning," p. 5.

26. *Detroit News*, June 6, 1956, p. 76.

27. *Detroit News*, June 7, 1956, p. 72 (quote), and June 8, 1956, p. 1; AIP statement in Blessing, "Challenge and Response," p. ii.

28. Charles Blessing, letter to Joe Waterson, June 6, 1963, Burton DCPC, Box 2, "Blessing Correspondence June–July 1963" folder; Charles Blessing, letter of recommendation to Harvard Graduate School of Design, January 27, 1965, Burton DCPC, Box 6, "Jan–April 1965" folder.

29. Cobo and Miriani examples from Blessing, interview, July 18, 1986. Additional details concerning Miriani's action to demolish components of city hall "in the darkness of the night" from Blessing, interview, September 19, 1986.

30. Charles Blessing, letter to Cavanagh, February 13, 1963, Burton DCPC, Box 3, "Civic Center Plaza" folder, '55–'65; "Memorandum of Conference," August 17, 1965; Charles McCafferty, memo to Charles Blessing, September 1, 1965; Charles Blessing, letter to Jerome Cavanagh, October 8, 1967.

31. Blessing, interview, July 18, 1986; DCPC minutes, April 21, 1965.

32. DCPC, "Renewal and Revenue," p. 42.

33. City of Detroit, "Detroit Cultural Center," circa 1965. See original text and letters in Burton DCPC, Box 4, "Cultural Center" folder.

34. Charles Blessing, letter to William Slayton, November 24, 1965, Burton DCPC; *Detroit Free Press*, April 22, 1965, p. 1A.

35. Fine, *Violence in the Model City*, p. 57.

36. City of Detroit press release, April 13, 1967, Phillips personal files and DCPC, minutes, December 7, 1967.

37. DCPC, minutes, December 7, 1967.

38. DCPC, minutes, January 26, 1971, and November 16, 1971.

39. Hilanius Phillips, interview, February 19, 1987.

40. Quintus Green, interview, May 22, 1995.

41. Institutions listed in paper authored by Hilanius Phillips, and in Medical Center Citizens District Council Reporter, June 1977, both in his personal files. See also *Detroit Free Press,* February 3, 1987, p. 1-C; *Detroit News,* March 13, 1979, p. 10-B; *Detroit News,* December 3, 1980, p. 1-B; Barat House in Francis Bennett, letter to Robert Toohey, August 13, 1965, Burton DCPC, Box 4, "Cultural Center" folder.

42. Hilanius Phillips, "The Detroit Cultural Center Brochure" commentary, undated looseleaf paper in author's personal files.

43. Hilanius Phillips, interview, February 19, 1987.

44. Ibid.

45. Martin and Carolyn Needleman, *Guerrillas in the Bureaucracy* (New York: Wiley, 1974); *Detroit News,* March 13, 1979, p. 10-B; Hilanius Phillips, interview, February 19, 1987.

46. Hilanius Phillips, interview, February 19, 1987; H. Phillips, memo to Carl Almblad, September 24, 1974, Phillips personal files; *Detroit Free Press,* March 10, 1971, p. A-6.

47. Madeline Cohen, "The 1963 and the 1988 Plans for Philadelphia's Center City: A Problem of Differing Planning Philosophies," paper presented to the Society for American City and Regional Planning History, December 1, 1989, p. 4; Edmund N. Bacon, "A Case Study in Urban Design," *Journal of the American Institute of Planners* 26 (1960): 224–35.

48. Philip Herrera, "Philadelphia: How Far Can Renewal Go?" *Architectural Forum* 121 (1964): 181; *Architectural Forum,* 120 (1964), Special Issue: Boston; *Journal of the American Institute of Planners,* 26 (1960), Special Issue: "Planning and Development in Philadelphia"; "Under the Knife, or All for Their Own Good," *Time,* November 6, 1964, pp. 69–75; Robert C. Weaver, "Planning in the Great Society: A Crisis of Involvement," *Planning 1966* (Chicago: ASPO, 1966), p. 6.

49. Julia Connolly, "An Identification of Communities in the U.S. Making the Greatest Progress in Comprehensive Planning and Development," report submitted to Urban Studies Program, Univ. of North Carolina, May 1961, Municipal Reference Library, Detroit Public Library, "DCPC" vertical file.

50. Harold Bellamy, interview, August 16, 1986, and Robert Marans, interview, March 1, 1988; Cohen, "The 1963 and the 1988 Plans"; Edmund N. Bacon, *The Design of Cities* (New York: Viking, 1968).

51. Jewel Bellush and Murray Hausknecht, "Entrepreneurs and Urban Renewal: New Men of Power," in *Urban Renewal,* ed. Bellush and Hausknecht, p. 223.

52. Holli and Jones, *Biographical Dictionary.*

53. Bellush and Hausknecht, "Entrepreneurs," p. 215.

54. Other cities' structures in Carl Almblad, memo to Charles Blessing, September 18, 1959, Burton DCPC, Box 5, "Urban Renewal" folder. See also "Under the Knife," *Time,* November 6, 1964, p. 71; Chester Hartman, *The Transformation of San Francisco* (Totowa, N.J.: Rowman & Allanheld, 1984), pp. 18–20; Caro, *The Power Broker,* p. 707.

55. Black, "Urban Renewal," pp. 45, 50–65.

56. Mollenkopf, *The Contested City,* pp. 165–66, 169.

57. Linda Ewen, *Corporate Power and Urban Crisis in Detroit* (Princeton: Princeton Univ. Press, 1978).

Chapter Six: Rising from the Fire

1. Kenneth Fox, *Metropolitan America: Urban Life and Urban Policy in the United States, 1940–1980* (New Brunswick: Rutgers Univ. Press, 1990).

2. Fine, *Violence in the Model City,* pp. 95, 117–18, 108(quote)–109.

3. Francis Kornegay, "Our Community: Seven Critical Problems Facing Us," October 17, 1962, Bentley Kornegay, Box 13, "Personal Speeches 1960–62" (quote).

4. Fine, *Violence in the Model City,* pp. 24–32, 40–70.

5. Detroit Commission on Community Relations, "Highlights of the Commission Meeting," August and October 1966, Reuther Detroit NAACP, Part 2, 10–7.

6. Fine, *Violence in the Model City,* pp. 299, 249.

7. *Report of the National Advisory Commission on Civil Disorders* (New York: Bantam, 1968).

8. Ze'ev Chafets, *Devil's Night: And Other True Tales of Detroit* (New York: Random House, 1990), p. 21.

9. Fine, *Violence in the Model City,* p. 384.

10. *Report of the National Advisory Commission,* p. 86–87; civil rights observer, Francis Kornegay, "Today's Social Revolution and Christian Action" (circa 1963), Bentley Kornegay, Box 13, "Personal Speeches 1960–63."

11. "Return to 12th Street: A Follow-up Survey of Attitudes of Detroit Negroes," *Detroit Free Press,* October, 1968, p. 7.

12. John C. Donovan, *The Politics of Poverty* (New York: Pegasus, 1967), pp. 24–38; Richard Cloward and Frances Fox Piven, *The Politics of Turmoil* (New York: Random House, Vintage Books, 1975).

13. Programs in Michigan Economic Opportunity Office, "Newsletter," September 1966, Reuther Detroit NAACP, Part 2, 23-12.

14. Greenleigh Associates, New York, "Home Interview Study of Low-Income Households," a special report prepared for Mayor Jerome Cavanagh, February 1965; Conot, *American Odyssey,* pp. 505–17.

15. Conot, *American Odyssey,* p. 481.

16. Detroit Community Renewal Program, "Detroit: The New City," pp. 2–4, and Mayor's Committee for Community Renewal, "Social Renewal Progress Report," Technical Report #15, June, 1966, pp. 5–10.

17. Mayor's Committee for Community Renewal, "Detroit's Community Renewal Program, 1967–68," March 1968, Burton DCPC, Box 21, pp. 3–5.

18. Jerome Cavanagh, "Understanding Human Needs with a Social Renewal Plan," remarks before the National League of Cities, July 26, 1965, p. 3, Burton, Jerome Cavanagh biography file.

19. Mumford, *The Urban Prospect,* pp. 241, 242.

20. Paul Davidoff, "A Rebuilt Ghetto Does Not a Model City Make," *Planning 1967* (Chicago: ASPO, 1967), p. 191.

21. Conot, *American Odyssey,* pp. 447–51, 490–91 (quote).

22. Ibid., p. 492, and Walter Reuther, memo to President Lyndon B. Johnson, May 13, 1965, Reuther Reuther, Box 406-4; Bernard Frieden and Mar-

shall Kaplan, *The Politics of Neglect: Urban Aid from Model Cities to Revenue Sharing* (Cambridge: MIT Press, 1975), pp. 286–89.

23. Frieden and Kaplan, *The Politics of Neglect.*

24. Mayor's Committee for Community Renewal, "Proposal for Progress," Sections II and III.

25. Harold Bellamy, interview, September 2, 1986.

26. Detroit Model Neighborhood Department, "Final Local Evaluation of Model Cities Program: Detroit, Michigan 1969–1975," March, 1975, pp. 44–46.

27. Ibid., p. 36; Detroit Model Neighborhood Department, Social Service Committee, Citizens' Governing Board, "Evaluation of Social Action Planning Project, Detroit City Plan Commission," May 1972, pp. 2–4.

28. Michigan Advisory Committee to the U.S. Commission on Civil Rights, "Civil Rights and the Housing and Community Development Act of 1974," Vol. II, "A Comparison with Model Cities," June, 1976, p. 29.

29. Michigan Advisory Committee, "Civil Rights," Vol. II, p. 103.

30. U.S. Comptroller General, "The Community Development Block Grant Program Can Be More Effective in Revitalizing the Nation's Cities," Report to the Ranking Minority Member, Committee on Appropriations, U.S. Senate, April 30, 1981, p. i.

31. Ibid., pp. 28–32.

32. U.S. Department of Health and Human Services, cited in *Detroit News/ Free Press,* June 20, 1993, p. 4B.

33. Mayor's Development Team, "Mayor's Development Team Report to Mayor Jerome P. Cavanagh," October, 1967, p. 8; June Thomas, "Racial Crisis and the Fall of the Detroit City Plan Commission," *Journal of the American Planning Association* 54 (1988): 148–61.

34. Harold Black, "Urban Renewal: A Program Involving a Multiplicity of Participants," Ph.D. diss., Univ. of Michigan, 1973; James Pickford, "The Local Planning Agency: Organization and Structure," in *Principles and Practice of Urban Planning,* ed. William Goodman and Eric Freund (Washington, D.C.: International City Managers' Association, 1968), pp. 523–45.

35. Quote from Charles Blessing, letter to Roland Foerster, October 11, 1967, Burton DCPC, Box 9, "Report to Mayor" folder; Charter Study Committee, "Report of the Charter Study Committee," November 14, 1969, Burton CRC, Box 9, "Report" folder.

36. Housing Committee, Model Neighborhood Citizen Governing Board, memo, August 19, 1969, Burton DCPC, Box 13, "Model Neighborhoods: Correspondence" folder.

37. Interview, June 18, 1989 [interviewee requested anonymity].

38. DCPC, "Affirmative Action Plan to Improve Employment Opportunities for Minority Groups and Women" (Detroit: DCPC, 1972).

39. June 7, 1971, minutes of Division Heads, Burton DCPC, Box 2, "Minutes of Division Heads Meeting, January 1971–April 1973" folder; DCPC minutes, August 26, September 2, and September 16, 1969.

40. "Statement of Opposition to the Mayor's Community Development Commission Proposal," May 23, 1972, Burton CRC, Box 26, "Housing and Urban Development 1972" folder.

41. Mel Ravitz, "The Power of Planning," keynote address to the American Society of Planning Officials, Detroit, April 16, 1972, pp. 1–6.

42. *Detroit News,* May 20, 1972.

43. Quintus Green, interview, May 22, 1995. Green was not the only interviewee to suggest that the entire purpose behind planning-related changes made by the charter commission was to curb Blessing's influence.

44. Detroit Charter Revision Commission, "Final Report, Housing, Urban Development, and Economic Development Committees," November, 1972, Burton CRC, Box 9, "Report" folder.

Chapter Seven: Coleman Young and Redevelopment

1. Fine, *Violence in the Model City,* p. 457.

2. "Black Mayors," *Black Enterprise,* June 1983, pp. 156–58.

3. Roger Williams, "America's Black Mayors: Are They Saving the Cities?" *Saturday Review,* May 4, 1974, p. 10.

4. Darden et al., *Detroit: Race and Uneven Development,* pp. 213–14.

5. Wilbur Rich, *Coleman Young and Detroit Politics: From Social Activity to Power Broker* (Detroit: Wayne State Univ. Press, 1989).

6. Williams, "America's Black Mayors," p. 10; Holli and Jones, *Biographical Dictionary,* p. 402.

7. Jon Teaford, *The Rough Road to Renaissance: Urban Revitalization in America, 1940–1985* (Baltimore: Johns Hopkins Univ. Press, 1990), p. 258.

8. Ibid., pp. 255–60.

9. Rich, *Coleman Young,* pp. 232–63; *Detroit Free Press,* April 16, 1993, p. 9A.

10. *Detroit Free Press,* November 1, 1981, p. 2B, cited in Teaford, *Rough Road to Renaissance,* p. 267.

11. Ibid., pp. 188–91, 259.

12. Williams, "America's Black Mayors," p. 11.

13. Patricia Edmonds, "The Women Behind the Mayor," *Detroit Free Press Magazine,* November 23, 1986, pp. 12–20.

14. *Detroit Free Press,* April 9, 1979, p. 1A; *Detroit News,* January 6, 1991, p. C1; *Lansing State Journal,* March 7, 1991, p. B2.

15. Bellush and Hausknecht, "Entrepreneurs," p. 223.

16. John Logan and Harvey Molotch, *Urban Fortunes* (Berkeley: Univ. of California Press, 1987), p. 50; Mollenkopf, *Contested City,* p. 4.

17. Clarence Stone, *Regime Politics: Governing Atlanta* (Lawrence: Univ. Press of Kansas, 1989).

18. Bryan Jones and Lynn Bachelor, *The Sustaining Hand: Community Leadership and Corporate Power,* 2d ed., revised (Lawrence: Univ. Press of Kansas, 1993), pp. 15–20.

19. City of Detroit, Mayor's Office, "Moving Detroit Forward: A Plan for Urban Economic Revitalization," April, 1975.

20. Ibid.; *Detroit News,* April 9, 1978, pp. 1B, 13B.

21. U.S. Advisory Commission on Intergovernmental Relations, "Community Development: The Workings of a Federal-Local Block Grant," (Washington, D.C.: ACIR, 1977), p. 45.

22. U.S. Comptroller General, "The Community Development Block Grant Program Can Be More Effective."

23. State of Michigan, "Cities in Transition: Report of the Urban Action Group to Michigan Governor William G. Milliken," December, 1977.

24. New Detroit, Inc., "New Detroit: What Has It Done? A Report" (Detroit: New Detroit, 1976).

25. Ewen, *Corporate Power,* pp. 210–12.

26. Darden et al., *Detroit: Race and Uneven Development,* pp. 46–54.

27. Ibid. and Marietta Baba, "Urban Redevelopment in Detroit: The 'Renaissance Center' Model of Private Investment and the Problems of Unemployment," (Detroit: Center for Urban Studies, Wayne State Univ., October, 1978).

28. Ewen, *Corporate Power;* Darden et. al, *Detroit: Race and Uneven Development.*

29. U.S. Department of Housing and Urban Development, "Consolidated Annual Report to Congress on Community Development Programs, 1982," pp. 60, 66, and "Report to Congress on Community Development Programs, 1989," pp. 53, 57.

30. City of Detroit, Planning Department, "UDAG Fact Sheet," April 1984, p. 3.

31. *Detroit Free Press,* September 23, 1991, p. 1A.

32. Ibid., June 29, 1980, p. 8.

33. Ibid., pp. 7 (quote), 8.

34. David Zurawik, "Power Politics on the Riverfront," *Monthly Detroit,* October 1982, pp. 127 (1st quote), 62 (2d quote).

35. *Detroit Free Press,* September 1, 1985, pp. 1A, 6A; various brochures, Rivertown Business Association.

36. City of Detroit, Downtown Development Authority, "1985 Annual Report," and Central Business District Association, "1988 Downtown Detroit Development Report," no page; City of Detroit, "Moving Detroit Forward: The Second Decade, Opportunities for Action," circa 1985, p. 8.

37. *Detroit Free Press,* October 23, 1988, pp. 1G, 2G; *Detroit Free Press Magazine,* October 27, 1991, pp. 6–17.

38. Rich, *Coleman Young,* pp. 192–204; *Detroit Free Press,* June 23, 1993, p. 10A.

39. *Detroit Free Press,* June 14, 1978, p. A-3, February 25, 1980, pp. 3A, 17A; City of Detroit, "Overall Economic Development Plan," 1979, pp. 2–3.

40. *Detroit Free Press,* May 13, 1980, p. 1A, 10A.

41. City of Detroit, "Economic Diversification and Revitalization Plan," 1980, p. 4; *Detroit Free Press,* December 8, 1979, p. 1A.

42. Charles K. Hyde, "'Dodge Main' and the Detroit Automobile Industry, 1910–1980," *Detroit in Perspective* 6 (1982): 16.

43. *Detroit Free Press,* May 31, 1979, p. 3A.

44. Ibid., May 13, 1980, p. 10A.

45. *Detroit News,* January 13, 1985, p. 8A; Rich, *Coleman Young,* p. 182.

46. Rod Stodghill II, "Coleman's Greatest Hits," *Detroit Free Press Magazine,* November 17, 1991, p. 17; Gary Blonston, "Poletown: The Profits, the Loss," *Detroit Free Press Magazine,* November 22, 1981, p. 14.

47. Margaret Wilder and Joyce Stigter, "Rethinking the Role of Judicial Scrutiny in Eminent Domain," *Journal of the American Planning Association* 55 (1989): 57–65.

48. Carter Wilson, "A Study of Organized Neighborhood Opposition to the General Motors Plant Redevelopment Project in Poletown," Ph.D. diss., Wayne State Univ., 1982; Jeanie Wylie, *Poletown: Community Betrayed* (Urbana: Univ. of Illinois Press, 1989).

49. Jones and Bachelor, *The Sustaining Hand,* pp. 121, 126.

50. Ibid., p. 119.

51. *Michigan Chronicle,* February 21, 1981, p. A4.

52. Jones and Bachelor, *The Sustaining Hand,* p. 161.

53. *Detroit News,* January 13, 1985, p. 1A; *Detroit Free Press,* February 3, 1986, p. 12A.

54. Jones and Bachelor, *The Sustaining Hand,* pp. 139–42.

55. Stodghill, "Coleman's Greatest Hits," p. 17; David Fasenfest, "Community Politics and Urban Redevelopment: Poletown, Detroit, and General Motors," *Urban Affairs Quarterly* 22 (1966): 101–23.

56. *Detroit Free Press,* September 24, 1986, p. 1A, September 21, 1988, p. 1A (tax abatement), November 16, 1991, p. 3A (Moten); Stodghill, "Coleman's Greatest Hits," p. 17.

57. Jones and Bachelor, *The Sustaining Hand,* pp. 229–32.

58. *Detroit Free Press,* December 13, 1987, p. 1A.

59. Ibid., May 13, 1980, pp. 1A, 10A.

60. Citizens' Research Council of Michigan, "Fiscal Trends of the City of Detroit," June 1991, pp. 2, 77; *Crain's Detroit Business,* December 27, 1993, p. 73.

61. *Michigan Chronicle,* May 4, 1985, p. A4, May 17, 1986, p. A1, May 9, 1987, p. A1; *Detroit Free Press,* September 23, 1991, pp. 1A, 7A.

62. *Detroit News,* August 29, 1985, p. 1E, September 5, 1985, p. 2B, September 26, 1985, p. 1C, October 3, 1985, p. 1C.

63. City of Detroit, "1990–91 CDBG Program Grantee Performance Report," p. 1.

64. *Detroit Free Press,* July 23, 1995, pp. 1E, 4E.

65. *Detroit News,* August 21, 1969, p. B4, September 21, 1978, p. A22; *Lansing State Journal,* November 24, 1983, p. 13B.

66. *Detroit Free Press,* September 23, 1991, p. 7A.

67. Ibid., August 27, 1990, pp. B1, B2; *Crain's Detroit Business,* Metrofacts, July 1, 1991, p. 10E (occupancy).

68. *Detroit News,* August 12, 1990, p. 10A. For retail sales: Citizens Research Council, "Fiscal Trends," pp. 69, 75.

69. David Halberstam, *The Reckoning* (New York: Morrow, 1986).

70. Richard Child Hill, "Crisis in the Motor City: The Politics of Economic Development in Detroit," in *Restructuring the City: the Political Economy of Urban Redevelopment,* by Susan Fainstein et al. (New York: Longman, 1983), p. 114.

71. Lynn Bachelor, "Flat Rock, Michigan, Trades a Ford for a Mazda: State Policy and the Evaluation of Plant Location Incentives," in *The Politics of Industrial Recruitment: Japanese Automobile Investment and Economic Developoment in the United States,* ed. Ernest Yanarella and William C. Green (New York: Greenwood, 1990), pp. 87–102.

72. *Detroit Free Press,* January 2, 1990, p. B1, July 2, 1993, p. A1; *Detroit News,* January 12, 1985, pp. 1A (quote), 6A.

73. *Detroit Free Press,* September 23, 1991, p. 7A.

74. Ibid., October 13, 1989, p. 11A.

75. City of Detroit, "Proposed Capital Agenda 1991–92 through 1995–96," p. 6.

76. Citizen Research Council, "Fiscal Trends," pp. 2–4.

77. Ibid.; *Detroit News,* February 2, 1986, p. 18A.

78. Chafets, *Devil's Night.*

79. William Julius Wilson, *The Truly Disadvantaged: The Inner City, the Underclass, and Public Policy* (Chicago: Univ. of Chicago Press, 1987).

80. *Detroit Free Press,* June 28, 1992, p. H1.

Chapter Eight: Planning a Better City

1. Jane Jacobs, *Life and Death of Great American Cities* (New York: Random House, Vintage Books, 1961); Herbert Gans, *Urban Villagers: Group and Class in the Life of Italian-Americans* (New York: Free Press, 1982).

2. Norman Krumholz and John Forester, *Making Equity Planning Work: Leadership in the Public Sector* (Philadelphia: Temple Univ. Press, 1990).

3. Robert Hoffman, interview, February 18, 1987.

4. Yates, *The Ungovernable City,* pp. 34–35, and Fainstein et al., "New Haven," pp. 52–55.

5. Marsha Bruhn, interview, July 8, 1994.

6. Neighborhood Opportunity Fund information from Detroit City Planning Commission, "Bi-Annual Report: 1988–1990," pp. 11 and 12, and separate sheet on "Neighborhood Opportunity Fund Grants: 1977 Through 1993–94."

7. Thomas, "Racial Crisis."

8. Hillanius Phillips, interview, February 19, 1987.

9. *Detroit News,* September 16, 1979, p. A22, May 26, 1983, p. F1.

10. Ibid., July 22, 1985, p. B4.

11. Quintus Green, interview, May 2, 1989.

12. Harold Smith, interview, January 28, 1987.

13. Harold Glover, letter to author, August 10, 1988.

14. Merle Hendrickson, interview, March 9, 1987.

15. Ed Hustoles, interview, February 4, 1987.

16. Harold Glover, letter to author, August 10, 1988.

17. Robert Mier, K. J. Moe, and I. Sherr, "Strategic Planning and the Pursuit of Reform, Economic Development, and Equity," *Journal of the American Planning Association* 52 (1986): 299–309.

18. *Detroit Free Press,* November 29, 1987, p. 12A.

19. *Detroit News,* April 5, 1990, p. 9A.

20. Ibid., December 18, 1983, p. 3A.

21. *Detroit Free Press,* December 12, 1983, p. 13 A.

22. *Detroit News,* December 18, 1983, p. 3A.

23. Ibid., September 27, 1982, p. 3A, 9A.

24. Ibid., December 18, 1983, p. 3A.

25. Ibid., April 5, 1990, pp. 1A, 9A; *Detroit Free Press,* December 12, 1983, p. 13A.

26. *Detroit News,* July 28, 1985, p. 19A.

27. *Detroit Free Press,* June 22, 1985, p. B1.

28. Ed Hustoles, interview, February 4, 1987.

29. Marsha Bruhn, interview, April 23, 1993.

30. *Detroit News,* April 5, 1990, pp. 1A, 9A.

31. City of Detroit, "Detroit Master Plan of Policies," March 1990 draft, Part III, pp. 135–36.

32. *Detroit Free Press,* December 12, 1983, p. 1A.

33. Jerome Kaufman and Harvey Jacobs, "A Public Planning Perspective on Strategic Planning," *Journal of the American Planning Association* 53 (1987): 23.

34. Ibid., pp. 23–33.

35. Frank So, quoted in William Lucy, *Close to Power: Setting Priorities with Elected Officials* (Chicago: Planners' Press, 1988), pp. 16, 19–21, 27–30.

36. Kaufman and Jacobs, "A Public Planning Perspective," p. 30.

37. *Detroit News,* October 21, 1986, p. 14A.

38. Mel Ravitz, interview, March 11, 1987; *Detroit News,* November 8, 1987, pp. 1A, 16A.

39. "The Report of the Detroit Strategic Planning Project: 'Choosing a Future for Us and for All Our Children,' " November, 1987.

40. *Detroit Free Press,* November 28, 1990, pp. 1C, 4C.

41. Ibid.

42. Jean Pogge and David Flax-Hatch, "The Invisible Lenders: The Role of Residential Credit in Community Economies," in *Challenging Uneven Development: An Urban Agenda for the 1990s,* ed. Philip W. Nyden and Wim Wiewel (New Brunswick: Rutgers Univ. Press, 1991), p. 86; *Detroit Free Press,* July 25, 1988, p. 1A, August 25, 1988, p. 13A.

43. "Michigan Housing Coalition News," Spring, 1990, pp. 1, 2.

44. *Detroit Free Press,* December 21, 1990, p. 3F; *Detroit News,* May 20, 1990, pp. 1C, 2C. Also available is a video, "A Neighborhood Redeemed," Public Broadcasting Stations (PBS), circa 1990.

45. *Detroit News,* March 31, 1991, p. 5A.

46. Ibid., and Gerald Luedtke and Associates, "Core City Neighborhoods, Inc., Plan," circa 1988.

47. Metropolitan Affairs Corporation, U–SNAP–BAC, and the Warren/Conner Development Coalition, "The Partnership for Economic Independence: An Initiative to Help the Chronically Jobless Attain Economic Independence," November, 1991.

48. Various Focus:HOPE brochures; *Detroit Free Press,* January 8, 1990, p. C1.

49. *Detroit Free Press,* January 18, 1994, p. 2E.

50. Elizabeth Gunn, "The Growth of Enterprise Zones: A Policy Transformation," *Policy Studies Journal* 21 (1993): 432–49; Marilyn M. Rubin, "Can Reorchestration of Historical Themes Reinvent Government? A Case Study of the Empowerment Zones and Enterprise Communities Act of 1993," *Public Administration Review* 54 (1994): 161–69.

51. This section drawn from the author's experiences as one of those temporary professionals. (While on sabbatical, I worked as strategic planning team manager for the application process.) See June Thomas, "Applying for Empowerment Zone Designation: A Tale of Woe and Triumph," *Economic Development Quarterly* 9 (1995):212–24.

52. Nancy Costello, "Teamwork Is Key," *Detroit Free Press,* December 22, 1994, pp. 10A, 11A.

Chapter Nine: Racial Disunity

1. Joe T. Darden, "Residential Segregation of Blacks in Metropolitan Areas of Michigan, 1960–1990," in *The State of Black Michigan 1992,* ed. Frances Thomas (East Lansing: Urban Affairs Programs, Michigan State Univ., 1992), p. 22.

2. *Detroit Free Press,* December 15, 1992, pp. 1A, 10A (survey data); Chafets, *Devil's Night,* pp. 127, 134.

3. Kim Trent, "City, Suburbs Hope to Bridge Great Divide," *The Detroit News,* January 2, 1994, p. 12 A; "Question and Answer: Mayor Dennis Archer, *Detroit Free Press,* March 23, 1995, p. 15A.

4. University of Michigan Detroit Area Study, reported in *Detroit News/*

Free Press, October 10, 1992, p. 10A; Charlotte Steeh and Reynolds Farley, "Detroit: A Metropolis Divided by Race? Report to Respondents" (Ann Arbor: Univ. of Michigan, Detroit Area Study, March 1993), p. 6.

5. *The Detroit News/Free Press*, June 20, 1993, p. 6A.

6. Wallace E. Lambert and Donald M. Taylor, *Coping with Cultural and Racial Diversity in Urban America* (New York: Praeger, 1990), pp. 80, 103, 128, 152.

7. Willie D. Davis, Jr., "Disparities in Health between Blacks and Whites in Michigan," in *The State of Black Michigan 1992*, ed. Frances Thomas (East Lansing: Urban Affairs Program, Michigan State University, 1992), p. 27.

8. Homer Hawkins, "Crack Cocaine," ibid., pp. 35, 36; Leland Ropp, Paul Visintainer, Jane Uman, and David Treloar, "Death in the City: An American Childhood Tragedy," *Journal of the American Medical Association* 267 (1992): 2909.

9. Chafets, *Devil's Night*, pp. 134–35.

10. *Detroit News*, March 4, 1986, p. 18C; Fox, *Metropolitan America*.

11. Wilson, *The Truly Disadvantaged*.

12. "Ties That Bind: Central Cities, Suburbs and the New Metropolitan Region," cited in *Detroit News*, July 19, 1992, p. 12A; David Rusk, *Cities Without Suburbs* (Baltimore: Johns Hopkins Univ. Press, 1993).

13. Metropolitan Affairs Corporation, "Economic Development in Southeast Michigan: Problems and Potentials," (Detroit: SEMCOG, September 1982), pp. 23–26; June Thomas and William Lontz, "Intergovernment Cooperation for Economic Development: Greater Detroit's Six Pack" (East Lansing: Michigan Partnership for Economic Development Assistance, 1991).

14. Citizens Research Council of Michigan, "Governmental Organization: Metropolitan Southeast Michigan, Summary of Staff Papers," (Detroit: Metropolitan Fund, Inc., May, 1965), pp. 35–36, 40, 47.

15. *Detroit Free Press*, December 29, 1975, pp. 3A, 9A; "The Regionalist Papers," 2d ed., ed. Kent Mathewson (Southfield, Mich.: Metropolitan Fund, Inc., 1978).

16. *Detroit Free Press*, December 29, 1975, p. 9A; see also Darden et al., *Detroit: Race and Uneven Development*, pp. 234–49.

17. Thomas and Lontz, "Intergovernment Cooperation," *Detroit News*, January 18, 1985, pp. 1A, 10A, January 15, 1985, pp. 1A, 14A, January 20, 1985, pp. 1A, 12A.

18. Hillel Levin, "City vs. Suburbans: Is It Really Black vs. White?" *Monthly Detroit*, August 1981, p. 43.

19. SEMCOG, "Social Impacts: Crime, Race, Education, 1990/2010," Regional Development Initiative Briefing Paper #2, February, 1991; SEMCOG, "Summary of Workshop #2, Social Impacts: Crime, Race, and Education," Regional Development Initiative, February, 1991.

20. SEMCOG, "Summary of Workshop #6, Management and Governance," Regional Development Initiative, June, 1991, pp. 25–30.

21. John Gallagher, "The Challenge of Regionalism," *Detroit Free Press*, "Business Monday," June 7, 1993, p. 6F; Rusk, *Cities without Suburbs*.

Chapter Ten: Conclusion: Moving toward a Finer City

1. John P. Kretzmann and John McKnight, "Building Specially Communities from the Inside Out: A Path Toward Finding and Mobilizing a Community's Assets" (Evanston: Center for Urban Affairs and Policy Research,

Northwestern Univ., 1993); Donald A. Softley, "New Ways of Thinking About Detroit," *Michigan Chronicle*, "Home Front" Magazine, May 30–June 6, 1995, p. 3.

2. Robert Mier and Howard M. McGary, Jr, "Social Justice and Public Policy," in Robert Mier, *Social Justice and Local Development Policy* (Newbury Park: Sage, 1993), p. 24.

3. For fullest description of the model, see Krumholz and Forester, *Making Equity Planning Work.* For case studies of other cities, see Norman Krumholz and Pierre Clavel, *Reinventing Cities: Equity Planners Tell Their Stories* (Philadelphia: Temple Univ. Press, 1994), chap. 1.

4. June Thomas, "Race, Poverty and Planning: An Academic Agenda," *Colloqui: Cornell Journal of Planning and Urban Issues.* VIII (Spring), pp. 34–36; see also allied articles in the same issue.

5. Larry Susskind and Jeffrey Cruikshank, *Breaking the Impasse: Consensual Approaches to Resolving Public Disputes* (New York: Basic Books, 1987).

6. Samuel G. Freedman, *Upon This Rock: The Miracles of a Black Church* (New York: HarperCollins, 1993); Jim Rooney, *Organizing the South Bronx* (Albany: State Univ. of New York Press, 1995).

7. See June Manning Thomas and Reynard Blake, Jr., "Faith-Based Community Development and African-American Neighborhoods," in *Urban Neighborhoods,* ed. Dennis Keating, Norman Krumholz, and Phil Starr (Lawrence: Univ. Press of Kansas, forthcoming 1996).

8. Krumholz and Forester, *Making Equity Planning Work,* chaps. 2, 14.

9. A new literature on professional values and ethics is growing that will be very helpful in this area. See, for example, Elizabeth Howe, *Acting on Ethics in City Planning* (New Brunswick, N.J.: Center for Urban Policy Research, 1994).

10. W. Dennis Keating, *The Suburban Racial Dilemma: Housing and Neighborhoods* (Philadelphia: Temple Univ. Press, 1994).

11. The principle of "both sides," based on mutual responsibility by both White and Black, is described in the Bahá'í writings. These writings form the basis for the workshops mentioned above, several of which the author has attended or helped conduct. See Shoghi Effendi, *The Advent of Divine Justice* (Wilmette, Ill.: Bahá'í Publishing Trust, 1969 [original 1939]), pp. 28–34.

12. Wilson, *The Truly Disadvantaged; Rusk, Cities Without Suburbs.*

13. Mark Alan Hughes, "Moving Up and Moving Out," *Urban Studies* 24 (1987): 503–17.

14. William Goldsmith and Edward J. Blakely, *Separate Societies: Poverty and Inequality in U.S. Cities* (Philadelphia: Temple Univ. Press, 1992), pp. 59, 158–72.

15. Cornel West, *Race Matters* (New York: Random House, Vintage Books, 1994), especially chap. 1; see also, by West, *Prophetic Fragments: Illuminations of the Crisis in American Religion and Culture* (Grand Rapids: William B. Eerdmans, 1988).

16. Lewis Mumford, *Faith for Living* (New York: Harcourt Brace, 1940).

17. The author, who has participated in training and offering technical assistance to faith-based community development organizations in Detroit, expands on these themes in Thomas and Blake, "Faith-Based Community Development."

18. "Residential Mobility Programs," in "Urban Policy Brief," a newsletter

of the Office of Policy Development and Research, U.S. Department of Housing and Urban Development, no volume, September, 1994, pp. 1–6.

19. Rusk, *Cities Without Suburbs*, pp. 90–120.

20. Catlin, *Racial Politics and Urban Planning*, pp. 110–46.

21. 'Abdu'l-Bahá, *The Secret of Divine Civilization* (Wilmette, Ill.: Bahá'í Publishing Trust, 1970), 67.

Postscript

1. Robert Marans and Byong-Suk Kweon, "The Quality of Life in Metro Detroit at the Beginning of the Millennium," in Robert Marans and Robert Stimson, eds. *Investigating Quality of Urban Life: Theory, Methods, and Empirical Research.* Social Indicators Research Series 45. (New York: Springer, 2011), pp. 163–83.

2. Camille Charles, "The Dynamics of Racial Residential Segregation," *Annual Review of Sociology* 29 (2003): 167–204.

3. Segregation indices at CensusScope, a service of the Social Science Data Analysis Network, at www.censusscope.org/us/rank_dissimilarity_white_black.html

4. Detroit Office of Foreclosure Prevention & Response, "Community Stabilization and the Impact of the Foreclosure Crisis in Detroit: Progress toward Recovery: June 2008–December 2011." www.foreclosuredetroit.org.

5. See various reports at www.detroitparcelsurvey.org

6. Rolf Pendall, Elizabeth Davies, Lesley Freiman, and Rob Pitingolo, "A Lost Decade: Neighborhood Poverty and the Urban Crisis of the 2000s," Report. Joint Center for Political and Economic Studies, September, 2011.

7. Lara Rusch, "Going Regional: The Evolution of an Organizing Strategy in Detroit." *City & Community* 11.1 (2012): 51–73.

8. See City of Detroit, Department of Planning and Development, Community Reinvestment Strategy reports at www.detroitmi.gov/Departments/PlanningDevelopmentDepartment/Planning/LongRangeandCommunityPlanning/1997CommunityReinvestmentStrategy/tabid/2084/Default.aspx

9. Eric Burnstein et al., "Engagement Works: Planning with Citizens for Detroit's Future." University of Michigan Urban and Regional Planning Program capstone report. May 2012. At http://sitemaker.umich.edu/urpoutreachreports/all_reports&mode=single&recordID=0000c0a8de10000007d51b0500000139d3b6ef19833f4545&nextMode=list

10. Detroit City Planning Commission, Biennial Report, 2001–2, p. 13.

11. Detroit City Planning Commission, Biennial Reports, 1996–98, 2001–2. See also 2010–11 work program at www.detroitmi.gov.

12. R. J. King, "Anatomy of the Deal," *DBusiness* 3, 6 (October, 2008), 66–73.

13. Draft strategies for Detroit Works and other background information are posted, as of 2012, at http://detroitworksproject.com/planning/strategies.

14. See June Thomas and Margaret Dewar, "Introduction," in Margaret Dewar and June Thomas, eds. *The City after Abandonment* (Philadelphia: University of Pennsylvania Press, 2012), 1–16.

15. Steven R. Holloway, Richard Wright, and Mark Ellis, "The Racially Fragmented City? Neighborhood Racial Segregation and Diversity Jointly Considered." *The Professional Geographer* 64.1 (2011): 63–82.

Index

Index

288